Akita:
Mother of God as Coredemptrix
Modern Miracles of Holy Eucharist

May 24, '97

Mutsuo Fukushima

Akita:
Mother of God as Coredemptrix
Modern Miracles of Holy Eucharist

Tears from the Statue of the Holy Virgin, Akita, Japan,
Prove Her Cooperation With Jesus' Work of Redemption

*Modern Eucharistic Miracles Emphasizing
the Real Presence of Jesus in the Holy Eucharist*

*Divine Revelations Concerning How
the Laity Should Receive the Holy Eucharist*

*Supernatural Authenticity Approved by the
Local Ordinary, Bishop Ito, in His Pastoral Letter
of April 22, 1984, Niigata Diocese, Japan*

*Messages and Miraculous Tears of
the Holy Mother Mary from 1973 until 1981*

by Francis Mutsuo Fukushima

Queenship
Publishing Company
P.O. Box 42028
Santa Barbara, Ca. 93140-2028
Phone (800) 647-9882 Fax (805) 569-3274

**I dedicate this book to the Sacred Heart
of Our Lord Jesus Christ and to the
Immaculate Heart of Mary**

Library of Congress No. 94-66312

ISBN: 1-882972-30-9

Published by:
Queenship Publishing
P.O. Box 42028
Santa Barbara, CA 93140-2028

Printed in the United States of America

Table of Contents

Preface

by Fr. Gerard McGinnity

OF THE MANY APPARITIONS taking place throughout the world at this time — some already fully or partially approved — those in Akita have aroused especial interest because of the outright authentication declared in the first instance by Bishop Ito prior to his resignation and subsequently by Bishop Sato his successor who, acknowledging the spiritual fruitfulness of the happenings, pledged himself to protect the convent from any persecution.

Like so many among clergy and laity, I welcome this declaration and I praise God for the discernment of both Bishops.

Happily, in God's arrangement of events the assessment of what took place in the diocese of Niigata was presided over with spiritual sensitivity and scientific skill.

Akita, however, compels our attention for another reason. It sparkles like a teardrop gem in the gorgeous web woven by the Queen of Heaven's presence across the globe of the world today.

There Our Blessed Mother has delivered the most important, perhaps, of all Her messages in recent times with a succinctness hardly found elsewhere. Whereas in other locations the Mother of God has reason to utilize the system of secrets while treating of the future of the Church and the world, in Akita, Her call is conveyed forthrightly in four extensive messages.

This studious work of Francis Mutsuo Fukushima is a remarkable accomplishment. It comes from the pen of an adept and thorough journalist whose prestige among his peers is indicated by the post of vice presidency he held until 1992 in the International Federation of Catholic Journalists, the 1992 World Press Institute Fellowship he won to study U.S. politics, and whose intrepid pursuit of truth before the highest powers in the land for the sake of victimized Chinese dissidents amply illustrates his exceptional integrity.

His treatment of the Akita happenings, though compact, is compelling and leads inexorably to conclusions which are inescapable.

His delicacy of description for the miraculous tears and bleeding wounds as well as the mystical meaning they represent;

the vigorous analysis offered by experts in medicine and science;

his magnificent management of wide-ranging testimonies;

his painstaking pursuit of the entire sequence of events;

his comprehensive examination of related incidents in the life of the visionary;

his presentation of historical and biographical background;

the theological depth of meaning contained in Fr. Yasuda's commentary — all serve to make *Akita: Mother of God as Coredemptrix, Modern Miracles of the Holy Eucharist,* a superlative book.

The human details of the life story of Sr. Agnes, the recipient of Marian messages, give a moving biographical dimension which Francis smoothly integrates in a way that powerfully enriches our understanding of the essential message of Akita.

For example, to impart Her very sensitive message about the profaning of the Holy Eucharist Our Lady spoke in Her wise and delicate manner, "Please pray amid your poverty in reparation for the ingratitude and insults toward the Lord by so many men." Yet, the sequence of miraculous events which follow in Sr. Agnes' experience is essential for the completion of Her meaning. Perhaps the reason for this wise method: that Our Lady wished to avoid unhelpful controversy and unenlightened opposition concerning the reception of Holy Communion. The Holy Spirit guided the sisters in Sr. Agnes' community, recognizing the dreadful reality of Eucharistic profanation — through the miraculous bleeding on the hands — to *choose* to receive on the tongue rather than on the hand. In this process, Our Lady's serious message was trenchantly conveyed — but deftly and irenically.

Since first studying Akita I have had many sad evidences of the abuse of Holy Communion. These were cases of abuse which could never have occurred were it not for the fact that the Sacred Host was taken by hand via children found playing with Hosts in the Church seats at the end of Mass; Hosts trampled into the ground; between pews; Hosts recovered from missalettes after Mass and Hosts placed in the pocket and carried out of Church to be profaned — not to mention the innumerable fragments lost through rough and casual treatment of the Host in hands that are never purified.

Observations of this sort need never cause tension within the Church for, as Our Lady Herself remarks, the very Church is itself in the peculiar difficulty of being, at this time, the subject of severe attack.

Mr. Fukushima's exploration of this very central theme in the Akita apparitions illustrates both his method and his talent. He is able to explore each theme incisively and comprehensively, elaborating appropriately from history and theology to draw the maximum enlightenment from this heavenly gift.

Introduction

THE OVERWHELMING FOOTAGE of Her sparkling tears was nationally-televised in Japan on January 4, 1992 — only three days before the then U.S. President George Bush initiated his globally spotlighted four-day visit to Japan.

Though some will inevitably find it incredible, tears were seen exuding from the eyes of the wooden statue of the Blessed Mother Mary located at a Catholic convent in the northern Japanese city of Akita.

The formal name of the convent, registered with the Holy See, is the Institute of the Handmaids of the Sacred Heart of Jesus in the Holy Eucharist. (Seitai Hoshikai in Japanese).

Nippon (Japan) Television Network, the Japanese counterpart of the United States' ABC *News,* broadcasted the astonishing film footage during an evening prime time documentary, which aired that evening between 6:30 and 9:00 p.m.

The audience rating was high as the program aired during one of the New Years' holidays, when even Japan's so-called salaried "workaholics" take days off to try to relax their overworked nerves. Most enjoyed themselves with family members, chatting over "osechi" — the New Year's special traditional dinner — together.

Silently, tears streamed down the cheeks of the statue of Mary before the eyes of hundreds of thousands, perhaps even millions, of viewers seated before their television sets in their homes that evening.

While, the documentary program entitled, *Wide Show; Decisive Scoops,* did not devote its entire two-and-a-half-hours of air time to the 1973 Marian apparition in Akita and the subsequent 101 episodes of the lachrymations (weepings) of the statue, it did include a live broadcast of life within the convent. The television station sent a 35-member camera crew and reporters to the convent, after formally obtaining the authorization for the live broadcast from the local bishop, Monsignor Francisco Keiichi Sato.

The bishop of the local diocese — under whose jurisdiction the convent falls — ordered the Mother Superior to cooperate with the filming. The bishop is the successor of Bishop John Shojiro Ito, who recognized and declared the supernatural character of the apparition by issuing his pastoral letter in 1984. Bishop Sato issued the order advising the crew that an annual New Year's spiritual retreat of the nuns not be disturbed by the filming. As the bishop cleverly anticipated, the nuns' solemn holy hours of prayer at their annual retreat were also broadcasted live during the program, along with footage of the convent's beautiful garden and natural surroundings covered by a New Year's snow.

Although the weeping was a main feature of the program, it also broadcast an assortment of various news-making items which drew international media attention in 1991, such as the eruption of Mt. Pinatubo in the Philippines and the hurricane that killed dozens of Japanese in the autumn of that year.

The statue's 101 weepings continued from 1975 until 1981 at irregular intervals beginning on January 4, 1975. Since the first weeping, more than 500 persons, both Christians and non-Christians, reported witnessing the flow of tears from the eyes of the statue of the Holy Mother at the Akita convent. The 500-strong eye-witnesses include the former non-Christian mayor of Akita City, Mr. Keiji Takada, as well as pilgrims of American, French, Brazilian, Korean, and Japanese nationalities. The eyewitnesses also include Carmelites, Trappistines, as well as the nuns of the convents of Maryknoll, Caritas, Sisters of Miyazaki, St. Joseph, the Holy Spirit, and the Mission Sisters of the Sacred Heart. The tears were scientifically analyzed by Dr. Kaoru Sagisaka, then assistant professor of Akita University's Medical Faculty. He identified the blood type of the tears as type AB on January 29, 1975. The eye-witnesses include even non-Christian journalists from Tokyo Channel 12 Television Station, who videotaped the flowing of the Holy Mother's tears on December 8, 1979.

The footage of the weeping statue of Mary aired on January 4, 1992, was recorded by chance with an 8 millimeter home-video camera on July 26, 1978, by Mr. and Mrs. Yoshinaka, a Catholic couple. The Yoshinakas brought with them the 8-millimeter camera to the convent on a pilgrimage they took with their students they were teaching at a cramming school they ran. They did not expect that God would give them such a precious chance of videotaping the Holy Mother's tears. Mrs. Yoshinaka told me in an interview, "We recorded the Holy Mother's weeping with love and faith, while asking Her in silent prayers to allow us to take the footage of Her precious tears." The same footage was shown to the American Catholic audience on March 8, 1994, during a "Family Night" interview program of the Eternal Word Television Network of Mother Angelica. The Japanese couple began visiting the convent on a regular basis after they were informed by other Japanese Catholics of the mysterious weeping incidents. The Yoshinakas complied with a request by the Nippon Television Network to allow its staff TV crews to convert their precious 8-mm film into videotape for the January 4 broadcast.

During the live broadcast from Akita, a chief commentator presided over the proceedings of the whole program and over the broadcast discussion from the station's Tokyo studio which was linked live by both radio and television from Akita.

During the discussion, a staff reporter of the Nippon Television Network, asked from the convent premise, "Why did Mary shed tears?" Then, the chief commentator, a non-Christian, added, "If Mary offered up Her sufferings and tears in reparation for our foolish ways of living, my heart is deeply moved."

The staff reporter at the convent premise, replied, "We, Japanese who reside in this materially-rich country, may also have done things, about which we have to feel remorseful." He also added, "In this New Year of 1992, we may have to make greater efforts to live an honest, kindhearted life based on peace while trying to distance ourselves from the (life of) darkness."

The broadcast sent shock waves to some quarters of the Japanese archipelago. In the ensuing 10 days until around January 15th, some 300 non-Christian Japanese pilgrims scrambled to join ordinary Catholic pilgrims in visiting the convent from all over Japan.

Moved by the tears, these non-Christians came to see the statue more closely and meditate upon their ways of life from a new more spiritual perspective.

Among these non-Christians was the four member family of a bus driver in his 40s, who brought his wife and two daughters. He arrived on January 12th from the prefecture of Iwate, located several hundred kilometers from the Akita convent.

A nun who greeted the bus driver at the convent quoted him as telling her, "Although I am not a Christian, I have familiarized myself with the Bible without attending any church. However, after we watched the statue of Mary weeping at this convent chapel on television on January 4, our whole family decided to accept baptism into the Christian Church. Please tell us, how we could receive baptism."

The nun said she replied, "It is necessary for you to first learn the catechism, which explains the teachings of the Catholic Church." The nun informed the family of the address of a Catholic church nearest their home in Iwate by looking up the address in a church directory for them.

The nun asked the family to begin "praying" to receive Divine guidance to foster their fresh determination to seek a new and more meaningful life based on the love of God and love of neighbor, saying, "Prayers help a person deepen an understanding of Divine love for each member of humanity."

The nun said in the telephone interview, "When I heard him explain the family's motivation that led them here, I thought it was the working of God and Holy Mother Mary which gave this grace to them. It seems to me that God and the Blessed Mother influenced the hearts of the people at the television station. It was They who motivated the television officials to broadcast this program, because They wanted to inform as many people as possible of Their work (of mercy) in Akita so as to bring people to salvation."

Another similar episode are the conversions of more than 20 family members and relatives of Mr. and Mrs. Yoichi Imatani. Mrs. Imatani, an oil painter, had long asked her husband Yoichi to accept baptism for many years, only in vain. However, after the husband witnessed the tears streaming from the Holy Mother's statue, on July 29 and 30, 1979, he decided to accept baptism. After his baptism, the whole family made the daily recitation of a family Rosary a firm habit. More than 20 family members and friends of the couple were led by the Holy Mother to accept baptism into the Catholic Church.

Mrs. Imatani said, "My greatest happiness is to give witness and testimony about the love of the Holy Mother of Akita which I experienced."

On July 25, 1993, Bishop Sato said during a sermon for more than 400 pilgrims to the convent of the Marian apparition, "I hope that this place will develop further as a place of pilgrimage." The sermon was the climax of a two-day celebration of the completion of a new convent building of the Institute of the Handmaids of the Holy Eucharist. On the previous day, the bishop and pilgrims participated in a rosary procession led by the miraculous statue of the Holy Mother.

When this author heard these true episodes, it immediately stirred within me the memory of a passage in a tender-hearted letter sent me by Cardinal John O' Connor of New York.

The Cardinal said in the November 2 1, 1 990, letter, "Clearly, there is a worldwide hunger for Mary in the human heart, to say nothing of the desperate need."

In his masterpiece novel, *The Power and Glory,* the now-deceased British novelist, Graham Greene, wrote the following words of wisdom about the essence of true Christian love: "Every child was born with some kind of knowledge of love. . . they took it with the milk at the breast: but on parents and friends depended the kind of love they knew — the saving or the damning kind."

Rev. Fr. William Everett, the Jesuit missionary who baptized me into the Catholic Church in 1980, concurred with Greene's thinking.

One of Fr. Everett's books, *The Philosophy of Love,* says, "Genuine love contains an intellectual component which insures that it is based on objective truth. It at times can be harsh, severe and critical because of its fidelity to the truth." This observation of wisdom also applies to the harsh messages which concern the sinful aspects of modern men's lives, delivered by the Blessed Virgin of Akita.

Love means positive care for the betterment of others. Love encourages us to do good for our neighbors, while dissuading us from doing that which is wrong. In this sense, we can say, there is an inestimably deep love behind the severe warnings and messages of the Blessed Virgin Mary at Akita.

When this author, a member of the Union Catholique Internationale de la Presse (UCIP) — French words for the International Union of Catholic Press — visited India to attend a UCIP Tri-annual Congress in 1986, I had the honor of becoming closely acquainted with Cardinal Jaime Sin of Manila, who was invited to the Congress as a major guest speaker. The Cardinal later sent me three letters, one of which said Catholic journalists with a genuine faith can be a powerful tool of God.

The Cardinal's letter, dated June 27, 1987, told me, "The apostolate of the mass media is an area in the apostolate that is very close to my heart. We need to bring the Good News of God's love to all corners of the world. We can only do it through the magic of mass communications."

Yes, spreading the good news of Divine love that caused various modern miracles concerning the Holy Mother and the Holy Eucharist in Akita is the very purpose of this book. Its purpose is to convey to the world true information about the supernatural Marian events in Akita — the information I have gathered as a professional journalist —— and to share the knowledge of how God and Mary planned to bolster our Catholic spirit of *truth, justice, and love of God and neighbor* through the Divine messages.

Cardinal Sin told me in his May 1, 1991, letter, "Mary is the perfect disciple of the Lord. May you continue to imitate Her virtues and follow Her holy example."

Mary's greatest virtue, then, is Her humble willingness to shoulder the cross and abandon herself to cooperate with God's Plan of love and salvation, whenever God willed that Mary should take on yet more sufferings in His plan of redemption — She willingly accepted. At the Annunciation of the Archangel Gabriel, the Virgin Mary said, "Fiat," (let it be done to me as you say) opening the way for the supreme power of the Holy Spirit to conceive in Her womb the Savior of all humanity.

Our Holy Father, Pope John Paul II, says Mary's readiness to shoulder Her daily crosses later led to the outpouring of an abundance of Divine graces into numerous souls. Mary's contributions in the Divine Plan of salvation began when she consented to become the Mother of God. Then, throughout her life, Mary continued to offer up her sacrifices, prayers and sufferings in accordance with God's plan of salvation because of Her "obedience of faith."

In Golgotha (Calvary), Jesus emptied himself and accepted death on the Cross to redeem mankind from Satan. Our Holy Father said in his 1987 encyclical letter *Mother of the Redeemer*, "At the foot of the Cross, Mary participated — through faith — in the amazing mystery of Her Divine Son's self-emptying... Through faith Mary participated in Her Son's death, which redeemed mankind.

May God, through our study of the events of Akita, help us learn from and follow our Virgin Mother's example as "Coredemptrix," who, out *of true Christian love,* offered up Her own sufferings, prayers and sacrifices thus cooperating with Her Son's work of redemption on the Cross.

Sr. Agnes has long "lived" this Marian message calling us to offer up our prayers, sufferings and sacrifices in reparations for the sins of humanity.

Fr. Stefano Gobbi, the founder of the Marian Movement of Priests, told a spiritual meeting (Cenaculum) in Tokyo's Mikawashima Catholic Church (Salesian church) on September 5, 1993, "The Marian apparition in Akita is true. The local bishop recognized and declared the supernatural character of the apparition there in accordance with canonical procedures. I am personally acquainted with Sr. Agnes who received the Marian messages. She is the nun emaciated and consumed by sufferings. She is leading a humble, hidden life. I think this humble, hidden life is a good sign."

Chapter 1

Dazzling light from Holy Eucharist
Stigmata forces Communion on the Tongue
Mary's Supernatural Tears

IN 1973, IN A CATHOLIC CONVENT in a suburb of the city of Akita in northern Japan, a Japanese nun reported receiving messages of serious implications for all mankind from the Mother of God, the Blessed Virgin Mary.

Sr. Agnes Katsuko Sasagawa, then 42, reported to Bishop John Shojiro Ito, that the Blessed Mother called for Roman Catholics to offer up fervent prayers, penance, and sacrifices. The Blessed Mother was also reported as calling for the mankind to repent of their sinful lifestyle and to amend themselves.

Bishop Ito, the ordinary of the diocese of Niigata wherein Akita lies, immediately initiated an investigation of the messages and related mysterious events that were observed by both Christian and non-Christian visitors.

According to the testimony of Sr. Agnes, the first mysterious event at Akita was that she saw a brilliant light from the Tabernacle on June 12, which animatedly conveyed the impression of the true presence of Jesus in the Holy Eucharist in the Tabernacle. During the five days of June 12, 13, 14, 28 and 29, 1973, Sr. Agnes observed luminous rays which emanated from the Tabernacle.

Sr. Agnes

In the "Spiritual Diary of Her Soul" — a collection of notebooks in which Bishop Ito ordered Sr. Agnes to record her mystical experiences and apparitions — she recalled that on June 12th (Tuesday), "When I approached softly to open the door of the Tabernacle, brilliant rays suddenly emanated from the Tabernacle. I prostrated myself there."

Bishop Ito had given this community of nuns the obligation of Adoration of the Blessed Sacrament in the spirit of atonement. To this end, permission was given to the responsible person to open the tabernacle door, whenever a priest was not available.

This day the members went out to attend a lecture so the person in charge commissioned Sr. Agnes to open the Tabernacle door for adoration, so that Sr. Agnes might worship Jesus present in the Holy Eucharist during their absence later in the day. All the other nuns were on their way to attend a meeting of catechists at Niigata, several hundred kilometers from Akita. Sr. Agnes was left alone to experience these first mystical events.

Tabernacle from which the Majestic Light emanated

Akita: Mother of God as Coredemptrix

The following is from Sister Agnes Sasagawa's spiritual diary; which recorded the events on June 12, 1973.

"Of course, I had no courage to open the Tabernacle door. Was it about one hour? Having been overcome by the majestic light, even after it disappeared, in awe, I could not raise my head. When I came to myself and reflected on what had happened, I thought to myself: Did Jesus in the Blessed Sacrament show Himself in the light to such a sinful one as me ... or was it a mental illusion — and I doubted."

"When I was working before as a catechist in Myoko Catholic Church, I used to open the Tabernacle door to make a loving act of adoration, but never had such an experience"

"I came out of Chapel, but then, went back in to think and pray over what had happened, wondering if perhaps it were possible that my mind was not somewhat odd. This time nothing happened. Since this was my first experience of such a happening, and since it was so strange to me, I did not tell anyone. Keeping a secret in my heart, I went to bed."

Chapel where these miracles of the Holy Eucharist took place.

"I awoke early the next morning, and could not get yesterday's event out of my mind. I thought to myself how fortunate it was to rise early. I went into the Chapel at five o'clock, I was alone. We usually say the morning prayer of the Divine Office together at six o'clock. Thinking that yesterday's event might be an illusion, I wanted to test myself, so I came close to the Tabernacle to open the door again. Suddenly, just as yesterday, I was struck by a dazzling light. In my surprise, I stepped back and prostrated in adoration. I thought, this was not an illusion nor a dream and had the firm confidence that Jesus who is truly in the Blessed Sacrament, had shown Himself. I remained prostrated for a long time even after that holy light disappeared. Soon, it was time to say the Divine Office, so the Sisters came into Chapel. I started to say the Office with everyone, since I was pierced through by that awesome majesty, I remember that I said my prayers absent-mindedly."

"The next day was Thursday, June 14th. While I was at adoration with the Sisters, I saw not only the shining majesty as I saw before, but as if to envelope the light from the Tabernacle, the red sanctuary lamp nearby was burning like a flame. The tip of the red flame was glittering like gold. It seemed as if the red flame was enveloping the whole Tabernacle. In that sudden phenomenon, I was astounded and trembled. I prostrated there for a while."

"I was surprised and taken up by what happened these three days. I was unable to think of anything but to adore and praise the Lord in Chapel. After I finished my adoration, I left Chapel and came to myself. I was then freed from that inexplicable, strange, inner sweetness. As I came back to my usual self, I repeated the same self-reflection, 'I wonder if something is wrong with me...' So I wanted to test if it was a true fact and see if I was normal. I was thinking how terrible it would be if my mind were abnormal and I was out of my mind. I also wondered if the other Sisters had seen the same phenomenon and felt a strong urge to find out. So at the breakfast table the next morning, I started to tell them about it. However, everyone's reaction was that they had seen nothing. So, I immediately held my tongue and said nothing. Then my Superior, Sr. Chie Ikeda, advised me to keep it a secret since it happened to me alone. I was startled by her advice."

"The first apparition of the light was on Tuesday June 12th, at 8:30 a.m., the second was the next day, the 13th at 5 a.m., and the third was on Thursday, June 14th, 8:30 to 9:30 a.m. This third phenomenon specially left me with the strongest impression and it was engraved deeply in my heart and breast. It was with me wherever I went. Since that time, whenever I went into the Chapel, I felt that light remained always in my heart. Even when the Blessed Sacrament was not exposed, my heart was naturally filled with adoration and praise for Lord. I came to consider the Chapel as the real Sanctuary and rejoiced to go to Chapel all the more. My feet were always directed there. Keeping these three days phenomena in my heart as I prayed, I could not stop my heart from burning with unspeakable interior sweetness and love for Him. Even now as I am writing this, something like a reverberation of joy is still within me which makes my heart burn with a mysterious longing for the Lord."

"On June 23rd, the Bishop came from Niigata to stay for a week and to celebrate the next day's feast of the Blessed Sacrament. In our life on the hill, we no longer had a spiritual director. Since June 5th, when Chaplain Fr. Mochizuki left on a new assignment, we had not had Mass in our convent. We had no idea as to when a new Priest would come. Sunday, the 24th, was the feast of the Blessed Sacrament, we attended the Bishop's Mass during which he gave us the admonition that, "Our Congregation is consecrated to the Blessed Sacrament and we therefore should deepen our devotion to the Sacred Heart of Jesus in the Blessed Sacrament." "On June 28 (Thursday) Adoration was arranged from 8 a.m., and the four of us made a Holy Hour of adoration together. After the Rosary, a hymn and some other prayers in common, we began our mental prayer. After a while, the light which I had seen three times before, appeared from the Blessed Sacrament, and as if to envelope that light, a kind of mist or cloud or smoke floated around it. Beside the light all around the altar, countless Angels were adoring the Holy Eucharist. I was taken up with the admirable sight, so I knelt, adoring from my heart in the direction of the light. Then I prostrated. The idea came to me that someone may have been making a fire outside and the natural smoke may have reflected onto the altar. I rose slowly and turned my eyes to the garden outside but I saw nothing like fire. The altar was bathed in the mystical light. I really could not stare directly at the majestic light, so I closed my eyes naturally and prostrated in adoration. When the hour of adoration had ended, I remained in Chapel until Sister Kotake tapped me on the back. Sister was going to go out for some shopping. When I arose and looked at the altar, the lovely sight of light and cloudy smoke had disappeared and it was the usual small Chapel. My heart longed to stay in that state. That day, only a guest catechist, the Bishop and myself were at home. I was asked to prepare the lunch. I decided to go to the work room until then. The sight I had just seen was so real and present before my eyes, that I did not progress much in my work. Yet, while I was meditating, I made an effort to work stitch by stitch."

"The time came when I was supposed to fix tea for the Bishop. So I went to him. I wondered if I should tell him about these things and ask for the proper direction. I hesitated for a while. I thought, if I don't tell him, I might lose my mind. Moreover, I was worried that perhaps I had already lost my mind and was seeing these strange events as a result. So I thought that it was proper to speak to him since I was in need of good judgment and direction. I thought how terrible it would be if I was losing myself through mental illusion or if I became a burden to my Sisters by being mentally sick. I decided to stir up my courage and tell the Bishop just who I am, and of everything just as I saw it, without hiding anything, nor making too much nor too little of it ... and ask for his direction leaving all to his prudent judgment. I started to speak to him rather timidly, the Bishop seemed to listen to me sincerely. I gradually gained peace and was able to tell him everything as it was. When I had finished, I thought it was very good to have done so, and felt as if a big heavy burden had been lifted from my shoulders. My heart became very light and I was very happy."

"After listening to my long story very quietly the Bishop told me this: "Since we are not yet certain about what you saw, don't speak to anyone about it. Be sufficiently careful not to be too much taken up with it. What we have to be most cautious about is not to be proud by saying to yourself, 'I alone could see such a phenomena as I am a special person.' You must try to be more and more humble from now on, and without clinging to it, try to live an ordinary life as every other Sister does. After listening to you, I feel that your words are not those of a person who had lost her mind. Do not be worried. These things do happen, you need not be troubled. You know that various apparitions took place to the shepherd children in Fatima. But in your case it is still not made clear. Try to live an ordinary life in silence. Please pray and meditate well on the Blessed Sacrament."

"I received these admonitions and was very happy. I was glad that I had told him everything. I retired in peace. My heart became very light and cheerful." (From Sr. Agnes' spiritual diary.)

Sr. Agnes' Stigmata

In the evening of, June 28, 1973, a cross-shaped wound, about 3 cm. by 2 cm., developed on the palm of her left hand, causing very sharp pain. From then on, the wound renewed itself every week for a month. On every Thursday the wound used to appear and assumed the appearance of pink blisters and started bleeding. On every Friday, the wound bled profusely, giving the intense pains to Sr. Agnes.

The bleeding lasted until 3:00 or 3:30 p.m. of each Friday. On each Sunday, the wound returned to its original appearance of pink blisters. The wound disappears by Sunday of each week. Therefore, the wound was non-existant on Sundays, Mondays, Tuesdays and Wednesdays of each week. It was of a color bordering on rose. Sr. Agnes said in an interview with this author, "Blood oozed from the central point at which two straight lines of the cross intersected. I thought the wound formed because of my sins." Sr. Agnes also said, "Sr. Katoke and Sr. Ikeda used to treat my wound with gauze and they witnessed blood welling up and flowing out of the wound." "Because the blood never clotted, the two superiors used to say they perceived the wound as mysterious and said the wound which sends forth the blood of beautiful red color may be carrying a serious meaning," according to the testimonies of Sr. Agnes.

Fr. Thomas Teiji Yasuda, who was appointed chaplain of the convent in early 1974, said these words of Sr. Agnes are indicative of her deep humility. The priest of the Society of Divine Word said that when he asked her what sins of hers she thought resulted in the formation of the wound, she replied it might have resulted from "my weakness of faith and my insufficient gratitude for Divine graces."

The mysterious phenomenon of the abrupt appearance and its disappearance of Sr. Agnes' wounds repeated themselves five times from June 28 (Thursday), 1973, until July 29 (Sunday) of that year.

In parallel with the bleedings of Sr. Agnes' hand, the statue of the Holy Mother Mary at the convent chapel also bled from the palm of its right hand, according to the testimonies of Bishop Ito, Sr. Agnes, Sr. Theresa Toshiko Kashiwagi, Sr. Saki Kotake and other eyewitnesses.

The blood from the statue's hand was wiped away on one of the occasions with a bleached white cotton cloth and a piece of gauze. This hard evidence is still preserved at the convent. The blood from the statue was scientifically analyzed by Dr. Kaoru Sagisaka of Akita University, who identified the blood type as B on January 29, 1975. The details of this analysis are described in the chapter 9.

Wound in the Palm of Holy Mother's Statue

On Thursdays and Fridays of this one-month period, the pain in Sr. Agnes' palm intensified so violently that the other nuns entreated her to desist from work. Nonetheless, she persisted in her tasks and her chapel chores as the designated sacristan. During this period, the heart of Sr. Agnes appears to have been led by the mysterious events happening about the Tabernacle to draw ever closer to the Eucharist. She set her steps quite readily toward the Tabernacle. Sr. Agnes wrote in her spiritual diary, "I was very unwilling to withdraw from the presence of the Holy Eucharist and to leave the chapel (after prayers).... My heart was consumed with love for the Lord wholeheartedly and was full of the wish to consecrate myself to the Lord." Then Sr. Kotake and Sr. Ikeda retired to their rooms.

Sr. Saki Kotake, the then novice mistress, testified of the wound on the night of July 5, 1973, as follows; "That evening we had been invited to eat at a house in town and we were to spend the night in one of our convents there, but I was preoccupied by the condition of Sr. Agnes Sasagawa, so I decided to return to the convent. I went directly to her room where I found her seated on her bed crocheting. At my request, she opened her hand with great difficulty and said to me with tears in her eyes, 'It hurts me so much that I decided to crochet.'"

"Sr. Agnes seemed in agony and appeared to think, 'Is this because my sins are great that the wound appeared?" Sr. Kotake went on to say, "I felt that God gave it to Sr. Agnes as a privileged gift." "I told Sr. Agnes, 'It seems to hurt you so very much, but try to bear it by thinking of the sufferings of the Lord. Excuse us for causing you to bear the consequences of the sins of us all. Then I brought Sr.

Ikeda to her room. The two of us treated her wound with gauze and bandaged the hand and asked her to awaken us if the pain increased."

On July 6, at approximately 3:00 a.m., Sr. Agnes could not sleep because of the excessive pain caused by her bleeding wound. While Sr. Agnes was in her room on the second floor of the convent, she arose from bed, changed the bandage on her own hand and began to pray. Suddenly, she heard a voice which came from where, she did not know. The voice said, "Be not afraid. Pray not only in reparation for your sins, but for the sins of all people. The world today wounds the Sacred Heart of Our Lord by its ingratitude and sacrileges. The wound on the palm of Mary is deeper and more painful than yours. Now let us go."

Suddenly a beautiful figure, what at first seemed like a woman, appeared and stood near Sr. Agnes' right shoulder. Then, seeing the figure, Sr. Agnes noticed such a striking resemblance to her deceased elder sister, Tomi, that she called the figure, "My sister." Sr. Agnes said that the figure shook its head negatively, and smiling tenderly, said, "I am the one who is with you and protects you." The figure thus identified itself as her guardian angel and beckoned her towards the chapel. Sr. Agnes dressed quickly and went out to the corridor. The angel then led her to the chapel through the dark long corridors of the convent and down the stairs. Upon reaching the chapel, the angel vanished. In deep adoration, Sr. Agnes first worshipped the Holy Eucharist in the Tabernacle of the altar.

The words of the angel, thus spoken, *still resounded* in her soul: "The wound in the palm of the Blessed Mother is deeper and more painful than yours." As Sr. Agnes came near the altar to examine the statue's hand more closely, it suddenly came to life, emanating a brilliant and dazzling light. Sr. Agnes could not endure to look at it and she immediately prostrated herself on the floor. It was then that Our Lady gave Sr. Agnes the first of three messages.

First Message of Holy Mother

Then what Sr. Agnes called a "voice of indescribable beauty," came from the direction of the statue of the Blessed Mother. The voice came to the "spiritual ears" of Sr. Agnes (who was physically totally deaf at this time). The voice said:

"My daughter, my novice, you have obeyed me well, abandoning all to follow me. Do you suffer much because of the handicap which deafness causes you? You will be assuredly healed. Be patient, It is the last trial. Does the wound in your hand give you pain? Pray in reparation for the sins of humanity. Each person in this community is my irreplaceable daughter.

"Pray very much for the pope, bishops, and priests. Since your baptism you have always prayed faithfully for them. Continue to pray very much... very much. Tell your superior all that passed today and obey him in everything that he will tell you. Your superior is wholeheartedly seeking prayers now."

Second Message Urges Reparations for Sins & Offering up of Sufferings

The second message was given to her in the same manner as the first, on the following first Friday, August 3, 1973. Beginning around 2:00 p.m., Sr. Agnes spent an hour in the chapel, meditating upon the Lord's passion and reciting the Rosary. Her guardian angel appeared and joined the recitation. A voice coming from the statue of the Blessed Mother told her:

"My daughter, my novice, do you love the Lord? If you love the Lord, listen to what I have to say to you."

"It is very important. Convey it to your superior."

"Many men in this world grieve the Lord. I seek souls to console Him. In order to appease the anger of the Heavenly Father, I wish, with my Son, for souls who will make reparation for sinners and the ungrateful by offering up their sufferings and poverty to God on their behalf."

"In order that the world might know the wrath of the Heavenly Father toward today's world, He is preparing to inflict a great chastisement on all mankind. With my son, many times I have tried to appease the wrath of the Heavenly Father. I have prevented the coming of the chastisement by offering Him the sufferings of His Son on the Cross, His Precious Blood, and the compassionate souls who console the Heavenly Father. A cohort of victim souls overflowing with love."

"Prayer, penance, honest poverty, and courageous acts of sacrifices can soften the anger of the Heavenly Father. I desire this also from your community: please make much of poverty, deepen repentance, and pray amid your poverty in reparation for the ingratitude and insults toward the Lord by so many men. Recite the prayer of the Handmaids of the Eucharist with awareness of its meaning; put it into practice; offer your life to God in reparation for sins. Let each one endeavor by making much of one's ability and position, to offer oneself entirely to the Lord."

"Even in a secular community, prayer is necessary. Already souls who wish to pray are on the way to being gathered in this community. Without

attaching too much attention to the form, pray fervently and steadfastly to console the Lord."

After a moment of silence She continued:

"Is what you think in your heart true? Are you truly prepared to become the rejected stone: My novice, you who wish to become the pure bride of the Lord. In order that you, the bride, become the spouse worthy of the Holy Bridegroom, make your vows with the hearty readiness to be fastened to the Cross with three nails. These three nails are honest poverty, chastity and obedience. Of the three obedience is the foundation. With total obedience follow your superior. Your superior will understand you well and guide you."

Third Message; "Two Weapons" for Catholics

The third and final message was given also by the voice coming from the statue of the Blessed Mother on October 13, 1973. During the day's early morning recitation of the Rosary, she had witnessed that majestic rays embodying the splendor of the Holy Eucharist. The rays filled the chapel.

Sr. Agnes visited the chapel alone after breakfast and after the other nuns went out. Sr. Agnes took up her rosary, making the sign of the Cross. Then, the voice of indescribable beauty came to her deaf ears. From the first word, Sr. Agnes prostrated herself onto the floor, concentrating all her attention.

"My dear daughter, listen well to what I have to say to you. And relay my messages to your superior."

After a moment's silence:

"As I told you, if men do not repent and better themselves, the Heavenly Father will inflict a great punishment on all humanity. It will definitely be a punishment greater than, the Deluge, such as has never been seen before."
"Fire will plunge from the sky and a large part of humanity will perish...

The good as well as the bad will perish, sparing neither priests nor the faithful. The survivors will find themselves plunged into such terrible hardships that they will envy the dead. The only arms which will remain for you will be the Rosary and the sign left by My Son (Eucharist)."

"Each day recite the prayers of the Rosary. With the Rosary pray for the bishops and priests. The work of the devil will infiltrate even into the Church One will see cardinals opposing other cardinals... and bishops confronting other bishops."

"The priests who venerate me will be scorned and condemned by their confreres; churches and altars will be sacked; the Church will be full of those who accept compromises and the demon will tempt many priests and religious to leave the service of the Lord."

"The demon is trying hard to influence souls consecrated to God. The thought of the perdition of so many souls is the cause of My sadness. If sins continue to be committed further, there will no longer be pardon for them."

"With courage, convey these messages to your superior. He will tell each one of you to continue prayers and acts of reparations for sins steadfastly, while ordering all of you to pray fervently. Pray very much the prayers of the Rosary. I alone am able still to help save you from the calamities which approach. Those who place their total confidence in Me will be given necessary help."

Bleeding from Statue's Hand

Many of the mystical events in Akita concern the wooden statue of the Holy Mother Mary. The hand carved statue of Mary, made of the wood of the "katsura" tree, stands protectively on a globe, assuming a posture of pouring out grace and peace. Its feet are bare and both arms are held wide open. The statue is about three feet tall from its pedestal to the upper edge of the Cross, which stands behind the statue. The Cross is connected to the back of Mary's figure from the heart downward, but there was no need for joints since both were carved from only one block of wood.

Akita: Mother of God as Coredemptrix

Fr. Thomas Yasuda said, "As of 1973, this statue in Akita was the only statue in the world depicting the Holy Mother Mary combined with the Cross behind it. The design of the Holy Virgin carrying the Cross has the profound connection with the upcoming dogma of the *Mother of God as Coredemptrix*. I think God selected this statue to effect the miracles of its 101 episodes of weeping as the hard evidence of the upcoming dogma with it." (Note: The deep link between the Akita apparitions and the dogma, which many serious church observers and theologians expect to be declared by the Holy See in coming years, will be clarified in chapter 8.)

The nuns, Bishop Ito, and several pilgrims as well, all reported witnessing a cross-shaped wound, which formed abruptly, in the palm of the right hand of the statue, as well as bleeding which issued forth from that wound for eight days from July 6 until July 27, 1973,

Although Sr. Agnes' stigmata disappeared on July 29 (Sunday), 1973, the wound in the palm of the statue remained until September 29, 1973.

Sr. Teresa Toshiko Kashiwagi, the Mother Superior of the Convent, said, "I witnessed the fresh blood flowing from the cross-shaped wound of the statue of the Holy Mother. The vivid red blood was moving along the palm of the statue's right hand. The wound underwent several transformations in a short span of time. Parts of the palm surrounding the cross-shaped wound assumed the aspect of human flesh and I witnessed the grain of the skin had the appearance of a fingerprint after one such transformation."

Sr. Teresa of the Infant Jesus Saki Kotake, then novice mistress, was another eye-witness to the bleeding of the statue's hand. She was one of the three founding nuns of the Institute of the Handmaids of the Eucharist on the hill of Yuzawadai.

Asked about her observation of the bleeding wound, Sr. Kotake said, "Suppose that you spray water at a point on a slanting wooden board. The water would naturally flow downward along the board at a fairly quick speed. The blood which oozed from the cross-shaped wound of the statue's palm flowed in that manner."

Sr. Kotake also said, "What was especially mysterious about the phenomenon was that the blood never fell to the floor. It simply vanished before dropping on the carpet. After the blood stream flowed from the wound to the lower edge of the palm, it vanished there. This continual repetition of the stream and vanishing were observed by everyone present." The wound of the statue vanished on September 29, 1973, the feastday of St. Michael the Archangel.

Sr. Agnes also said, "Strangely, the blood that appeared on the hand of the statue, never fell to the ground. Even when Sr. Kotake had alerted me with tears in her eyes about the statue's speedy abundant bleeding while praying the Rosary with Bishop Ito and Sr. Ikeda on their knees on the morning of July 26, 1973, the blood did not drop onto the floor, remaining in its palm." "Furthermore, in my case also, I felt that the blood accumulated in my palm when I was praying in the chapel, but it never soiled the floor even a single time," she said.

Bishop Ito and the nuns also reported witnessing and wiping away with gauze and cotton, abundant perspiration which had a fragrance of ineffable sweetness. This perspiration exuded from the statue daily between September 29 and October 15, 1973. The fragrance was said to be reminiscent of a combination of those of roses, lilies, violets, and all such blossoms. A nun was quoted as joyfully exclaiming:

"Even the most exquisite perfume in the world cannot emit this fragrance!" So profuse was the perspiration, that the gauze and cotton used to wipe it away became completely saturated.

Akita: Mother of God as Coredemptrix

The 101 Episodes of the Statue's Weepings

About fifteen months after the third message of Akita was delivered the wooden statue of the Holy Mother started weeping, according to the hard evidence of videotaped weepings and the testimonies of many eyewitnesses I interviewed.

In a March 13, 1982 episcopal report to Cardinal Joseph Ratzinger, Prefect of the Congregation of the Doctrine of Faith, Bishop Ito reported that he himself witnessed the weepings of the statue four times.

The bishop's report says, "The wooden statue shed tears for 101 times, starting from January 4, 1975 until September, 15, 1981, the date which corresponded to the feast day of the Lady of Seven Sorrows,... Usually such phenomenon would be regarded as the result of mischief or trickery by someone. However, I can declare in front of God that the phenomenon was not trickery, as I am an eye-witness of the very phenomenon."

The mother superior of the convent, Sr. Theresa Toshiko Kashiwagi, is one of several nuns who witnessed almost all occasions of the 101 lachrymations (weepings) of the statue. She wrote in one of her letters to this author, "The number of the eye-witnesses exceeded 500. If we count each of the repeated experiences of witnessing the statue's tears by a same person, the aggregate number of the eye-witnesses exceeded 2,000. This is the objective fact." (Note: The detailed records of the 101 weepings of the statue of the Holy Mother, such as their dates, times and number of witnesses are attached to this book as Appendix _.)

Among some 500 eye-witnesses, there are some prominent non-Christians. The former Buddhist mayor of Akita, Mr. Keiji Takada, witnessed the tears from the statue on June 23, 1979, along with other 39 witnesses when he was still the incumbent mayor. He retired in 1990 after serving as the mayor for 16 years. My friend, Mr. John Bird, a noted British film producer, and I, jointly interviewed the mayor when he was still in his mayoral office.

The weeping statue.

The mayor said, "Yes, I witnessed the tears of the statue of Mary with my own eyes. When I entered the convent chapel, I saw the tears remaining on the face of the statue after it had shed tears for awhile. I witnessed them on the occasion when my friend, Mr. Kazaemon Kudo, proposed visiting the convent with me to enjoy seeing beautiful roses blooming then in the big Japanese-style garden in the convent premise."

Mr. Kudo, the mayor's friend and Akita Prefecture Assembly legislator, said, "I observed the tears resting on the face and chin of the statue of the Holy Mother in the convent of the Seitai Hoshikai. (The Institute of the Handmaids of the Sacred Heart of Jesus in the Holy Eucharist). The drops of tears, which appeared to have flowed for awhile before the mayor and I entered the chapel, were clinging to the chin of the statue. I noticed that there remained a trace of the stream of tears from one of the eyes of the statue alongside the nose to the chin, as well as the one from the chin to the neck."

The legislator went on to say, "I was moved by the tears. The impression of the tears still remains in my heart."

He added, "Although, I as a Buddhist cannot accept baptism because of my family's strong traditional ties with a local Buddhist temple, I believe the Holy Mother of Christians wept, because she was saddened by the lives of the great majority of mankind who are leading egocentric and arrogant lives, while forgetting the need to help the downtrodden, the underprivileged and suffering people."

Bishop John Shojiro Ito continued his study of canon law at Washington Catholic University from 1952, after being consecrated to the priesthood in 1938. The bishop was appointed as the first bishop of the Niigata diocese in 1962 by Pope John XXIII.

The bishop witnessed the weeping of the statue at 6:45 p.m. on January 4, 1975, — the third of the day's three episodes of its weepings (It was the very day when the 101 weepings started) — then on August 22, 1981 and on two other occasions.

Bishop Ito Approves the Apparitions
in his 1984 Pastoral Letter

About ten years and 6 months after the series of mysterious incidents at the convent, — during which time the bishop made a thorough investigation — Bishop Ito issued a pastoral letter recognizing and declaring the supernatural authenticity of the Marian messages and apparitions in Akita.

Bishop John Ito

Akita: Mother of God as Coredemptrix

In the April 22, 1984 pastoral letter, — issued to the faithful on behalf of the universal Catholic Church — the bishop described the 101 episodes of weeping of the wooden statue of the Holy Mother at the convent chapel as the "most remarkable fact." Because of the importance of the weepings, the author decided to quote a part of the pastoral letter here. (The whole text of the pastoral letter is presented in the appendix C.)

The bishop said in the pastoral letter as follows:

"The most remarkable fact, in my opinion, and the most evident, is the overflowing of an aqueous liquid, similar to human tears from the eyes of the statue of Our Holy Mother."

"This began on the 4th of January, 1975 (Holy Year) and some tears flowed 101 times, until the 15th of September, 1981, Feast of Our Lady of the Seven Sorrows. I was able myself to witness four lachrymations (weepings). About 500 persons have also been eyewitnesses. I twice tasted this liquid. It was salty and seemed to me truly human tears. The scientific examination of Professor Kaoru Sagisaka, specialist in legal medicine in the faculty of Medicine at the University of Akita, has proved that this liquid is indeed identical to human tears."

"It is beyond human powers to produce water out of nothingness, and I believe that to do this requires the intervention of a force that transcends that of human beings."

"Moreover, it is not the question of pure water, but of a liquid identical to that secreted by human body. It flowed only from the eyes of the statue, as tears flow, and that more than 100 times over a period of several years and before numerous witnesses. It has been established that it could not have been by trickery or human maneuvers."

Bishop Ito's 1982 Report to Cardinal Ratzinger

Bishop Ito reported these weepings of the statue of the Holy Mother in his 1982 March 13 report to Cardinal Joseph Ratzinger, Prefect (Secretary) of the Congregation of the Doctrine of Faith. I was given two copies of this 19 page report by the Bishop. One copy is the bishop's Japanese hand-writing. The other is its French translation, which was actually sent to Cardinal Ratzinger.

The bishop said in the report, "Usually, these phenomenon of weepings of a statue would be regarded as the result of a mischief or trickery by someone. However, I can declare in front of God that the phenomenon were not trickery as I am an eye-witness of the very phenomenon."

"The reasons why I concluded as above are as follows:

1. I, who am Bishop, witnessed the weepings of the statue four times. I observed tears well up and overflow from the eyes of the statue and stream down just as a human being shed tears. I watched the tears stream down the statue's cheek, accumulate on the chin, then flowing down the statue's garment, reaching the feet and then flowing along the globe on which the statue stands. Then the tears reached the pedestal that supports the globe and statue."

   "I can never forget the profound emotion I experienced when I first watched the tears from the statue. I was so strongly touched at the sight that I felt like wiping away the tears by bringing cotton. In actuality, I wiped away the tears from the statue of the Holy Mother. Twice, I tasted the tears, which tasted salty just like human tears."

2. "The statue shed tears 101 times from 1975 until 1981 and more than 400 persons witnessed these weepings. If these weepings had been performed by someone as trickery, it

would have been discovered and uncovered such as during this long period."

3. "The Faculty of Medicine at the University of Gifu officially analyzed and examined the tears which were collected with absorbent cotton. The university identified the tears as human fluid and proved that the blood type of the tears is type 0. Therefore, it is an impossibility to arrange for the statue to shed tears of a human being in such a large quantity."

(The above is a precise translation of what the bishop wrote down in his 1982 report to Cardinal Ratzinger)

Sr. Agnes' Stigmata and its result

Bishop Ito, in his report to Cardinal Ratzinger, also reported that he observed a cross-shaped wound — 3 cm. long by 2 cm. wide. His report said the wound first formed in the palm of the left hand of Sr. Agnes on June 28, 1973, the eve of the Feast of the Sacred Heart of Jesus.

Sr. Agnes also said, in an interview with this author, that the wound caused "almost unbearable pain," renewing itself each week, appearing in the form of a cross and beginning to shed blood on Thursdays. Profuse bleeding occurred on Fridays. The wound would return to its cross-shaped pink blister appearance on Saturdays.

The episodes of profuse bleeding of her hand occurred on July 6, 13, 20, and 27 of 1973. This testimony coincided with the testimonies of the bishop and the other eye-witnesses. Bishop Ito said in an interview with this author, on January 20, 1991, "The Cross shaped wound in her palm was made of two straight lines. I witnessed the mysterious change of the wound on Thursdays, Fridays and Saturdays. When I saw the bleeding wound, I thought this must be a stigmata. The wound resembled that of the statue very closely."

According to the testimonies of Sr. Agnes, the bishop and other nuns, the aspect of the wound was very different from what one would usually see in a wound of this type. It did not seem to have been caused by any sort of blade. It was as if a cross, made of two straight lines, had been engraved in the skin. Of a color bordering on rose, it was not repulsive like other wounds. Rather, it seemed to give off a certain beauty.

Sr. Agnes said, in an interview with this author, "In the painful moments, I felt as if a drill was twisting in the flesh of my palm to force the wound open further."

The following is the vital testimony of Sr. Agnes taken from her spiritual diary.

Thursday, July 26th, 1973, the feast of St. Anne.

"The Mass that day was at 5 p.m., and we had the renewal of vows of Sister Yoko Ishikawa. About 3 p.m., Sister Ishikawa came to my room looking for Sister Saki Kotake. Since she could not find her, I went to the Chapel to look for her there. In the Chapel, Sister Chie Ikeda and Sister Kotake were praying the Rosary very fervently. I hesitated a little, but finally I called Sister Kotake. Sister Kotake's eyes were filled with tears as she said to me, "There is more bleeding from Holy Mother Mary's hand. Today it is even more profuse than the last time. It is very dark and looks painful. Would you pray here in place of me?" Then she left and went to Sister Ishikawa. I was astounded when I heard the news, and for a while, no words of prayer came to me. I was too afraid to go near the Holy Mother Mary's statue. Coming to myself, as I joined Sister Ikeda in the Rosary, my left palm began to ache very much. Up until this time, it usually started to ache every Thursday about Vespers time. But today it is a little earlier... I wonder why it is so? Bearing the pain, I continued to pray."

Akita: Mother of God as Coredemptrix

"Mass started a little after 5. Just as Sister Ishikawa was renewing her vows, my hand started to ache almost unbearably. I almost screamed. It was bleeding and ached just as if someone had pierced my palm all the way to the back with a nail. I tried with my whole strength to bear it. My forehead was in a greasy sweat. At that moment, clinging to our Lady's medal, I prayed, " Mary, help me!" I tried to endure the pain by thinking of the sufferings of Jesus on the Cross. This all took place in just a short time, but when I was bearing the pain, it seemed like a very long time. I still cannot forget it. At Holy Communion, everyone received in their hands, but since I could not open my palm, because of the pain, I received in my mouth."

(The profound meaning of this testimony will be clarified in chapter 7 by using quotations from Popes and theologians.)

After dinner, Sr. Agnes was summoned by Bishop Ito who wished to examine her hand more closely. As she opened the palm of her hand with great difficulty, he observed the very deep puncture. About this examination, she recalled that, "The bishop told me my wound appeared to risk passing from the palm to the back of the hand." She also quoted the bishop as saying, "Go to the hospital of Dr. Iwabuchi to have your hand treated."

Although neither the nuns nor the bishop disclosed anything to the press, rumors of the extraordinary events in Akita spread, especially after the weeping of the statue started in 1975 — about two years after the first mysterious events and Eucharistic miracles. Pilgrims began trekking to this remote hamlet from various districts of Japan and from more than 24 countries including Argentina, Austria, Australia, Brazil, Britain, Canada. Czechoslovakia, Denmark, France, Ireland, Italy, Malaysia, the Netherlands, Nepal, Singapore, Switzerland, South Korea, Tanzania, the Philippines, Poland, Portugal, Puerto Rico, Taiwan, Venezuela, and the U.S.A.

Bishop Ito told me in an interview that "the wooden material from which the statue is made is very dry. The statue cannot hold water ample enough within its wood so as to stream out of it in such abundant quantity, as I myself have witnessed. Besides, we should note that the tears came out of the statue's eyes alone. There is no natural way to explain it."

"Only God can cause water to come out of nothingness. Even the Blessed Mother can not do so by Herself. Satan also cannot cause water to flow out of nothingness. This is the ultimate source of my conviction that the phenomenon is supernatural and the messages are from God."

Interview with the Sculptor of the Statue

The wooden statue of the Blessed Mother was carved in 1965 by a Buddhist sculptor, Saburo Wakasa, then 45,

The Sculptor, Saburo Wakasa

at the request of the community. Mr. Wakasa, a citizen of Akita, is a member of the Japan Sculptors' Association and his artistic works are displayed every year at various exhibitions. Surrounded by his beautifuly carved sculptures and Buddhist statues at his atelier (artist's studio), Mr. Wakasa told me in an interview that he "sculptured the whole statue of Mary, globe, and the Cross from the same block of wood so there are no joints in the statue. I devoted myself entirely to sculpturing the statue of Mary, just as I do in carving my works to submit to exhibitors."

"Whenever I sculpt, I always put my whole heart into the project. The statue of Mary was my first work connected with Christianity. Of my various statues, it is only with the statue of Mary at the hamlet of Yuzawadai that mysterious events have occurred." Questioned as to whether he regards the reported shedding of tears from his carved statue of Mary as a "miracle," he replied as follows:

"Fushigidesu... (It is beyond my understanding). The wood from which I carved the statue of Mary was very dry and rather hard. It took three months to carve the statue and no extraordinary events took place while I was carving it. Nothing could be farther from the truth than the false allegations that I put a trick device into the eyes of the statue.

Sparkling Tears of Mary

Fr. Joseph Marie Jacq of the Paris Foreign Mission Society, was one of the eye-witnesses and a theologian who came to know deeply about the spiritual condition of the nuns at Akita. After guiding a retreat there and making more than 20 pilgrimages there, he wrote on his first pilgrimage to the convent of apparitions in Akita as follows:

"The community of the convent in Akita is warmed by a charity and poverty of a truly evangelical quality. Indeed, everything speaks of poverty, humility, and littleness there. The cracks and holes in the walls and doors were so many that the screen partitions chattered in the drafts. Everyday, I bumped my head against the low frames of the hallway, partitions and doors."

Fr. Joseph, a devout missionary who served the Japanese people for 33 years, wrote about the first (on January 24, 1979) of the four episodes of weeping which he personally witnessed as follows:

Father Joseph Marie Jacq

"We gathered in the refectory for supper at about seven o'clock in the evening. A short while after we started eating, we were interrupted by a nun who came to announce, 'Father Joseph, come quickly, the Blessed Mother is all in tears!'"

"I rose from the table and hastened to the separate room of the statue, followed by a young layman from Kyoto, the entire community of the nuns, and Father Yasuda. We found the face of the Blessed Mother freshly bathed in tears. This had been the twenty-third such occurrence."

"I fixed my gaze on the appealing, though immobile and impassive, countenance of the statue. I contemplated the holy tears, so clear and bright, sparkling like crystal, as dew on a morning rose, evocative of the Mystical Rose of Her Litany. Tears so silent... yet so eloquent! Warm, mysterious, and insistent tears! True human tears, just like those of all mothers."

"We then began to recite the Rosary with Fr. Yasuda leading the first decade of the Sorrowful Mysteries of the Rosary. As the third decade was recited, the tears which had collected at the base of the neck and in the folds of the raiment of the statue, started to flow most slowly down the bosom to the waistband, marking brilliant, moist traces."

"A large teardrop paused on the cheek below the right eye, seemingly about to fall, but it remained sparkling about to fall, like a gem throughout the Rosary. At the corner of the left eye, a smaller teardrop pearled, but it also stayed, as if the Mother of the God were restraining its fall. A very large teardrop swelled below the point of the chin, but it also remained for more than an hour, suggesting by its brilliance and clarity the transparence of the Immaculate Heart itself."

"The inspiration to record by photograph the tears of Our Lady, then took hold of me. After asking Her in mental prayer to excuse my juvenile familiarity as I intended no irreverence, I took a few moments to take some pictures, using a flash borrowed from Sr. Marguerite Ito."

"Fr. Yasuda said that the weeping of the statue in Akita can dispel, in the eyes of logical minds, any doubts concerning the celestial authority and supernatural authenticity of the messages confided to Sr. Agnes."

Chapter 2

Sister Agnes Sasagawa, Vessel of Suffering

SR. THERESE TOSHIKO KASHIWAGI, the mother superior, told me in an interview; "Sr. Agnes has a prayerful spirit. She loves to pray for others."

Sr. Agnes related her method of prayer in an interview with me. Sr. Agnes said, "When I pray, the numerous faces of people for whom I promised to pray appear on the screen of my heart and I concentrate my attention on each of them. Each time I recite one Ave Maria on one Rosary bead, I put an intention for the person in the prayer. During the prayers, I hold and press the Rosary bead firmly and strongly with my fingers."

"As the spiritual needs of those I carry in my intentions draw all my attention completely, there is no time for my mind and heart to be distracted by capricious ideas and thoughts. Many pilgrims ask me to pray for them and I promise to do so. If I should neglect my prayers for them, I would regard it as a sin of breaking a promise. If I neglect them, I imagine my heart would feel guilty for neglecting the prayers for those for whom I promised to pray. Providing lip service of praying for someone else is not a good thing, is it? It is because God is watching our hearts."

"I have always drawn encouragement and consolation from the part of the message of the Blessed Mother who said here, *'Prayer, penance, and courageous acts of sacrifices can soften the Heavenly Father's anger.'*"

During this interview, this author noticed that her many years of praying the Rosary has created a big callous on the forefinger of her right hand. At my request, Sr. Agnes shyly allowed me to touch the callous.

As the interview progressed, I asked her how she felt about Pope John Paul II. To this Sr. Agnes replied, "I like the Pontiff very much. I think that his humility is his most wonderful characteristic. His complete trust in the Blessed Mother is quite evident. I believe the Pontiff considers all human beings, especially Christians, as his spiritual children. I admire this characteristic in him "

Baptism of Sr. Agnes and Her Spiritual History

Sr. Agnes Katsuko Sasagawa was born on May 28, 1931, in Joetsu City in the prefecture of Niigata. Surrounded by affectionate family members, she was brought up in a happy warm-hearted home. Highly intelligent, but physically weak, she underwent many surgical operations. In April, 1949, at the age of 19, she had an appendectomy during which a doctor gave her a spinal anesthesis (i.e., anesthesia injected into a body part near her spine). The injection paralyzed her lower limbs making her bedridden for nearly 10 years.

Neighbors urged her father to file a lawsuit demanding compensation against the doctor who administered the spinal anesthesia. However, her pious Buddhist father rejected the neighbors' recommendation. Sr. Agnes quoted her father as saying at that time, "Human beings should not harbor any grudge or any feelings of vengeance against others. Besides, the doctor made a mistake in trying to cure my daughter's sickness." This father imparted the spirit of forgiveness, compassion, and kindness for others to Sr. Agnes from her childhood.

Immobilized in a hospital bed, Sr. Agnes, who had been a celebrated student with a splendid memory and fine reasoning ability, was plunged into a life of uncertainty and instability, transferring from one hospital to another.

But it was precisely in these bleak circumstances that Divine Providence pursued her. In the Myoko Hospital at which she was hospitalized on September 15 or 16, 1958, in the prefecture of Niigata, she befriended a kindhearted Catholic nurse by the name of Miss Haru Watanabe, who gave her a book on the Catholic teaching of the love of God, written by Fr. Drouar De Lezey of the Paris Foreign Mission Society, entitled, *Shrinri no Hongen (The Source of Truth)*.

Concerning this book, Sr. Agnes said, "*The Source of Truth* was so wonderful that I read it three times." She was also influenced by books written by Professor Takashi Nagai, a saintly Catholic radiologist who threw himself and his medical skills into the service of the victims of the atomic bombing in 1945 in Nagasaki despite his own fatal radiation disease stemming from his exposure to A-bomb radiation and X-rays, that shortly took his life.

These books led Sr. Agnes to further studies of the Catholic faith until finally she officially began her catechesis from a Salesian missionary priest named Fr. Julien Sleuyter. Sr. Agnes said, "I was very moved by the great love of Fr. Sleuyter, who came to the Myoko Hospital every day for 40 consecutive days during that summer vacation season to teach me catechism."

After Fr. Sleuyter left, Fr. Camillo Concari, an Italian Franciscan, came to the hospital to teach her catechism once or twice a week. Fr. Concari spoke better Japanese. After seeing Sr. Agnes acquire a deep understanding of Catholic teachings, Fr. Concari agreed to baptize her into the Catholic Church around December in 1959.

Then, doctors at the hospital told her they decided to allow her to leave the hospital in October or November of 1959 in view of her physical improvement.

Around this time, Fr. Concari had a second thought and told Sr. Agnes, "I came to know your pure character and love for God. Judging from your character you would come to attend Mass every Sunday throughout the cold winter of this region despite your still-weak body. So let's wait for spring to come and bring a warmer air."

So, her baptism was postponed for five to six months until the severe cold winter of Niigata Prefecture passed.

Sr. Agnes told me, "When I was waiting for spring to come to receive my baptism, I was meditating upon the feelings of people of the Old Testament who had waited so fervently and patiently for the Savior to come."

"I felt as if I came to understand the feeling of the people of the Old Testament who waited for their Savior's coming fervently and patiently," she said.

The religion of her family was Buddhism. A Buddhist sect followed by her family was founded by Shinran, in the 13th century. Shinran, a Buddhist priest-cum-philosopher, taught a high-level ethical and moral teaching.

So, the family used to have close acquaintances among Buddhist priests.

When she was waiting for her baptism, a Buddhist priest, who learnd of her plan to accept baptism into the Catholic Church, came to visit her home to investigate her plan.

The priest asked her, "Why are you planning to accept baptism into the Catholic Church?"

Sr. Agnes replied, "Catholic teachings enabled me to understand the meaning of life very clearly, with the same clarity with which mathematical questions are solved. I came to know that even Shinran and Buddha were creatures of God and I came to believe it is right and ethical for a human being to believe and love the Creator of everything of the Universe."

Sister Agnes Sasagawa, Vessel of Suffering

The Buddhist priest then told Sr. Agnes, "I understood your feelings. Please pray for me, too." Then, he left. Sr. Agnes was baptized into the Catholic Church on April 17, 1960, at the age of 33 at the Naoetsu Catholic Church in Naoetsu City, Niigata Prefecture. The name of this city was later changed into Joetsu City.

Miss Watanabe, the nurse who introduced Christianity to Sr. Agnes during her bed-ridden years, said of Sr. Agnes in a direct conversation with this author, "I knew her pain and character. If I had been placed in her position of having to suffer so terribly, I would have committed suicide, unable to endure such extreme pain. Her noble spirit enabled her to endure the pain. Her spirit of nobility is distinct from our mediocre spirits."

Up to this time, Sr. Agnes underwent a total of 11 surgical operations on various parts of her body. At one time, she had her left collarbone separated in an operation designed to revive her numbed hand. Due to insufficient union of the separated collarbone, another operation had to be performed to insert a metal rod into her body which would hold the bones together. When I asked her to give us some advice for all the suffering people who may read this book, she said: "God never places a burden upon you which you cannot bear. Entrust and offer yourself up to God. Then God will support you and give you strength to stand the trial. *This trust and belief is the key.* Please live by drawing strength from faith. You are covered and protected by the hands of God, even while in your agony."

Awakened to the love of God, she was eager to serve God and neighbors. She wished to become a nun. Agnes was admitted to the convent of Junshin (Sisters of The Immaculate Heart of Mary) of Nagasaki on February, 28, 1962. However, four months after Sr. Agnes entered the convent, her physical illness gripped her again, causing her to become unconsious for 4 days. She was transferred to the Myoko Hospital in Niigata Prefecture again for treatment and rehabilitation. After she recovered fairly well after more than a year of rehabilitation training, she fell in a hospital bathroom and became unconscious for 10 days, starting on January 24, 1964. However, Divine Providence would work through her again. Some Lourdes water was sent from the convent in Nagasaki to the Myoko Hospital. The Lourdes water had been brought to the Nagasaki convent from France beforehand, probably, by a Divine arrangement. As the Lourdes water entered the mouth of the unconscious sister, she regained consciousness and her paralyzed limbs became mobile. The cure took place on February 2, 1964.

Her Years as Cathechist

Sr. Agnes was allowed to leave the hospital in 1965 following her recovery. Afterwards, she received an urgent request made by Fr. Stacchini Bernardo of the Takada Catholic Church in Joetsu City to work as a catechist at a newly-built mission church.

Fr. Bernardo, a Franciscan missionary, acted as a leader of the Legio Marie in China in the 1940's before coming to Japan. He was jailed for more than two years by the Chinese Communist Party from 1948.

Sr. Agnes agreed to comply with Fr. Bernardo's request after getting permission to do so from the mother superior of the Junshin convent, in Nagasaki, Sr. Yasu Esumi. Sr. Esumi told Sr. Agnes in a letter in responding to Sr. Agnes' question on how to reply to Fr. Bernardo, "Our convent is ready to accept you back. However, if God's plan for you is that you work there at the mission church, then you have to comply with Fr. Bernardo's request. If the time comes when you cannot make a living there, you are always welcome back at the convent."

Sr. Esumi was an example of love of neighbors for Sr. Agnes. When she had an encounter with Sr. Esumi on January 30, 1962, Sr. Esumi soon recognized the deep love for God in the soul of Sr. Agnes and decided to admit her to her convent on the spot. Sr. Esumi told Sr. Agnes, "Although our convent does not have a precedent of accepting someone who had been bedridden for over 10 years, what we want to accept are souls with the will to offer themselves entirely to God."

Sr. Yasu Esumi was a saintly nun who survived the 1955 atomic-bombing attack on Nagasaki. While suffering from the after-effects of radiation from the A-bomb, the nun continued to work hard for the underprivileged and the Catholic Church. She maintained deep devotion to Our Lady of Guadalupe.

In the autumn of 1975, two years after Sr. Agnes was admitted to the Institute of Handmaids of the Holy Eucharist, Sr. Esumi traveled all the way to Akita to give encouragement to Sr. Agnes. She gave Sr. Agnes her cherished wooden rosary.

On April 28, 1965, Sr. Agnes began working as a catechist at the Myoko Catholic Church in a borough near Joetsu City in the diocese of Niigata. She prayed much, worked hard as a catechist, and helped to prepare 70 catechumens to accept baptism into the Catholic Church.

Her mother, a Buddhist, came to visit Sr. Agnes repeatedly and stayed in the circuit church with her. When Sr. Agnes was teaching catechism to catechumens, her mother used to listen to her daughter's explanations of Catholic teachings in the same room, while making lace with a needle or was sitting at other needlework.

One day in 1965, her mother told Sr. Agnes, "I want to receive baptism into the Catholic Church."

Sr. Agnes was surprised at this sudden request from her own mother and asked, "Well, mother, why did you say such a thing?" Her mother replied, "Well, Kako-chan (nickname of Sr. Agnes), when I was listening to your explanations of God's teachings every day, while doing needlework, I became convinced of the truth of Catholic teachings."

Her mother was baptized into the Catholic Church on the Christmas of 1965. Her father also accepted baptism much later. Fr. Yasuda of the Akita convent baptized her father.

Akita: Mother of God as Coredemptrix

In her spiritual diary, (parts of which this author was able to obtain) Sr. Agnes wrote:

"My supreme joy was in being able to lead souls to God. I could forget any toil and labor whenever I saw the joyful faces of catechumens who had been baptized and started to lead a new life (of faith and love)."

She lived alone at the mission church structure, and on three different occasions she was forced to face burglars. One day, two knife wielding burglars broke into the church and demanding food, saying, "We were just freed from prison. Call and bring a bishop here!" Smiling her trepidation away, Sr. Agnes asked them to come to the kitchen. In an interview in 1991, Sr. Agnes said,

"I spoke to them while praying to God to soften their hardened hearts. Even when they pointed daggers at me, I had the conviction that, should they go so far as to kill me, God would support and save my soul. My constant yearning was to remain with God at every possible moment."

"I was convinced that God is really present in the Holy Eucharist in the chapel's tabernacle and that He never ceases watching and loving me. I was also determined to protect and defend the Holy Eucharist in the tabernacle... and God protected me from the danger."

Disarmed by her "fearless" attitude, they left. Sr. Agnes later related, "I wonder how I could have faced them with a smile. Yet, at the very moment they confronted me, I felt no fear." After watching them go, Sr. Agnes rushed to a neighbor's house, and on seeing the neighbor, belatedly became petrified with fright.

On another occasion, a burglar broke into the church and tried to scare her into handing over money and food. Sr. Agnes, responding very honestly to the burglar's demands said, "I have nothing but this." She then emptied a bag of sweets and offered them to him saying that she would bring him some tea.

Moved by her kindness, the robber grabbed her hands, started to weep and left with the confectioneries. On the third occasion, a burglar tried to threaten her into handing over money. As a poor catechist, she did not have the amount he demanded. Instead, she willingly handed him 20 yen out of her near-empty purse and told him, "You can buy a piece of milkbread with this money." The robber thanked her and left muttering, "...this woman who has nothing willingly gave me 20 yen... but others refused to give anything."

When a policeman finally arrived after being alerted by a neighbor, he asked her whether she really lived alone in the church building. Sr. Agnes answered, "Yes" and then added out of her usual honesty, "But I live here with God." Hearing her answer, the policeman seemed a little bewildered and appeared to be at a loss as to what to say to her.

Before entering the mother house of the Institute of the Handmaids of the Eucharist on May 12, 1973, Sr. Agnes had become a member of the institute on August 15, 1969 and continued her work as a catechist in the Myoko Catholic Church remaining spiritually united with the nuns at the mother house through deep prayer.

On March 16, 1973, she lost her hearing. In the morning, there was a phone call from the mother house of the Akita convent. She went to answer the call putting the receiver to her ear. She heard the bell, but in the next instant, when she placed the receiver on her ear, she realized that she had lost her hearing completely and found herself plunged into total silence.

When she was sitting on the floor in surprise at the sudden loss of her hearing, Fr. Camillo Concari visited the circuit church by chance to encourage her. Noticing her condition, Fr. Concari brought her to the Niigata Rosai Hospital for medical treatment and examination. She was hospitalized there around March 20.

Dr. Katsuro Sawada of the hospital diagnosed her deafness as "incurable" and completed legal document formalities for her, so that she can start receiving the government's medical allowances for the handicapped, such as deafness.

She was hospitalized for 47 days and learned lip-reading. Upon entering her new world of silence, she remembered the words Job uttered in grief when he lost everything. "The Lord gives, and now He has taken away. May His name be praised."

Sr. Agnes later said she felt her heart to be strengthened when she calmly thought she would offer up the suffering of her deafness for the love of God in accordance with the holy will of God.

Fr. Yasuda, said, "I think God allowed her to lose her hearing to help her concentrate and meditate upon the word of God ONLY, and not the words of human beings, to prepare her soul for her upcoming encounter with the Marian apparition during which she received the Divine messages."

Despite her deafness, Sr. Agnes received a letter from the Akita convent telling her she had been accepted as a member of the mother house of the convent. When she arrived at the convent on May 12, 1973, she was welcomed by the six nuns of the convent as if she were a family member.

On March 28, 1993, this author had a telephone interview with Dr. Tadahiko Yasuda, a medical doctor. Dr. Yasuda is a nephew of Fr. Yasuda. Dr. Yasuda lives in the city of Akita and has served as the doctor in charge of Sr. Agnes for many years,

He often comes to the convent of the Institute of the Handmaids of the Eucharist, whenever Sr. Agnes suffers from her physical sickness. He has diagnosed her for many years and knows her physical situation more deeply than any other doctor at present.

Sister Agnes Sasagawa, Vessel of Suffering

*(The following is the result of my interview
with this medical scientific expert.)*

Dr. Yasuda's Testimony

Dr. Yasuda said, "The physical sickness of Sr. Agnes Sasagawa is beyond any efforts to explain it scientifically. It is a mystery for me, who have accumulated experiences by diagnosing more than 200,000 patients over the past 30 years. She is special. Her body's temperature is very low and blood pressure is also very low. She takes only a small amount of water and beverages, I have not seen such a patient in my career as a doctor. Her invalidity is also beyond the reach of scientific explanation."

"Since she lost her eye-sight and consciousness last August 29, 1992, I went to the convent almost every day to treat her as a doctor. I regard her sickness and subsequent recovery of her eye-sight on October 2 as something which is beyond any scientific explanations."

"Yes, it is true that her body is weak, but Sr. Agnes does not show any traces or symptoms of being preoccupied with hallucination. She has not shown any paranoiac tendency. She does not show symptoms of hysteria. Her physical sickness has nothing to do with any hysteria."

"Hysteria essentially results from the desire to escape from the hard, tough and disagreeable realities. It is a temporary reaction. In contrast, her physical sickness has lasted long. We have to reject any allegation of a hysteria as something to explain her condition."

"When I think of her case, it revives the memory of a passage from Blaise Pascal's Pansees. Pascal said, 'we had better bet on an assumption that God exists and we live by that assumption.' When I feel like accepting Pascal's recommendation, I regard what happened to her and her physical conditions as something resulting from a supernatural intervention."

"I have a feeling that God's hand is working behind her physical conditions and behind what happened through her."

"I do not believe her current sickness and invalidity have any link or tie with her anterior series of physical sickness. I cannot believe her current physical situation is some type of after-effect of something of her past."

"I observed that Sr. Agnes has a kind, noble attitude for others. Futhermore, as a human, when other people offer their kindness to her, she accepts such kindness with gratitude. In this regard, she is quite an ordinary person."

"In the past, I have told my uncle (Fr. Yasuda) if a person tries to explain something which cannot be understood with human intellect alone, such efforts will only draw misunderstanding and prejudice against such mysterious events."

"If anyone tries hard to explain the mysterious events at the convent on the basis of science, then such efforts will prompt many critics and skeptics to try to suppress such efforts."

"I have heard that when Marian apparitions took place in Fatima or Lourdes, people did not have to explain the events scientifically."

"What is beyond the ability of human intellect and reason cannot be understood with human intellect and reason. It seems to me that the weepings of Mary's statue at the convent are the result of Divine efforts to help people understand the seriousness of sin and egoism tarnishing today's world."

"We have to clear up our souls and hearts and maybe we have grieved Mary. So I believe it is primarily important to reflect upon the meaning of the tears of Mary, rather than wasting time by trying to explain what happened in Akita scientifically."

The Poem of a Noble Soul

Sr. Agnes likes composing "haiku" poetry — traditional Japanese verses consisting of only 17 syllables with a seasonal reference. In such austere simple structure, the haiku poetry carries rich emotions and abundant implications, although the poetry does not rhyme. Edwin Reischauer, former U.S. Ambassador to Tokyo and noted Japanologist, once praised the haiku of the famous 17-century poet Basho, who could "conjure up a whole scene with all its emotional overtones in a simple phrase," as Mr. Reischauer put it.

One of Sr. Agnes' acquaintances who loves the beauty of her haiku poems offered to publish them in a book of 470 poems (selected out of some 2,000 haiku poems) which was published on July 26, 1985, under the title, *"The Dawn of Roses."* After publication, her haiku drew praise from a former veteran journalist of the Asahi Shimbun newspaper, Mr. Toshiyuki Miyamoto, who is deeply knowledgeable about the art of haiku poetry. In his review, Miyamoto said, "When I read Sr. Agnes' haiku, I could see the sincerity and nobility of her spirit, even though, technically speaking, her skill of haiku writing is still somewhat insufficient."

The following are some of the examples of her haiku poems and my English translations of them. It is extremely difficult to convey the beauty of the Japanese expressions used in these poems.

      Osanasae/   Ippo noboran/
Kurisumasu

(During Christmas, I meditated upon the teaching of my Lord, who told us to learn from children's pure and trustful hearts. I will make a sincere effort to attain the goal of attaining such virtues.)

      Danbono/   Heyani himotoku/
Junkyoshi

(In this convent room warmed by a heater, I read a book on the history of the martyrdom of the early Japanese Christian martyrs who endured bloody persecution. I want to learn from their faith)

Akita: Mother of God as Coredemptrix

Ainikuni/   Sakai nashitoshiru/
Ave Maria

(While reciting the Ave Maria in the Rosary with some South Korean pilgrims, I realized there are no national boundaries in people's love for God and the Blessed Virgin.)

Fudehajime/   Kamitokaki mata/
Aitokaki

(On this New Year's day, I took out a calligraphy brush and wrote the word "God, " then wrote the word "Love" all with two brush strokes on a white sheet of paper.)

Kamoshikano/   Nakamagaoshite/
Nozokiiru

(While at supper in the dining room, an antelope from a forest came into the convent and into the room, as though it were our friend.)

Yikiwakete/   Kamoshikaasobu/
Seiboen

(Passing through fields covered with snow, antelopes came to play at the Maria Garden of our convent.)

Sr. Kashiwagi said "Although Fr. Evangelista (the priest who wrote the report of the first investigative commission of the Akita events) alleged that Sr. Agnes is a psychopath, I believe these beautiful haiku poems evidence the healthiness and beauty of her spirit and mind."

The lengthy and profound psychoanalysis conducted by the Faculty of Medicine of the Akita University also verified in an official report that "there are no traces and tendency of mental diseases in the examined (Sr. Agnes) in her past and the present."

Dr. Masahiro Kuba issued this document of psychoanalysis. The psychiatrist said in an interview with this author in 1993, "I issued the document of psychoanalysis about Sr. Agnes Sasagawa officially as the medical doctor of Akita University."

Dr. Kuba now works as the chief of the Psychiatry Department of The Kakunodate Public General hospital, a large hospital in the city of Kakunodate in Akita Prefecture.

Cure of Deafness Comes Though Holy Eucharist

In the first message, the Blessed Mother promised the absolute healing of Sr. Agnes' deafness. (After a temporary cure, which lasted for 5 months from Oct. 13 of 1974, she relapsed into deafness on March 10, 1975.)

Fr. Thomas Yasuda, S.V.D., said, "The miraculous healing of her deaf ears, on October 13, has a profound meaning. The 'triple coincidence' of the date of the cure and the date of the third message of Akita and the date of the last Marian apparition in Fatima, it gave the Divine authentication of the truth of the message of the Holy Mother of Akita on October 13, 1973."

The date of the miraculous healing also revealed the profound connection between Akita and Fatima, where the Holy Mother gave her last message on October 13, 1917. Because so many Catholics ignore or downplay the importance of the messages of Fatima, God appeared to have drawn attention to the messages by sending the Holy Mother and an angel to Akita 56 years after the apparitions in Fatima. Akita events and messages also provide a clarification of the Fatima messages for reasons I will explain in this book.

The Holy Mother said in Akita on October 13, 1973 . *"If men do not repent and better themselves, the Heavenly Father will inflict a great punishment on all humanity... Fire will plunge from the sky and a large part of humanity will perish. The good as well as the bad will perish sparing neither priests nor the faithful."*

Akita: Mother of God as Coredemptrix

In Fatima, on October 13, 1917 some eye-witnesses of the "Miracle of the Sun" reported being given a vision of the Sun coming down above our heads.

It seems to me that this "Heavenly chastisement" predicted in Fatima and Akita is something which would be imposed as the result of a widespread denial of true Catholic doctrine and teachings, as well as sinful and immoral lifestyles of the many members of modern humanity who refuse to live up to the ten commandments of God.

Pope John Paul II said in his encyclical, "Veritatis Splendor," (Splendor of the Truth) released in October 5, 1993, "Today, it seems necessary to reflect on the whole of the Church's moral teaching, with the precise goal of recalling certain fundamental truths of Catholic doctrine, which, in the present circumstances, risk being distorted or denied."

The Pontiff also called on bishops to take "appropriate measures to ensure that the faithful are guarded from every doctrine and theory contrary to" the church's genuine moral teaching.

Before God cured the deafness of Sr. Agnes, her guardian angel appeared to her and predicted the upcoming healing in an apparent bid to call for attention and deep reflection about the profound meaning of the miraculous cure.

On May 18, 1974, the guardian angel told Sr. Agnes — among other things — *"Your ears will be opened in August or in October. You will hear, you will be healed. But that will last for only a short period because the Lord still wishes this offering and you will become deaf again. In seeing that your ears are restored again, the heart of those who still harbor various doubts will melt and they will believe."*

Sr. Agnes conveyed this angelic message to Fr. Yasuda in accordance with the angelic instruction to *"report what I have told you to him who directs you. But speak of it to no one else until it takes place."*

On September 21 of that year, the guardian angel told Sr. Agnes — among other things *"Today or tomorrow begin a novena, one of your choice, and then continue repeating it. During the course of three novenas, your ears will be opened and you will hear during your adoration of the Lord truly present in the Holy Eucharist. The first thing that you will hear will be the chant of the Ave Maria which you are accustomed to singing. Then you will hear the sound of the bell ringing for the Benediction of the Most Blessed Sacrament."*

"After the Benediction, ask calmly the one who directs you to have a Canticle of Thanksgiving sung. Then it will be known that your ears hear again. At that moment your body also will be healed and the Lord will be glorified."

"When your Superior (Bishop Ito) is informed of this cure, he will be filled with courage, his heart will be cleared and he will bear witness."

"However, the more all of you sisters offer with good intention, the more there will be difficulties and obstacles. To overcome these exterior obstacles, pray with more confidence with the solidarity of the community. (of the sisters) *You will be protected, be sure."*

After a silence, the angel added, *"Your ears will hear only for a short period. They will not yet be totally cured. You will become deaf again, because the Lord still wishes this offering. Report what I have told you to him who directs you."*

The healing came on the 22rd day after Sr. Agnes began the three rounds of novenas. This October 13 fell on the fourth day of her third novena. In the evening of October 13, (Sunday) the convent held the adoration of the Blessed Sacrament. Fr. Yasuda wrote as follows: "That evening exposing the Blessed Sacrament and incensing the altar, a thought crossed my mind: Could this not be the day? After the prayer of contrition, I returned to my place and joined in the Rosary. Then came the chant of the *Ave Maria* ... it was towards the end of the chant, Sr. Agnes prostrated herself on the floor and I saw that she was weeping. After the silent meditation and the usual prayers of Vespers came the moment of the blessing with the Holy Eucharist. One heard the sharp tingle of the bell rung by one of the sisters. Raising the monstrance, I traced the Sign of the Cross praying, "Lord, give Your grace according to Your Will!"

"Then kneeling before the Blessed Sacrament exposed, I began the litany of divine praises, "Blessed be God..." At the end as I was getting ready to indicate a hymn, Sr. Agnes, to whom I had turned my back, spoke, "My Father, may we sing the *Te Deum*, hymn #12!"

"I immediately turned around and said, "Do you hear again?"

"Yes, I have just received this grace," she answered, without need of having to read my lips.

Therefore, I told the congregation. (On Sunday, there were also lay Catholic people from outside who came to attend the Benediction) "Today, as the angel had predicted two times in May and in September, the ears of Sr. Agnes have been restored to hearing; this has just happened. In thanksgiving let us sing the *Te Deum.*"

The news of her healing seemed to have produced a strong impression on those present who were unable to believe their ears. Some sobs were heard when the congregation were singing the *Te Deum* in an atmosphere charged with emotion, according to Fr. Yasuda.

Sr. Agnes said as follows about the occasion of her healing, "At the moment of Benediction of the Blessed Sacrament, as the angel had predicted before, I first heard the voices singing the Ave Maria as though in the distance, as though in a dream. I heard only the voices and nothing else. Then there were some moments of silent meditation followed by the usual evening prayers, but of those I heard absolutely nothing. At the very instant when Father gave the blessing with the Blessed Sacrament, I clearly heard the sound of the bell. Then I heard him begin, "Blessed be God... " It was the first time I was hearing his voice."

"In the beginning when I heard the singing of the *Ave Maria,* an immense feeling of gratitude filled my heart at the thought that God had leaned down to so small a thing as I. I was so overcome that I prostrated myself weeping. Finally, able to stifle my voice, I no longer even found words for prayer."

"During the year and seven months that I had been plunged into a world of total silence, my parents were desolate and it was for me a tension renewed with each day. Even now that my hearing was restored, I knew that a day would come when I would have to suffer the privation of hearing once again and I fortified myself, thinking that it was necessary to continue to pray with more faith."

Immediately, a telephone call was made to Bishop Ito to give him the wonderful news. Sr. Agnes herself, told the bishop everything and answered his questions. She was also able to telephone her parents and close relatives to tell them of her unbelievable cure.

On the instruction from the bishop, Fr. Yasuda accompanied Sr. Agnes to the hospital of the Red Cross and to the Municipal Hospital of Akita to have the hospitals conduct a medical examination of her ears the following day (October 14). Both hospitals issued medical certificates verifying that her ears were now normal.

Bishop Ito reported this miracle to Cardinal Ratzinger, along with other details, in his March 13, 1982 report.

In the 19-page report, whose copy the bishop gave me, the bishop said, "On October 13, 1974, by which one year and three months had elapsed since the first Marian apparition on July 6, 1973, when the Holy Mother predicted the healing, Sr. Agnes' ears revived their hearing ability suddenly. In the evening, she made a telephone call from Akita to me in Niigata City, and we engaged in normal conversation over the phone."

Her miraculous cure encouraged the bishop very much. Shedding his hesitancy, the bishop decided to request a serious study of the mysterious events and messages by theologians by bringing to them some one hundred pages of manuscripts written by Fr. Yasuda on the basis of the analysis of Sr. Agnes' spiritual diary and, based on Fr. Yasuda's interview with Sr. Agnes and other nuns of the community.

Akita: Mother of God as Coredemptrix

This cure proved to be the first major development which led the bishop to take the action, thereby bringing the apparition of the Holy Mother at Akita to the knowledge of the public.

Before this cure was effected, Bishop Ito was troubled by his doubt that the third Marian message of Akita about the Heavenly chastisement might have been a repeated version of what had been reported to be the third secret of Fatima. He suspected that Sr. Agnes might have obtained knowledge of this message at Fatima by reading leaflets about it in the past.

When Fr. Yasuda asked her about this, Sr. Agnes answered without ambiguity that she had never seen anything of this kind. The doubt of the bishop was alleviated when the miraculous cure of her ears took place on October 13, which is the anniversary of the final message of Fatima.

The bishop was aware that arranging the coincidence of the date of the cure and the date of the messages of Fatima and Akita is completely beyond human power.

In his 1982 report to Cardinal Ratzinger, Bishop Ito noted this coincidence of the date of two happenings. He wrote, "The third message of Akita was delivered on October 13, which corresponds to the date of the final apparition in Fatima."

When the bishop decided to request the inquiry by theologians, following the encouraging miraculous cure, he decided to make no change in the text of the third message and submit it to examination by theologians.

It was on November 4, 1973, that Sr. Agnes could communicate the third message of Akita to the bishop, who visited the convent on that day. Because Sr. Agnes did not know the meaning of the word, "cardinal," she asked the bishop, "What does that mean 'cardinal?'" Sr. Agnes was referring to the Western-language word, 'cardinal,' used by the Holy Mother when the Holy Mother said, "The work of the devil will infiltrate even into the Church in such a way

that one will see cardinals opposing cardinals, bishops against the other bishops."

Bishop Ito was impressed by her question, and answered, "The word means 'sukikyo' (Cardinal in Japanese)." She said then, "Ah good! Then that was it?" She had finally understood. "Yes, 'sukikyo' I learned that word in my catechism, but I had never heard that Western language word and I was asking what that could be."

This simple detail shows that Sr. Agnes was completely incapable of having invented the text of the messages.

About 7 years and 5 months after the initial cure of her deafness was brought about by Jesus in the Holy Eucharist, the complete, permanent healing was effected again by Jesus in the Eucharist on May 30, 1982, according to the medical certificates issued by scientists and the bishop's pastoral letter.

On March 25, 1982, before her permanent cure was effected, an angel had announced to Sr. Agnes as follows:

"Your deafness causes you to suffer, doesn't it? The moment of the promised cure approaches. By the intercession of the Holy and Immaculate Virgin, exactly as the last time, before Him who is truly present in the Eucharist, your ears will be definitely cured in order that the work of the Most High may be accomplished. There will still be many difficulties, sufferings and obstacles coming from outside. You have nothing to fear. If you endure those difficulties and offer up those sufferings to God, you will be assuredly protected. Pray well by offering up everything to God. Convey what I said to the priest who guides you spiritually and ask for his guidance and prayers."

Finally, on the last Sunday of the month of Mary, the 30th of May, 1982, (Feast of Pentecost) at the moment of Benediction of the Blessed Sacrament, her ears were instantly and completely cured.

On May 31, Sr. Agnes went to the Red Cross Hospital at Akita to have her ears examined precisely and thoroughly by Dr. Tatsuhiko Arai of its Ear, Nose and Throat Section. The examination verified that her ears were cured perfectly. The doctor, moved by the cure, stood up with all the nurses at the section and bowed his head deeply toward her, saying, "Congratulations for your cure."

On June 14, Bishop Ito visited Dr. Tatsuhiko Arai at the hospital at Akita. The doctor had diagnosed Sr. Agnes' deafness as total, from the time when she had moved to Akita nine years earlier. The bishop asked about his current opinion about the total care. Seeing her now entirely cured Dr. Arai told the bishop that he regards it as a "miraculous cure," but the "custom of modern medicine" bans him from using the word "miracle" in the certificate he issued. (Note: See Appendix _ for this medical certificate.)

Medical Certificate of Her Cure

Meanwhile, another Japanese medical scientist, Dr. Katsuro Sawada, the physician who had first examined her at the Rosai Hospital of Joetsu City, also issued a medical certificate, dated June 3, 1982, attesting that the minute examination of her auditive capacities proved that there was no further anomaly in the two ears of Sr. Agnes Sasagawa.

Here, I want to call readers' attention to an episode in 1986 that teaches us what great consolation God gives to a humble soul on fire with love for God.

Years ago, Sr. Agnes had lost the wooden rosary given to her by Sr. Yasu Esumi, the mother superior of Nagasaki's Junshin convent somewhere in the spacious premise of the convent surrounded by the woods of the Hill of Yuzawadai.

Sr. Esumi gave the rosary to Sr. Agnes in the autumn of 1975, when she paid a visit to the Akita convent and stayed for a few days after travelling more than 1,000 kilometers from her convent in Nagasaki.

She was saddened very much at the loss of the cherished rosary given by her spiritual benefactor. A few years had passed since she got a new rosary to pray with in lieu of the wooden rosary. Meanwhile, it was Sr. Agnes' habit to feed birds that fly to her window-sill every morning by placing some remaining crumbs of bread from nuns' breakfast table on a brown plastic plate on the windowsill. The birds liked Sr. Agnes, judging from the fact that the birds used to enter her second-floor room at the wooden convent after Sr. Agnes went to bed.

Sr. Agnes had to close the window of her second-floor room if she wants to have a sound sleep, as the birds used to kiss her cheek or arms with their beaks awakening her. Among the birds there was a couple of robins that are a bit bigger than other small birds.

In recent years, Sr. Agnes usually gets up at 3:00 to 3:30 a.m. and starts praying. After the personal prayers, she joins the reciting in choir of Divine offices and morning prayers at the convent, that start at 6:00 a.m.

On June 15, 1986, Sr. Agnes was awakened — before 5:00 a.m. by the noise made by the pair of robins outside her windows. Sr. Agnes used to name the pair "Peasuku and Peako."

Sr. Maria Therese Kazuko Kaizu said, "The pair of birds twittered to Sr. Agnes in such a tender way that I wondered why the wild birds could cause such a commotion." Sr. Maria has been a close friend of Sr. Agnes. On the morning of June 15, she was also awakened by the noise made by the birds' beaks, along with Sr. Agnes, as Sr. Maria's room is next to that of Sr. Agnes. Then, Sr. Maria was listening, as the following event took place in Sr. Agnes' room.

Puzzled at the unusual early-morning visit by the pair, Sr. Agnes left her bed and approached the window pane, saying, "What are you doing this early morning, Peasuku and Peako? Are you hungry?"

The robins, their wings vibrating, were seen suspended in one place in mid-air outside her window.

Then, Sr. Agnes noticed there was something glittering on the windowsill. Sr. Agnes wondered, "What is this?"

The tiny glittering object was the small "miraculous medal" she used to attach and tie to her long-lost wooden rosary.

Along with the medal, she found her long-lost rosary on the windowsill. It was the rosary which Sr. Esumi gave to Sr. Agnes eleven years ago. Surprised, Sr. Agnes asked the birds, "Oh, did you bring the rosary back to me?" Sr. Agnes started weeping at the mysterious Divine providence and the tenderness of the birds. Then, she noticed that some red blood was clinging to the beak of "Peako," which apparently had to open its beak wide to pinch the rosary in carrying it back to the windowsill of the second floor room of Sr. Agnes.

After confirming that Sr. Agnes picked up the rosary, tarnished by the soil, the pair of robins flew away and have never returned since.

The rosary and the miraculous medal is still kept at the convent as a precious reminder of how kind God is to a soul who loves Him and His Holy Mother with all its might.

Nuns at the convent call it the "Tori no rosario" or "The rosary of the bird." It may be another encouragement that God gave to inspire people to recite the rosary more often to receive ample Divine blessings through the devotion.

Chapter 3

Position of Catholic Church
Authority to Judge Apparitions

IN 1976, BISHOP ITO asked the Archbishop of Tokyo, Monsignor Peter Seiichi Shirayanagi, to establish the first commission of Inquiry into the Marian apparitions in Akita. The archbishop created the first commission and became its president. Two years later, the commission issued a conclusion written solely by Fr. Garcia Evangelista questioning the supernatural character of the apparition in Akita.

However, the bishop learned from Archbishop Jerome Hamer, then deputy Prefect of the Congregation of the Doctrine of Faith, that the Holy See primarily gives the authority to judge the apparitions to the local ordinary (*Ordinarius Loci*).

In this case, the local ordinary was Bishop Ito himself. Fr. Evangelista was a mere member of the first commission that does not have any authority regarding judgments on apparitions. The first six-member commission did not even include Bishop Ito, the very prelate with the highest primary authority on this issue.

Fr. John Masayuki Shirieda, a Salesian, and a member of the Pontifical Commission on Inter-religious Dialogue, told the bishop and me when this author accompanied the bishop to the Holy See in 1988 as the bishop's secretary, as follows;

Fr. Shirieda said, "The first commission of inquiry does not have any canonical legality, because the authority to hand down a conclusion regarding the authenticity of any Marian apparition is given canonically to the ordinary of the local diocese where the apparition took place — In the case of Akita, the very ordinary is you, bishop!"

Vatican Document on Judgment of Apparitions

The Holy See's guidelines regarding judgment of the genuineness of Marian apparitions was issued in writing in 1978 by the Congregation for the Doctrine of Faith. Its complete name in Latin is, "Normae S. Congregationis Pro Doctrina Fidei Modo Procedenti In Diudicandis Praesuptis Apparitionibus ac Revelationibus." In English, this literally is translated as "The guidelines and norms of the Congregation of the Doctrine of Faith regarding the Methods and Procedures for Judging the Alleged Apparitions and Revelations."

This guideline document is signed by Cardinal Franjo Seper, then the Prefect (chief) of the Congregation. Cardinal Seper, a Croation, was a wise advisor to Pope Paul VI.

The document says, "Officium invigilandi vel interviendi praeprimis competit Ordinario loci." Translated, this means, "The responsibility and work to constantly watch the developments of an apparition and INTERVENE come primarily under the authority and jurisdiction of the local bishop."

Archbishop Francis Xavier Kaname Shimamoto of Nagasaki concurred with the view of Fr. Shirieda, the Vatican official whose heartfelt books are extensively read by both Christians and non-Christians in Japan. The archbishop said in an interview with this author, "A Catholic church guideline regarding the procedures to judge the truthfulness of an apparition gives the authority to judge the supernatural character of an apparition to the local bishop of the diocese in which the apparition in question takes place. Therefore, I believe what Bishop Ito declared in his pastoral letter on the Marian apparition in Akita."

Archbishop Shimamoto, the current president of the Catholic Bishops' Conference of Japan (CBC Japan), also said, "Someday I myself may make a pilgrimage to Akita. A recent foreign Catholic press allegation which gave the impression that the Japanese episcopal conference is in opposition to the apparition in Akita is an exaggeration."

Unconvinced by the negative conclusion of the first commission of inquiry, Bishop Ito went to Rome in 1979 to meet with Cardinal Franjo Seper, who advised him to impanel "the second commission of inquiry," with the authority given to the bishop by the universal Catholic Church.

Thus, in 1979, upon the advice of the Holy See, the bishop established the seven-member second commission of inquiry. Unlike the first commission, this commission came to a positive conclusion.

On September 12, 1981, the commission of inquiry, after three years of investigation, voted to approve the supernatural character of the messages of the Blessed Mother and the mysterious events in Akita in a 4 to 3 ruling.

On the very day, the statue of the Blessed Mother shed tears for the 100th time at 8:44 a.m. before 13 eye-witnesses including two visiting nuns of the Nerima convent of the Caritas Sisters of Miyazaki in Japan.

The news of the 100th weeping was immediately conveyed by telephone by Sr. Therese Kasiwagi, the mother superior, to the commission at its final meeting, and which was on the verge of its vote concerning the authenticity of the apparitions. Still, an unconvinced member told the committee:

"We should not recognize the tears from the statue of the Blessed Mother as an important evidence of miracle. Unless a miracle more spectacular than the miracle of the weepings takes place, we should not recognize the supernatural character of the apparitions in Akita."

However, the seven-member commission voted to recognize and approve their authenticity.

Fr. Yasuda wrote in his book, "The more weak the faith, the more one requires spectacular signs. The numerous miracles operated by Christ were also denied by many Jews who refused to accept the divinity of Jesus. It may not be surprising that the statue of Mary weeping a hundred times was dismissed by some as not being sufficient enough evidence for them to accept the supernatural authenticity of the apparition."

On April 22 of 1984 (Easter Sunday), — after an investigation of more than 10 years — Bishop Ito solemnly issued a pastoral letter, in which he recognized and proclaimed the supernatural character of the apparition and messages of the Blessed Mother Mary and the guardian angel of Sr. Agnes.

The bishop declared the celestial authenticity of the Marian apparition in Akita on the strength of the power given to him by the Congregation of the Doctrine of Faith's guidelines on the judgments of apparitions.

In the conclusion of the pastoral letter, the bishop wrote, "After the investigation conducted up to the present day, I cannot deny the supernatural character of a series of mysterious events concerning the statue of the Holy Mother Mary which is found in the convent of the Institute of the Handmaids of the Sacred Heart of Jesus in the Holy Eucharist at Yuzawadai, Soegawa, Akita. I do not find in these events any elements which are contrary to Catholic faith and morals. Consequently, I authorize throughout the entire diocese, with which I am charged, the veneration of the Holy Mother of Akita, while awaiting that the Holy See's definitive judgment on the matter."

Position of Bishop Francisco Sato, Current Ordinary

Bishop Ito resigned as the local ordinary of the diocese on June 9, 1985 — more than 13 months after the issuance of the pastoral letter on the Akita apparitions.

The current ordinary of the diocese of Niigata is Bishop Francisco Keiichi Sato, a Franciscan. He assumed the post of Ordinarius Loci on the same day — on June 9, 1985.

Bishop Aloysius Nobuo Soma, the chairman of the Peace and Justice Committee of the Japanese Episcopal Conference, told me, "Now, we have to listen to the thoughts of Bishop Sato on the apparition matter, as he is the ordinary of the Niigata diocese."

On July 24th and 25th of 1993, Bishop Sato joined various forms of devotion and worship at the convent of the apparition in Akita, along with some 400 pilgrims who traveled to Akita to attend the ceremony marking the completion and consecration by the bishop of a new convent building there. On July 24, the bishop and pilgrims joined the rosary procession led by the miraculous statue of the Holy Mother placed on a beautiful flower-decorated palanquin which was carried by several faithful.

While reciting five decades of the holy rosary, the procession departed from the convent, followed beautiful village paths and then returning to the Maria Garden of the convent, a spacious traditional Japanese-style garden for Christian meditation and prayers.

Shinji Nishimura, a pilgrim from Chiba, south of Tokyo, said, "When people made the rosary procession, I was one of those who carried the palanquin of the Holy Mother Mary. I was so happy that I felt as if I were dreaming a happy dream."

On July 25, Bishop Sato presided over a Mass he concelebrated with Fr. Yasuda and five other priests. During the Mass at the Maria Garden, 35 pilgrims joined the convent's third order comprising some 7,000 Japanese and foreign associate members.

Akita: Mother of God as Coredemptrix

In a homily Bishop Sato delivered to the pilgrims and nuns, he expressed hope that Akita will develop further as an international place of pilgrimage. The bishop said the examples of nuns' and the Japanese faithful of kneeling in front of God and trusting God's love would draw God's graces further.

"Through our example of living (as a good Christian), I hope that this place will develop further as a place of pilgrimage." the bishop said in the homily in front of some 400 Japanese and foreign pilgrims.

After the morning Mass, the bishop, nuns and the pilgrims shared their joy at a luncheon banquet accompanied by various singings and recreations. Bishop Sato himself sang solo, while playing his accordion. When Fr. John Hayashi, a member of the Marian Movements of Priests, and some members from his Maruyama Church sang an old pop song, the bishop played the accompaniment on his accordion without the scores."

Then, the nuns sang a Polish folk song to the accompaniment of two guitars played by two of the nuns.

In the afternoon, the bishop celebrated the "Benediction" at the convent chapel, beginning the litany of divine praises in front of the monstrance he placed on the altar, and chanting, "Blessed be God" in the solemn devotion that wrapped up the two-day ceremony.

The fact that the bishop told the 400 pilgrims and nuns that "I hope this place will develop further as a place of pilgrimage" carries the profound providential significance. The episcopal declaration and expression of his hope for further development of Akita as an oasis of Divine graces for international pilgrims was the Divine gift for the universal Catholic Church.

When we ponder on the following provision of the Holy See's guideline and norms of the episcopal judgments on the authenticity of a certain Marian apparition, the significance of this episcopal declaration will be made clear.

The Position of the Church

The Congregation of the Doctrine of Faith's "Normae De Modo Procedenti in Dijudicandis Praesumptis Apparitionibas ac Revelationibus" says, "Deinde, Si hoc examen favorabile habuerit, permittere aliquas manifestationes publicas cultus vel devotionis simulque super eas magna cum prudentia invigilare. (quod aequivalet formulare pro nunc nihil obstare.)"

These Latin sentences are translated as follows: "If a bishop (of the diocese where the apparition took place) reached the conclusion that the apparition is favorable for the faithful, the Ordinarius Loci (the local bishop) is authorized by the Church to permit various public manifestations of worship and devotions (at the site of the apparition) while continuing to observe the situation always with the maximum prudence. Such episcopal permission is tantamount to declaring the apparition is "nihil obstare" (i.e. corresponds with Catholic faith and morals) in the form of a written document."

In accordance with the Holy See guidelines and norms, Bishop Sato authorized the public manifestation of devotion to the Marian apparition in Akita and the bishop himself joined various devotional activities, such as the Rosary procession along with the miraculous statue, the Mass and Benediction on July 24 and 25, 1993. Bishop Sato was the chief celebrant at the Mass and Benediction. (See the photos of Bishop Francisco Sato.)

Bishop Sato's Letter to Japanese Bishops

On top of this, Bishop Francisco Sato sent a letter in September, 1990 to Archbishop Peter Seiichi Shirayanagi, then the President of the Catholic Bishops' Conference of Japan (CBC Japan).

In the official letter of grave importance, Bishop Sato declared that he decided to continue to uphold and maintain Bishop Ito's authorization of the veneration of the Holy Mother of Akita.

Bishop Ito concluded in his pastoral letter that the mysterious events in Akita are supernatural and, therefore, Catholics should be authorized to express their veneration for the Holy Mother Mary of Akita.

The letter of Bishop Sato to the archbishop of Tokyo also pointed to conversions and miraculous cures that have taken place among pilgrims to the convent of the apparition, according to Bishop Ito.

Archbishop Shirayanagi received this letter in September, 1990. Two months later — on November 29, 1990, — the archbishop, as then president of the episcopal conference, read out the letter to all the seven bishops and archbishops of the Standing Committee of the Episcopal Conference.

The attendants at the conference included the present President of the Episcopal Conference, Archbishop Francisco Kaname Shimamoto, and Archbishop Hisao Yasuda of Osaka, Bishop Nobuo Soma, Bishop Satoshi Fukahori, Bishop Chisato Sato, Bishop Fumio Hamao, as well as Bishop Ito.

Bishop Ito later told the Akita International Conference in 1992, attended by 150 bishops, theologians, priests and the faithful from 80 dioceses from around the world, as follows:

"This meeting (of the Catholic Bishops' Conference of Japan) took place on November 29, 1990, with all the members of the Standing Committee in attendance. While we discussed the phenomenon, Archbishop Shirayanag of Tokyo, read a letter from Bishop Francisco Keiichi Sato, the Bishop of Niigata."

"Bishop Sato, who accepted my pastoral letter, remarked that there are numerous pilgrimages to the site in Akita and that conversions and miraculous cures have taken place there," he said.

After knowing the contents of the letter from Bishop Sato, the Standing Committee, the decision-making panel of the Catholic Bishops' Conference of Japan (CBC Japan), decided to "obey unanimously" the judgment of Bishop Sato during the session of the conference on November 29, 1990, according to the official records of the conference. The decision was issued in the form of a printed statement from the General Secretariat of the CBC Japan on December 4, 1990, which carries the seal of the Chairman of the CBC-Japan's standing committee, Archbishop Shirayanagi.

The official statement said the episcopal conference decided to obey Bishop Sato's decision to authorize the veneration of the Blessed Mother of Akita in accordance with "Normae de modo Procedenti in dijudicandis praesumptis apparitionibus ac revelationibus" issued by the Holy See's Congregation of the Doctrine of Faith in February, 1978.

The "Normae" says a national episcopal conference can intervene in the judgment of the authenticity of an apparition only if a local bishop agrees to such intervention.

The original Latin text says "Conferentia Episcopalis regionalis vel nationalis intervenire potest; (a) si Ordinarius loci, postquam suam egerit partem, ad ipsam recurrat ad tutius rem diudicandam; (b) si res ad ambitum nationalem aut regionalem iam pertineat," "Semper tamen praevio consensu Ordinarii loci."

These sentences translate as follows: "The national or regional Episcopal Conference may intervene under the following conditions, but the conferences must always obtain the approval of the local bishop for such interventions."

(a) "If the Episcopal Conference believe they have to request the review of the local bishop's judgment, after the local bishop invoked his authority to judge."
(b) "If the alleged apparition has already, become a national or regional issue."

In the case of Akita, Bishop Sato, the current ordinary of the Niigata diocese, declared, in the letter to the President of the CBC Japan, that he decided to take over the conclusion of his predecessor Bishop Ito, who authorized the veneration of the Blessed Virgin

Akita: Mother of God as Coredemptrix

Mary of Akita. Therefore, the CBC Japan said it decided to "obey unanimously" the judgment of Bishop Sato in accordance with the "Normae" of the Holy See.

The "Normae" says: "Officium invigilandi vel interveniendi praeprimis competit Ordinario Loci." This means: "The responsibility and work to constantly watch the developments of an apparition and intervene come primarily under the authority and jurisdiction of the local bishop."

When the Marian apparitions occurred in Lourdes and Fatima, the Holy See respected the judgments of the local ordinaries of the dioceses of those places. Although the Holy See never issued any official documents confirming the authenticity of these apparitions, the local bishop's judgments automatically became the position of the Holy See, as in the case of Akita.

For example, in the case of Fatima, the local ordinary of the diocese of Leiria-Fatima, Bishop Jose Correia Da Silva, issued a pastoral letter on October 13, 1930, declaring that he, using the jurisdiction over the matter given him by the Catholic Church, authorized the veneration of the Our Lady of Fatima.

Thirteen years had elapsed after the first apparition when this declaration was issued by the bishop of Fatima.

It is well-known that Pope John Paul II made pilgrimages to Fatima on May 13, 1982 and 1991, to thank Mary for protecting his life from the bullet of an assassin, who shot him on May 1 3, the anniversary of the first of the 1917 Marian apparitions in Fatima.

Before episcopal recognition was given to the Fatima apparitions in 1930 by the local bishop (and, thus, automatically by the universal Catholic Church) the three visionary children, Lucia, Jacinta and Francisco, used to suffer terrible slander, opposition and persecution. In response to these ordeals, the shepherd children offered up their sufferings to God in cooperation with the Divine work of salvation.

It is not surprising, then, that the apparition in Akita also came under slander and persecution. In Fatima and Lourdes also, Satan used both skeptical Roman Catholics and agnostic people to oppose and discredit the apparitions in these two holy places.

Undoubtedly, Satan is well aware of the great spiritual benefits that would stream into a person's soul should the soul make a pilgrimage to one of these places of apparition, humbly accept the messages of the Heavenly Mother, and begin applying the Heavenly instructions to their lives. Naturally, Satan will do his utmost to discredit such fountains of grace.

On the contrary, it seems to me that such Satan-induced human opposition actually gives credence to the authenticity of the apparitions in Akita. So, too, does it authenticate the greatness of the divine gifts prepared by God for numerous Roman Catholics and others through an ongoing process towards the full flowering of devotion to the Our Lady of Akita.

During the Marian year on September 15, 1987, His Excellency Archbishop William Aquin Carew, Apostolic Nuncio to Tokyo, visited the convent, accompanied by Bishop Francis Keiichi Sato, the present ordinary of the Niigata diocese, Bishop John Shojiro Ito, Fr. Taisuke Ishibashi, then provincial of the Japanese branch of the Society of the Divine Word, and three other priests.

The Apostolic Nuncio, during his 40-minute stay at the convent, first went to the chapel and prayed kneeling before the Holy Eucharist in the chapel's beautiful tabernacle. The statue of the Blessed Mother, which, by then had wept its total of 101 times, stood at the tabernacle's right.

The ambassador then addressed the nuns at the Akita convent. In the address, Archbishop Carew encouraged the nuns to continue following in the footsteps of Christ by bearing the crosses which God has given to each of the nuns by patiently enduring their daily sufferings, offering them with love to God. The archbishop also encouraged the nuns to make much of their sacred vocations, for which the Lord invited the nuns to serve Him. Sr. Theresa Toshiko Kashiwagi, the mother superior, later wrote in the convent's monthly bulletin, dated October 1, 1987, "All the nuns were deeply touched by the archbishop's warm kindness and encouragement."

Sometime after the speech, Archbishop Carew and his entourage were accompanied by Sr. Kashwagi on a tour of the convent. As they passed through the garden's archway of grape vines, Sr. Kashiwagi informed the archbishop that the archway was called the "Via Dolorosa" (Way of Sorrow). The archbishop then remarked to his entourage that the very date of this visit, September 15, is the feast day of the Our Lady of Sorrows. Then Bishop Ito remarked that the very date of the archbishop's visitation also fell "by coincidence" on the sixth anniversary of the last weeping of the wooden statue of the Blessed Mother of Akita, September 15, 1981, the 101st weeping. Before the archbishop left the convent, he gave the nuns his blessing. Remembering his blessing, Sr. Sumako Sugawara remarked,

"I still remember the archbishop's blessing. Coupled with his encouraging words, it strongly bolstered my spirit." In mid-November, two months later, the archbishop's heartfelt letter arrived at the convent, giving great joy to all the nuns. The letter stated, "It is a special grace to visit you and to see the place venerated by so many pilgrims gathered to honor Our Lady, Queen of the Universe and Mother of the Church. May Mary cherish and protect you and all visitors during this Marian Year, and bring each and every one to the everlasting Kingdom of Her Son."

Chapter 4

Testimonies of Eye-witnesses of Tears and Pilgrims

PILGRIMS OFTEN SAY that they are moved by the lives of these nuns who are totally devoted to the Eucharist. Their love is expressed in all of their daily activities and is seen in their genuine piety, evangelical poverty, cheerful dispositions and in their warm-hearted kindness. The key to their spiritual success is their deep prayer life which

Sisters working

is firmly centered in and around the presence of the Eucharist and which consists of silent prayer, common prayer, pious practices, the daily recitation of two Rosaries in common, and a holy hour after Mass.

The nuns pray together in choir for at least four hours a day. Other hours of the day are filled with personal prayer, looking after the needs of pilgrims, preparing meals and accommodations for them if they wish to stay for more than one day. In addition to these duties, they also make visits to the sick, teach catechism, perform their regular housekeeping chores and run errands into town. They also tend a small field where they grow vegetables and fruit, such as potatoes, pumpkins and apricots which are served as food to the pilgrims.

The nuns appear to have acquired a profound spirit of love and prayerfulness. Regarding the strong need for prayer, Sr. Kashiwagi, the mother superior said, "I pray to God that pilgrims, first of all, learn to love to pray." Fr. Joseph Marie Jacq likened the little convent to a "silent beehive, industrious and fervent, as was the House of Nazareth."

Five of 20 nuns of the Akita convent as well as Fr. Yasuda, witnessed nearly all the 101 weeping episodes of the statue. These five nuns are Sr. Theresa Toshiko Kashiwagi, Sr. Chie Ikeda (now-deceased mother superior), Sr. Saki Kotake (former novice mistress), Sr. Hiroko Owada and Sr. Agnes Katsuko Sasagawa.

Here, let me explain the brief history of the convent itself. Sr. Chie Ikeda and Sr. Saki Kotake were among the three founding nuns of the convent.

The pair and Sr. Agnes Sumako Sugawara asked Bishop Ito to approve their request to form a Pious Union in 1962, when the bishop was appointed to the ordinary of the Niigata diocese.

Around that time, Bishop Ito received a letter from Cardinal Gregorio Agagianian, then Prefect of the Congregation for the Propagation of the Faith, which was later renamed the Congregation of

Evangelization Cardinal Agagianian recommended the bishop establish a group of pious Japanese Catholic women to assist with the work of evangelization in his diocese. The Cardinal told the Bishop such a group would be useful in helping missionaries and Japanese priests evangelize the Niigata diocese, where the number of Catholic priests were very limited.

Inspired and encouraged by the cardinal's letter, Bishop Ito approved the foundation of this convent community on September 8, 1970. On this day, the bishop consecrated the convent's building in a ceremony attended by Catholic clergies and faithful in the Akita region. The convent started as a Pious Union with about 12 members.

The Marian apparition started on July 6, 1973... about three years after the episcopal approval of the foundation of the convent.

In the autumn of 1975, the intentionally acclaimed Japanese Catholic novelist, Shusaku Endo, visited the convent. Several million copies of Endo's novels have sold in more than 11 languages.

Based on his real experiences at the convent and interviews with eye-witnesses, the novelist later wrote two essays dealing with the apparition in Akita. In them, Endo expressed his opinions favorable to the apparitions and the life of honest poverty of the nuns.

In a 1991 interview in his condominium in Tokyo, Mr. Endo told me that he himself experienced a "fragrance of indescribable sweetness" from a Rosary brought by a pilgrim into the convent chapel, which became soaked with tears shed by the statue of Mary. Mr. Endo told me, "I still have the Rosary here in my study."

Mr. Endo said the Rosary beads were given to him by his friend, Mrs. Yoko Yamazaki and that the fragrance was transferred from the tears wept by the statue to the rosary beads when Mrs. Yamazaki's younger sister, Mrs. Nobuko Oshima, made a pilgrimage to the Akita convent. Mrs. Oshima handed over the rosary to her sister, who is also a talented writer.

Akita: Mother of God as Coredemptrix

This phenomenon of the fragrant Rosary beads inspired Mr. Endo to make a personal visit to the convent to learn more about the events there.

During his stay in Akita, Mr. Endo held several interviews with eye-witnesses, including Professor Eiji Okuhara, a Catholic physician in the Department of Biochemistry of the Faculty of Medicine of Akita University. Professor Okuhara is a former Rockefeller Foundation fellow. He conducted his advanced study of biochemistry in Columbia University in New York and then in Michigan State University in Lansing from 1959 to 1962.

Professor Okuhara had asked his colleague, Assistant Professor Kaoru Sagisaka, on January 24, 1975, to analyze the tears and blood which had been collected from the statue.

Professor Okuhara said he did not tell Associate Professor Sagisaka that the tears and blood were collected from the wooden statue. Prof. Okuhara said that he asked for the analysis by his non-Christian colleague to ensure objectivity.

In the autumn of 1975, Dr. Okuhara contributed an article to a newspaper for intellectuals and journalists. Dr. Okuhara lent a copy of the paper entitled "Journalists" to this author. The edition is dated September 15, 1975. Dr. Okuhara said in the article, "The scientific analysis proved that the specimen containing the blood from the wooden statue is stuck by real blood, moreover, by the blood of a human being. The test also proved that the tears collected from the statue is a human body fluid."

"I cannot help saying that I perceive as truly mysterious the fact that these series of phenomenon were observed by people who can be trusted most deeply and these specimens were scientifically identified as containing the ingredients identical to those of a human body liquid,"

This author had an interview with Dr. Okuhara on August 16, 1993. The scientist told me, "I found Sr. Agnes an ordinary person, just like Bernadette of Lourdes. Sr. Agnes' soul is full of Divine grace, probably from the time of her birth, like that of Bernadette. These two sisters can be compared to an empty vessel used by God," he said. "Both Bernadette and Sr. Agnes heard the voice of the Holy

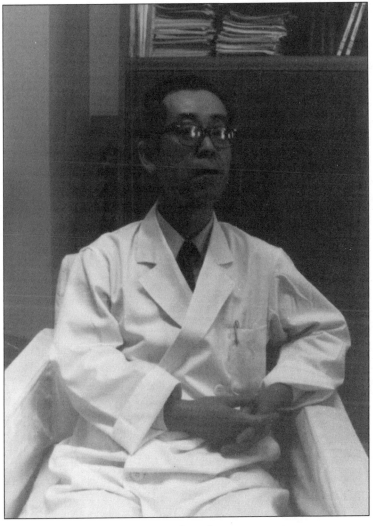

Dr. Sagisaka

Mother Mary, disregarding their intentions or efforts," he said. "I myself repeatedly observed the statue of Mary in the convent shedding tears," he said. He became an eyewitness after the initial scientific examination by Dr. Sagisaka was completed.

Dr. Okuhara told me on a separate occasion, "Associate Professor Sagisaka said if someone questioned the truth of the scientific tests and his medical appraisal documents (carrying the findings of the tests,) he is ready to anser any questions from anyone and defend the accuracy of the medical appraisal documents, because he has strong confidence in the scientific documents he wrote down."

Associate Processor Sagisaka made this statement after he was informed that the tears and blood were shed by the wooden statue following the issuance of his medical appraisal document concerning the tears and blood," Dr. Okuhara said.

After returning to Tokyo, Mr. Endo jotted down his reflections on "the fragrance of the Blessed Mother" he said he smelled from the rosary soaked with the tears from the statue, in one of his books:

Mr. Endo wrote, "If compassionate tenderness in a human heart had a fragrance, it would emit exactly this fragrance. It was the fragrance I knew of my mother during my childhood before she passed away. It was the fragrance of the compassionate tenderness which my heart has been without for a long time."

Mr. Endo is internationally renowned as the author of the bestselling novel, *Silence* — a story which vividly portrays the efforts of three Portuguese missionaries who smuggle themselves into 17th-century Japan to encourage the persecuted flock of Japanese Catholics and give sacraments to them.

In the interview with this author, Mr. Endo made it clear his two essays about his visit to the convent of the apparition are the reports of the real experiences of his own, rather than the fictitious product of his imagination.

Mr. Endo humbly wrote at the concluding sentence of his own report on Akita, "When I went to the convent, the Blessed Mother did not give me Her sweet fragrance. It seemed to me, it seemed as if Her failure to give it to me reflected Her judgment on my arrogant life and faith."

He continues, "I think the Blessed Mother of Akita called for people to repent and amend their lives, just as She did in Fatima and Lourdes."

Graham Greene once called Endo "one of the world's finest living novelists." (Greene is the famous British Catholic novelist whose novels entail profound theological or philosophical themes. As in the novels of Dostoevsky, Green's novels deal with sin and with the final victory of God's grace in the salvation for lonely souls enmeshed in such sins and temptations.)

When interviewed regarding the Marian messages given in Akita, Mr. Endo said:

"Because contemporary (and atheistic) academics and science have led people to neglect the true values which are most important to human beings,...and because people no longer have a sense of awe and reverence for God, they neglect the importance of showing true compassion and tenderness for others."

When asked as to whether he felt the Marian messages in Akita were an appeal for people to restore such compassionate tenderness in their hearts, the novelist answered, "Yes, I think so."

Dr. Teresa Chen-Tze Wei, M.D., a Catholic medical doctor who later obtained U.S. citizenship in the State of Kansas, acknowledged witnessing the Akita statue weep on September 15, 1978, when she made a pilgrimage to the convent. (She had long practiced medicine as a U.S. citizen in Japan.) Dr. Wei said:

"I am a doctor and a scientist. I will always maintain the truth of the statue's weeping, even if I'm called to witness before the most elevated of dignitaries." She survived the atomic-bomb in Hiroshima in 1945, and has long suffered from malignant myeloma (a type of tumor which occurs in the bone marrow) due to her past exposure to the A-bomb's deadly radiation. Dr. Wei had also sustained a compressive fracture of her eighth vertebrae. In spite of these ailments, she still works as a medical doctor for volunteer services in Taiwan, a home country of her husband, to which she moved in the spring of 1994.

Dr. Wei used to serve as a catechist for patients and medical staff in the hospital and for children at the church she attends. Through visits to Akita, she came to love the prayer of the Rosary deeply. About her devotion, she relates, "Whenever I faced various sufferings of my life, I learned to pray, crying for help to the Blessed Mother."

Using her own resources, she has built two mission churches in remote rural areas, "so that Catholics in these under populated areas can attend Mass on Sundays." She said her resolve to undertake such active gospel-like sacrifices strengthened "after visiting the Akita convent for the first time and coming to know the deep spiritual lives of Sr. Agnes and other nuns, who are full of love for God and neighbors in need."

"My sickness (malignant myeloma) is incurable," she states, "but I believe God and the Blessed Mother allowed me to recover my health temporarily, so that I can earn money to support the mission church in Murakami and provide a poor Chinese student with his school expenses. This is a small return to God for what He has given to me." As a scientist who has worked with many patients with mental diseases and psychological problems, Dr. Wei testified:

"I spent six days with Sr. Agnes at the convent and knew her character through intimate conversation and observance of her daily life. She is a perfectly normal person who does not have any psychological diseases. She has a compassionate character and is leading a holy life based on a genuinely deep love for the Holy Trinity."

"Sr. Agnes is a victim soul who joins with others in making reparation for the sins of the world by offering up sufferings to God. Many pilgrims ask for her prayers, and because of her holiness, I believe that God answers her prayers with special efficacy."

Dr. Wei also said, "I cannot agree to some Catholics' assertions that the Blessed Mother's stern prophecy of a Divine chastisement upon a corrupt mankind contradicts the Catholic teachings of Divine Mercy. What a strange assertion! Prophets in the Old Testament often warned that Divine Justice would strike the wicked. Jesus Himself said justice would be imposed at the last Judgment and declared that a Divine chastisement would strike the corrupt world. Such Catholics have only to read the Gospel of Saint Matthew and the prophesies of Isaiah and Jeremiah."

Another pilgrim, Mrs. Tamae Tominari, a Japanese housewife, and a devout mother of six children, said she believes that "the Blessed Mother, as the true mother of all people, is saddened by the wicked lives of many people. Her messages, stern as they seem, come from God's love. I think God wants people to make reparation for their sins, because He wants them to come to Heaven. Many people, even many Catholics, are reluctant to admit that they are leading sinful lives."

Mrs. Tominari went on to say, "People who condemn the messages of the Blessed Mother probably do not want to acknowledge the predicted perdition of the stubborn souls who refuse to amend their egotistic lives." She was referring to a part of the message given to Sr. Agnes on October 13, 1973, which says, *"The thought of the perdition of so many souls is the cause of My sadness. "*

Mrs. Haruko Tashiro, 77, a Japanese Catholic housewife who frequents the Akita convent, said that she and her husband, Fujio Tashiro, Emeritus Professor of the Tohoku University, along with other pilgrims, have witnessed large teardrops streaming down the statue's cheeks late in the afternoon of July 20, 1979. Mrs. Tashiro said the statue continued to weep tears throughout the recitation of five decades of the Rosary by the fourteen eye-witnesses. She expressed that she "was completely dumbfounded" as she gazed at the tears.

Akita: Mother of God as Coredemptrix

She continued, "I think the Blessed Mother's messages imply a call urging us to pray for world peace and for people suffering from famine and war, because the people suffering are our brothers and sisters of the same human family."

Fr. Daniel McCoy, a Jesuit professor at Sophia University in Tokyo, who visited the convent twice, said: "I think the message of the Blessed Virgin in Akita is neither grim nor dark, contrary to the assertions of some people. The message is one of warning, just as are her messages in Fatima and Medjugorje. "

"Her message admonishing Christians is true, because Christians are not praying enough to God and are not leading good enough lives these days. However, She is the Mother of all and She spoke to everyone. Each time I go there, I realize Her message more and more by meditating upon it."

"I was happy to see the humility of Sr. Agnes. She does not behave like a prima donna."

Sr. Mitten Maureen, an American Maryknoll sister working in Kyoto as a missionary, expressed her feelings:

"I was very very touched with the whole experience in Akita. I was impressed by the life of the sisters there."

Mrs. Mary-Arden Leeke from Swarthmore, PA, U.S.A., said:

"I have visited clinics and orphanages run by the Missionaries of Charity (of Mother Teresa), Maryknolls and Jesuits in Ethiopia and India, bringing such items as medicines and Rosaries."

"I noticed that the spirituality of the nuns in Akita was the same as that of Mother Teresa. The nuns treat each individual person and pilgrim with respect, so pilgrims feel comfortable and at home. Their deep love of their fellow human beings comes from their love of God and Mary."

"The nuns carry their love of Jesus into their work of prayer and serving pilgrims. Soon I will visit Ethiopia again as a volunteer. I think I will be able to transfer greater love and service to the people of Ethiopia, with my faith strengthened through my two visits to Akita."

Fr. Stanley Smolenski of the diocese of Hartford, Connecticut, expressed his sentiments as follows:

"I was impressed by the whole community's atmosphere, which was created by the nuns' simplicity and deep faith, joy and devotion to Our Lady and the Holy Eucharist as well as the uncomplicated truth of the seer. Much joy and peace fill the House of Mary (the convent's house accommodating pilgrims). It's a peace which the world can't give. The nuns have taken and integrated Japanese qualities of hospitality and graciousness with the Christian discipline of great spirituality."

Fr. Gerard McGinnity, an Irish priest, who holds a Doctorate in Patrology, and who is a veteran expert of contemporary Marian manifestations, said:

"My visit here was a once-in-a-lifetime experience for me. Each time I saw and heard the nuns' prayers, I sensed and detected a great sense of the presence of God here. The great respect and reverence for God and deep spiritual sensibility towards the presence of the Lord in the Tabernacle applies to every nun here. I have guided many retreats in Europe and have never been so impressed."

The parishioners of a church in Childs, Maryland, where Fr. John Conmy, OSFS, is Pastor, presented him with a pilgrimage tour to Akita as a birthday gift for his 80th birthday to expressed their gratitude for his long years of devout pastoral service. Fr. Conmy said that the trip to Akita was the best birthday gift he had ever received in his life.

Akita: Mother of God as Coredemptrix

Mr. Masahide Kanayama, who is both a Catholic and former Japanese Ambassador to Poland and South Korea, visited the convent in mid-February, 1988. Mr. Kanayama told me in a telephone interview, "Because God loves us, we should first change our egocentric hearts into more righteous ones and reflect on whether we really love God, before fearing or complaining about the sternness of the messages (predicting the coming of a chastisement). The messages are a warning about the present sinful world conditions."

"The Blessed Mother appears to be calling on all of us to plead for the actualization and rule of the Kingdom of the Heavenly Father on this earth through our personal prayer. It is unthinkable that the sisters of the community are telling lies about the truthfulness of the apparitions at the convent," he said. Mr. Kanayama also served as a Japanese diplomat in the Vatican during World War II.

Mrs. Mairead Maguire, a Nobel Peace Prize laureate and Irish Catholic, said in a telephone interview when she was staying at the convent overnight on October 28, 1990, "I believe the Blessed Mother is the Lady of All Nations and our Heavenly Mother is calling on all of us to form a worldwide network of prayer." Mrs. Maguire was awarded the prestigious prize in 1977 for her non-violent civic movement calling for reconciliation in divided Northern Ireland.

Mrs. Maguire recited the rosary often with the Akita nuns during her overnight stay. Mrs. Maguire met Sr. Agnes in person and asked her to pray hard for her peace movement in Ireland. After that, they sat together holding each other's hands with perfect silent understanding of each other.

A Californian pilgrim, Ms. Erika Volhontseff, wrote in a thank you note to the nuns as follows:

"My first impression of the Institute of the Handmaids of the Holy Eucharist was one of peace, love and beauty. The guest house, chapel and the park-like (traditional Japanese-style) garden (Maria

Garden) are a wonderful retreat from the busy world outside. Prayer and meditation come more easily and one feels an interior peace."

Ms. Ju Jong Seon, a South Korean Catholic, wrote in a note to the nuns before leaving for her home country:
"When I stood before the statue of the Blessed Mother, I deeply felt the compassion, warmth and goodness emanating from the Immaculate Heart of Mary. This impression moved me to love Jesus more and more deeply. I felt there can be no national boundaries in the presence of Jesus and Mary. I received many spiritual gifts during my stay there."

Fr. Roland Jolicoeur, a French Canadian priest, who visited Akita with a group of 20 pilgrims from Quebec, stated:
"Through my visit to Akita, I realized the Catholic faithful must pray more for their priests." He works ardently for a Catholic TV and radio evangelical movement called *Torch for Hearts,* which broadcasts a program which focuses on the evangelistic message of the Gospel in Japanese society.

Broadcasts of Mary's Tears by Secular Media

Sr. Theresa Toshiko Kashiwagi, the mother superior, said the influx of pilgrimage is gathering momentum and the numbers of pilgrims has increased sharply in recent years.

Millions of non-Christian Japanese have also been informed of these extraordinary events by the print and broadcast media, after some major television stations sent their reporters and camera crews to cover the mysterious phenomena at the convent.

In mid-December 1979, the videotaped phenomenon of the statue's tears was shown on the evening documentary TV program by "Television Tokyo Channel 12," a broadcasting network covering all of metropolitan Tokyo and adjacent five prefectures... an area of some 12 million people.

Akita: Mother of God as Coredemptrix

Another major TV station "Fuji Television Network" with its nationwide network also broadcast the phenomena of the weeping and the testimony of several eye-witnesses during an evening investigative documentary entitled, "Mystery in Our Modern Days," in June 1981.

The number of non-Japanese people who watched the videotaped weeping with their own eyes has continued to increase dramatically since April 1990, when a British documentary about the Marian apparition in Akita entitled, *Hill of Redemption,* made its debut in Ireland and the U.S. This film carries footage of the weepings with excellent resolution.

The Producer of the film, Mr. John Bird said he believes that various apparitions seem to have a central theme. He said the central theme of the Marian messages in Fatima was Faith; in Medjugorje, Hope; whereas, in Akita, the central theme of the message of the Blessed Mother seems to be "Divine Love for mankind."

The pilgrimages show signs of increasing even more. In early 1991, an American Catholic documentary film producer, Mr. Drew Mariani from Marian Video Productions, released his film entitled, *Marian Apparitions of the 20th Century* which included the footage of the weeping statue in Akita. Mr. Mariani interviewed key witnesses of the apparition during his filming in Akita.

In December 1974, the *CatholicGraph,* a now defunct monthly magazine, carried many color and black-and-white photographs of the weeping statue, as well as a series of investigative reports. It had been the first to report on the mysterious events.

Mr. Keisuke Yamauchi, once an editor for the Catholic Graph, and his wife went to the convent on May 13, 1976, and were fortunate enough to watch the tears shed by the statue of the Holy Mother. He was able to closely examine the entire room and an adjacent sacristy room trying to find a trick device, if any. "There were no trick devices," he declared. Mr. Yamauchi, a respected member of the prestigious Catholic Journalists' Club of Japan, wrote in his book, *Faith of Man*. He checked the ceiling above the statue and found there are "no traces" of raindrops, which he initially suspected might have moistened the ceiling. The inspection alleviated his doubts on the spot.

"I witnessed tears which flowed from the statue of the Blessed Mother of Akita. The reported phenomena (of the weepings) are factual!"

"I approached the statue of the Holy Mother and observed the teardrops by bringing my face to a position some 30 centimeters, then some 10 centimeters from the statue's face. A teardrop was glistening in front of my face. The teardrop was rather big and round, clinging to the right cheek of the statue's face. The right eye of the statue, moistened by the tears, was glistening. I saw a trace of teardrops remaining from the lower eyelid of the right eye to the right cheek, then to the chin of the statue. I also found another large teardrop clinging to the chin. Its throat was also wet with tears," Mr. Yamauchi wrote.

Akita: Mother of God as Coredemptrix

Chapter 5

*Miraculous Cure of South
Korean Woman From Brain Cancer*

ON EASTER SUNDAY, APRIL 22, 1984, (about one year
before the expiration of his tenure as ordinary of the Niigata diocese) Bishop Ito issued a pastoral letter in which he recognized and
proclaimed the supernatural character of the apparitions and messages of the Holy Mother Mary and the guardian angel of Sr. Agnes.

In the pastoral letter that described in detail the apparitions in
Akita, the bishop cited an objective evidence of the supernatural
character of the apparitions among other evidence. This evidence
took the form of a miraculous healing on August 4, 1981, of a South
Korean woman, Mrs. Teresa Chun Sun Ho. The woman was healed
of brain cancer through the intercession of Our Lady of Akita on
the 32nd day since she lapsed into a coma. Mrs. Chun, a mother of
four children, was 43 years old at that time.

The apparition of the Holy Mother and Her messages in Akita
have become widely known thanks to the activities of Fr. Joseph
Oh Ki Seon, a South Korean priest who witnessed the statue of the
Holy Mother weep on May 26, 1979 during his visit to Akita.

Mrs. Anastasia Chun Ock Seoun, the elder sister of Mrs. Chun,
who had obtained a copy of the photograph of the weeping statue,
decided to implore the Lady of Akita to heal her younger sister miraculously.

Akita: Mother of God as Coredemptrix

The pastoral letter of Bishop Ito said as follows:

"This patient, Mrs. Chun, lapsed into a coma in July, 1981 and was reduced to merely a vegetative existence on account of a cancerous tumor in her brain . The Blessed Mother of Akita appeared to her, telling her that she would no longer need to remain bedridden and that soon she would be able to rise — and that is precisely what happened."

"Shortly afterwards, she rose completely cured of her illness. This favor was obtained through the prayers of Korean priests and women, who implored the Blessed Mother of Akita to heal this patient and who prayed to Her to effect this miracle, as a preliminary condition to the canonization of the Korean martyrs."

"Computerized tomography scan radiographs of her brain show the complete cure of this patient even to non-professionals. The authenticity of the two radiographs (X-ray photos), taken during her illness and after her healing, are attested to by Dr. Tong Woo Kim, M.D., of the Saint Paul's Hospital in Seoul, who took these radiographs."

"Fr. Roman Theisan, a Maryknoll priest, who is the president of the Ecclesiastical Tribunal of the Archdiocese of Seoul issued an official certification of the authenticity of the radiographs. All the records have been forwarded to Rome. I (the bishop) went to Seoul last year, where I was able to meet with this woman and to verify the authenticity of her miraculous cure. In turn, she came to Akita on a pilgrimage of thanksgiving."

In 1983, an ecclesiastical commission appointed by South Korean church authorities officially acknowledged the authenticity of the miraculous cure of Mrs. Chun, for whom her family, along with Catholic priests and nuns, prayed for several weeks imploring the Blessed Mother of Akita to heal her. They placed a **photograph of the weeping statue of Akita** at her bedside, during the period of their joint supplications.

Left to right: *Mrs. Anastasia, Ms. Veronica and Mrs. Chun.*

After Mrs. Chun was cured and recovered the ability to communicate with others, she told her elder sister Chun Ock Seoun Anastasia, that the Blessed Mother appeared to her and healed her.

Then Mrs. Anastasia showed her two pictures of the Blessed Mother — that of Lourdes and that of Akita — and asked her which image was identical to that of the Blessed Mother who appeared to her. Immediately Mrs. Chun pointed to the picture of the Blessed Mother of Akita.

On October 15, 1983 — the very year when the South Korean church authorities forwarded official documents attesting to the authenticity of the miraculous cure of Mrs. Chun to Rome — Mrs. Chun, Mrs. Anastasia, Mrs. Veronica Whang, her godmother, Fr. Oh Ki Seon and Fr. Roman Theisan flew to Akita on a pilgrimage of thanksgiving for her miraculous cure.

When this author was in Seoul in 1988, I interviewed Mrs. Chun and she told me that when the Blessed Mother appeared to her,

Akita: Mother of God as Coredemptrix

Our Lady appeared to be made of a golden-colored wood and Her figure was a little bit smaller than that of a human being. This testimony immediately drew my attention to the common features of the Blessed Mother of Akita, as seen in various photographs with a yellowish golden color, shedding beautiful sparkling tears.

Mrs. Chun told me in an interview in Seoul on October 21, 1988, "Although I can only receive holy communion once a week because of my clothes-retail business to support my poor household, I eagerly await the coming of every Sunday, when I can receive my Lord Jesus present in the Holy Eucharist, by counting the number of weekdays I have to pass before the coming of each Sunday."

It seems to me (the author) that this spiritual hunger for the Holy Eucharist is very edifying and necessary to produce a Catholic with deep love of neighbors.

Cardinal Stephen Kim of Seoul and the Ecclesiastical Commission forwarded the documents attesting to her miraculous cure to Rome, in 1983 . Of these, Bishop Ito said:

"A canonical norm regarding judgment of the authenticity of such a miraculous cure requires a five-year continuation of the cure before its authenticity is approved."

In 1990, nine years after her healing, Mrs. Chun is healthy and has been working hard looking after her husband and four children. Together they recite five decades of the family Rosary every evening at 9:00 p.m. My first encounter with Mrs. Chun and her elder sister, Anastasia, took place on October 21, 1988, but I met them again when I went to Seoul on December 10, 1990. Thus, I was able to personally confirm the nine-year continuation of her miraculous cure. They told me that Mrs. Chun "has not even caught a single cold" since her healing from the brain cancer.

Miraculous Cure From Brain Cancer

Interview and Report on South Korean, Mrs. Teresa Chun Sun Ho

(The following report is based on my interview on October 21, 1988, with a South Korean woman, Mrs. Teresa Chun Sun Ho, then 51 years old, who was miraculously healed in 1981 from brain cancer by the mediation of the Holy Mother Mary of Akita.)

Among many miraculous healings effected by the mediation of the Holy Virgin of Akita there is one prominent case of a South Korean Catholic woman named Teresa Chun Sun Ho, who currently lives in Seoul in perfect health who looks after her husband and four children.

In 1983, an ecclesiastical commission appointed by South Korean Catholic Church authorities officially acknowledged the authenticity of her miraculous recovery from brain cancer that had reduced her existence to a vegetative state beginning July 4, 1981. After Mrs. Chun lapsed into a coma, her family, relatives, friends, Catholic priests and nuns prayed for 40 days imploring the Blessed Mother Mary of Akita to heal her.

Their prayers to the Blessed Mother Mary of Akita for a miraculous healing were also directed toward obtaining the proof of the supernatural virtues of the Korean martyrs, because such a miraculous cure is a prerequisite for the canonization of martyrs.

At that time, Korean Catholics were praying intently for such miraculous healings so that the Vatican would canonize 103 South Korean martyrs in view of the Pontiff's visit to South Korea slated for 1984.

After Mrs. Chun's miraculous cure took place, His Eminence Stephen Cardinal Kim, Maryknoll Father Roman Theisen, S.T.D., head of the Archdiocesan Tribunal of the See of Seoul, and the Ecclesiastical Commission forwarded the pertinent documents and X-ray photos of her brain attesting to her miraculous healing to the Vatican to ask for the canonization of the Korean martyrs. This miracle was effected by the mediation of the Blessed Mother of Akita as the "proof of the supernatural virtues of the martyrs." In this canonization process, in which various cures were examined by church authorities, Mrs. Chun's healing was the sole case whose supernatural character was verified by medical evidence of the X-ray photos.

Pope John Paul II finally canonized the martyrs during his visit to South Korea on May 6, 1984.

Here, let's examine the factual details of Mrs. Teresa Chun's supernatural healing and its causal relations with the Blessed Mother of Akita:

Mrs. Teresa Chun was baptized on April 11, 1981. Only about three months after her baptism, on July 4, 1981, she lapsed into a coma, because of the cancerous tumors that had developed in her brain. During an interview I conducted in Seoul on October 21, 1988, her elder sister, Mrs. Anastasia Chun, clearly described Mrs. Chun's condition stating, "Her existence was the same as that of the ball-point pen you hold now," she said, pointing to the pen I held in my right hand as I was taking my notes.

The X-rays taken at that time using the CTS (computerized tomography scan) method, clearly showed that large cancerous tumors had formed in the left frontal area of her brain. These photos were taken on July 18 at St. Paul Hospital in Seoul.

During the interview, Mrs. Anastasia, a Korean, who acted as an interpreter for Mrs. Teresa Chun, answered my questions in Japanese, having learned the language during the harsh 30 year, pre-World War II, colonial rule of the Korean Peninsula by Japanese military imperialists.

Miraculous Cure From Brain Cancer

At that time, Japan had forced all Koreans to learn Japanese prohibiting the use of the Korean language in order to integrate Korea into Japan's militant empire. On July 4, 1981, Dr. Kim Jung Jae, M.D., of the Medical Department of the Catholic University of Kyung Hee in Seoul diagnosed the disease of Mrs. Chun as a cerebral cancerous tumor (brain cancer). The professor diagnosed it as incurable. Dr. Kim found that she was also suffering from extreme malnutrition. Mrs. Chun was, then, working very hard to fight severe poverty and to feed her sick, unemployed husband and four children. She was only able to eat tiny amounts of coarse food. Neither had she, then, any knowledge of the mysterious events regarding the wooden statue of the Blessed Mother Mary at Akita. She has neither seen the photographs nor the drawings of the Blessed Mother of Akita.

All her family members, her godmother and two sisters lamented in bitter tears over Mrs. Chun's illness. Mrs. Chun had lapsed into a coma after shouting, "Jesus will heal me." Her vegetative existence lasted for 42 days. Her family could not afford to buy her the needed medicines nor injections.

Her elder sister, Mrs. Anastasia, proposed imploring the Blessed Mother of Akita to heal Mrs. Chun. All the family members, godmother, several Catholic priests and some Carmelites and other Catholic Order nuns, the Korean members of the "Legion de Marie" (Legion of Mary) and the Blue Army, prayed the Rosary seeking the intercession of the Holy Mother of Akita.

Especially her sister and family members prayed the Rosary intently placing the photograph of the statue of the Virgin of Akita close to Mrs. Chun's pillow every night with their "hands and the Rosary lifted up to Heaven," — a posture of penance — according to Mrs. Anastasia. Some of these faithful also fasted to invoke Divine mercy.

Akita: Mother of God as Coredemptrix

Earlier, Mrs. Anastasia had come to know about the Blessed Mother of Akita through the activities of Fr. Joseph Oh. Ki Seon, who was then the president of the Institute for Korean Martyrs' Research and Shrine Development, situated at the Catholic Center adjacent to the Myong Dong Cathedral. Fr. Oh passed away a few years ago.

On May 26, 1979, Fr. Oh had visited Akita and witnessed the weeping from the statue of Mary from 4:30 p.m. until 5:10 p.m. Deeply moved by his encounter with the Blessed Mother of Akita, he brought the photograph of the weeping statue back to South Korea, published it, and distributed some 100,000 copies of the original throughout that country.

Fr. Oh later translated into Korean Fr. Yasuda's 362-page Japanese book, *Our Lady of Akita*. Bishop Keiichi Sato, the present ordinary of the diocese of Niigata, had given permission to publish the Japanese book.

Cardinal Kim of Seoul gave his permission to publish the Korean translation and the book was published. At present, many of the Korean faithful believe the apparitions and messages of Mary at Akita.

Speaking with me through her sister Anastasia as an interpreter in an interview on October 21, 1988, Mrs. Chun said that the Blessed Mother appeared to her at around 3:00 a.m. on August 4, 1981, holding a white lamb in Her arms.

She reported the Blessed Mother was dressed in gold, breathing upon the lamb as white as snow and upon Mrs. Chun's own forehead three times strongly. Mrs. Anastasia heard her sister cry out from her coma "Lamb, Lamb, Lamb."

Mrs. Chun could see the lamb's wool flutter and sway from the breath of Mary, according to her own account. Trying to accurately describe Mary's actions before my eyes, Mrs. Chun gestured in the imitation of Mary's manner of breathing.

Fr. Yasuda said this incident means that the grace of her c\
given by the Holy Eucharist, which is Jesus Christ Himself, th
of God, by the intercession of the Holy Mother of Akita. The
lamb in the arms of the Holy Mother symbolizes the white
Eucharist, the ultimate source of the grace of the cure, Fr. Y.
said.

After experiencing this apparition, Mrs. Chun relapsed into a
sleep. Then, eleven days later, on August 15, she experienced
other Marian apparition at around 5:00 a.m. — this time in the fo
of a "dream."

"According to Mrs. Chun, Mary said to her, "Let's say a morn.
prayer," and then told her, "Teresa, wake up." Upon receiving t
order, Mrs. Chun woke up. Her sister Anastasia was asleep at h
bedside having exhausted herself from a long night's nursing. Mr
Chun asked her sister, "Why are you still asleep? It's time to say
morning prayer. Let's pray together."

Mrs. Anastasia then woke up helping her sister sit up on the bed.
Later, Mrs. Chun was able to walk with the support of her elder
sister.

After her healing was effected, Mrs. Chun described for her sister the Marian apparitions she experienced. Mrs. Anastasia then
showed her two pictures — that of Our Lady of Lourdes and that of
the Virgin Mother of Akita.

Mrs. Anastasia questioned her sister as to whether either image
was identical to that of Mary who had appeared to her. Mrs. Chun
immediately pointed to the picture of the Virgin Mother of Akita.

Mrs. Chun said in the interview, "To the end of my life, I will
never forget the kindness of the Blessed Mother Mary who cured
me of the disease."

A third apparition took place on December 9, 1981, when Mrs.
Chun was undergoing scientific tests in the X-ray room at St. Paul's
Hospital. Doctors were again taking a computerized tomography
scan (CTS) of her brain to check the conditions of the brain cancer.

The Blessed Mother, dressed in shining white, smiled to Mrs. Chun radiantly, then ascended to Heaven.

The CTS photographs taken that day, revealed the complete disappearance of cancerous tumors in her brain. The cure was attested to by both Dr. Tong-Woo Kim, M.D. and Dr. Gil Song Lee M.D., of St. Paul's Hospital in the form of a medical certificate.

Medical Appraisal Certificate Regarding the Cure of Mrs. Teresa Chun Sun Ho

(The following is the medical certificate issued by Dr. Gil Song Lee:)

Name: Chun Sun Ho,
Age: 43
Sex: Female
Address: (No. 1367-432 Sin-dang dong,
           Chung-ku, No. 202-25
           Htong-3 Pan, Seoul, Korea)

"This 43-year-old female patient was admitted to our hospital with a headache and right hemiplegia on July 18th in 1981. CT scan revealed a space taking lesion on the left frontal area with displacement and enlargement of the right lateral ventricle."

"However, the above abnormal findings have disappeared returning all to normal on the CT scan checked 5 months later (1981. 12. 9)."

1981. 12. 9
CMC St. Paul's Hospital
(Signed) N. S. Gil Song Lee, M.D.

Mrs. Chun After Her Healing

All the records, including this medical certificate and those CTS photographs, were forwarded to the Congregation of the Doctrine of the Faith in Rome. A part of these documents is carried as an appendix.

Both Mrs. Chun and Fr. Oh said she has not caught even a cold since the healing from the brain cancer in 1981. Mrs. Anastasia said that at present, her sister is still the main bread winner for her family and works hard each day selling children's underwear, socks, and women's' stockings while looking after her family. Her entire family lives a poor but faithful life, following Christ's teaching of kindness and prayer. She takes seriously the Holy Father's call for daily family prayer. Each day, her family recites the Rosary at 9:00 p.m.

Mrs. Chun stated, "I want to live a good, righteous life which will please God, throughout my life. Such a way of life is my greatest joy. My wish is to live a faithful life contemplating the mercy of God and the kindness of the Blessed Mother Mary until the day when God calls me (to His heavenly home)."

Since then, her family's financial condition has recently begun to improve, as two of her children graduated from schools and have started to assist the family financially. The family members love and cooperate with each other in solidarity, according to Mrs. Anastasia.

Mrs. Anastasia said, "Generally speaking, South Korean women work hard for their family. My sister works three times as much as an ordinary South Korean woman. She is very busy cooking, cleaning up rooms, washing clothes, looking after her family members and selling clothes."

"When she fell into a coma in 1981, my sister used to suffer malnutrition as she used to feed her four children primarily and then eat what her kids left on the table, along with 'kimuchi' (pickled cabbage soaked with red pepper.)" Mrs. Anastasia said.

Mrs. Chun gave me the impression of being a completely normal person who carried a kind and bright disposition. We held the interview in a pretty garden at the foot of the Choldu-san, a hill on which a museum and church are located in commemoration of the recently canonized Korean martyrs. Later, Mrs. Chun and Anastasia accompanied me to Seoul's Kimpo International Airport before I departed back to Japan. There, I found time to ask some additional questions at one of the airport restaurants.

There, I discovered that on October 15, 1983, Mrs. Chun and Anastasia visited Akita for the first time to offer prayers of thanksgiving for her healing. They came as members of a pilgrimage led by Fr. Oh.

In an interview with this author, Mrs. Chun said that, at the very moment she saw the actual statue of the Blessed Virgin of Akita for the first time, she realized it was exactly identical to the image of the Holy Mother Mary she saw during her experiences of the apparitions.

An ecclesiastical guideline of the Vatican regarding a miraculous cure states that it requires a five-year continuation of the cure of mysterious nature before canonical approval of the supernatural character of such a healing is established. As of October 21, 1988, when I first interviewed Mrs. Chun, seven years had already elapsed since her healing.

Two years later, I had a reunion with Mrs. Teresa Chun in Seoul on December 10, 1990. She was healthy and leading a kind prayerful life as an edifying Christian.

Chapter 6

Fr. Joseph, A French Missionary Loved by Holy Mother of Akita

BEFORE GOING DEEPLY into the meaning of Akita, I must first relate the background of a French missionary priest, who was integrated by God into the core of the mystery of the apparitions in Akita. The missionary was sent to Japan by the Foreign Mission Society of Paris in 1949. His name is Fr. Joseph Marie Jacq, M.E.P., whom I have already mentioned several times in the preceding chapters. Fr. Jacq is an edifying Roman Catholic priest whom Divine Providence brought to Akita on more than 20 pilgrimages, so that he be integrated into the heart of the mystery of the Divine Love manifested in Akita. He was born on April 18, 1923, in Brittany of France, and was ordained on June 29, 1947. In January 1953, Fr. Joseph was appointed as the chief pastor of St. Ann Church in Fujieda City, Shizuoka Prefecture, central Japan. He served for 33 years as a missionary in Japan.

His Encounter with Akita

During the years of his dedicated service in Japan, Fr. Joseph completely gave himself to the Japanese people and the Catholic Church there. After coming back to France, he wrote two books on the

Akita: Mother of God as Coredemptrix

Marian apparitions in Akita basing them upon his extensive investigations of the mysterious events and conversations with Sr. Agnes and other witnesses. He himself witnessed the weeping of the statue of the Blessed Mother on four different occasions — on January 24, 1979 (the 23rd weeping), August 22, 1981 (99th), September 12, 1981 (100th) and September 15, 1981 (101st).

It was through a layman in his church that Fr. Joseph heard for the first time of the occurrences of the mysterious events in Akita. One Sunday at Mass in 1975, a layman announced that the statue of the Blessed Virgin Mary had started weeping in Akita. This was the first year when the statue's lachrymations started. The parishioner expressed his gratitude to the Blessed Mother, saying the Mother of God vouchsafed to come particularly to Japan from Heaven, in order to summon humanity to prayer, repentance, and conversion. This layman's joy soon engulfed the entire assembly of St. Ann Church.

The highly positive reaction of these Fujieda parishioners was an average initial reaction to the apparition among practicing Japanese Catholics — perhaps the fruit of their lives consisting of diligent labor (for bread), prayers, and works of charity for others.

Fr. Joseph visited the Akita convent later in autumn of the same year. A raging hurricane had pounded out the Akita Prefecture and adjacent districts during the day he arrived. The hurricane had suspended all airline and railway transportation. The resultant disruption of transportation meant delaying his return to his parish for three days.

The hurricane, in effect, held Fr. Joseph captive, a prisoner of the Blessed Mother of Akita in Her sanctuary on the suburban hill abounding in natural beauty. This unexpected captivity gave him an excellent opportunity to become more than acquainted with the string of mysterious events occurring at Akita. It was at this time that he was introduced to Sr. Agnes, Fr. Yasuda and all the other prayerful nuns.

Fr. Joseph

This captivity in the domain of the Blessed Mother led him to intimately share in the daily work and prayer life of the handmaids of the Holy Eucharist and to become a knowledgeable witness to the community itself.

Soon, Fr. Joseph became close friends with Fr. Yasuda and Sr. Agnes. Ms. Gemma Chie Masuda, a kindergarten superior director and Japanese Catholic, a friend of both Fr. Joseph and Sr. Agnes, said, "God formed a special spiritual bond between Fr. Joseph and Sr. Agnes." The two are like spiritual twins in that they share the common spirituality of offering their sacrifices, sufferings and prayers to God to join in the work of making reparations for the sins of humanity.

It was during Fr. Joseph's third visit to Akita on January 24, 1979, that he first witnessed the weeping of the statue. It was his description of his first encounter with the weeping statue that I used in Chapter 1, because the description is so detailed and lively.

Fr. Joseph has spoken with his theological profundity about the Holy Eucharist and the prayer of the Rosary. He used to tell his parishioners, "The Mass exceeds everything in value. The Holy Eucharist is Jesus Christ himself, and the tremendous power of love of neighbor is contained in a single particle of the Holy Eucharist for release into human souls. Therefore, if a Catholic continued to receive Holy Communion with true humility, the communions would gradually transform the recipient into another Christ-like person whose heart would overflow with love of neighbor." With many other Saints, he has stated, "Holy Communion and the prayer of the Rosary are the two most powerful weapons to defeat Satan."

The True Spirit of a Missionary

Fr. Joseph may be properly described as around-the-clock love itself clad in Roman Catholic priestly vestments. He always cared for, and loved; many suffering and under-privileged people through and in his actions. In tending to these, he never worried about his own comfort. As pastor of St. Ann's Church, he would sleep on a wooden floor in his presbytery with merely a blanket.

Fr. Joseph was noted for his motorcycle that he rode to visit catechumens and the sick in the neighboring towns and villages as part of his missionary activities. A parishioner once lightheartedly called him, "The adventurous missionary motorcycle-rider." While evoking the humorous imagery, Fr. Joseph literally risked his life for missionary activities and would brave torrential rains and winds to visit people in need when he was convinced that such a visit would help save a soul.

One day, he went out on his motorcycle amid an approaching hurricane to visit the home of a catechumen named, Morita, to teach his family members weekly catechism lessons. The catechumen expected the missionary to give up the day's lesson amid the raging winds and rains. Nonetheless, he had a suspicious inkling that the priest just might. A family member of the catechumen later testified before the assembly of the parishioners at St. Ann's Church, "We bored a small hole in the wooden front board of a (traditional Japanese-style) anti-rain shutter at our entrance and were waiting indoors for an appearance, while peeping through the hole in the door. To our surprise, he appeared on his motorcycle as usual."

The catechumen was amazed and moved by the strength of Fr. Joseph's love for souls. His actions spoke louder than any sermon could have about the true nature of Christian love.

Noble Sacrifice

This author was also a parishioner at his church. In 1980, the year I graduated from Jesuit-run Sophia University, I took a job as a high school teacher of English at his parish. This was during the years before I initiated my career as a journalist. It was on October 19, in that year, that I accepted baptism from a Jesuit professor at Sophia University and began attending Fr. Joseph's church. Fr. Joseph encouraged me to attend daily morning Mass — at 6:00 a.m. — so that I would draw spiritual strength from holy communion and grow in the Christian spirit of love. Initially, I declined the suggestion, telling Fr. Joseph, "I cannot get up early in the morning because my shoulders tend to be oversensitive to the cold morning air."

Fr. Joseph replied, "My shoulders are also sensitive to cold air. That is why I often wrap this shawl around my shoulders," pointing to his black woolen shawl.

From that time on, I began to notice that Fr. Joseph no longer wore his shawl. Without revealing his motivation for it, he had thrown it away offering up the sacrifice of enduring the coldness that affected his shoulders. Only later did I understand that he did it to be an example for me and so that God would help me realize the importance of daily communion.

Fr. Joseph deeply admired the life of St. Therese of Lisieux, and let it serve as an example for him. Like St. Therese, Fr. Joseph's life was an endless string of silent sacrifices offered up with beautiful smiles. A Catholic once called him an "apostle of the smile."

Japanese Catholics and non-Christians in Fujieda both liked and loved this warm-hearted priest. When he celebrated his last Mass in Japan before going back to France in January 1983, the chapel was overcrowded with crying Japanese Catholics and the children of the four Catholic kindergartens he had founded.

The Japanese flocks he had shepherded reciprocated by loving him so deeply. Many wept over his departure that night. His last Mass in Japan was celebrated at the Okabe Sacred Hearts of Jesus and Mary Church, which he and his parishioners had literally built with their hands. This church was one of the four churches he built during his 33 years in Japan.

Thousands of non-Christian Japanese kindergartners and their mothers encountered Christianity when they entered into these Catholic schools. However, they came to learn of God's love through their contact with Fr. Joseph. For the first time in their lives, they heard about the redemption brought to them through Jesus and many eventually came to accept baptism into the Catholic Church.

There are many examples that show how deeply the Japanese Catholics loved Fr. Joseph. On one occasion, when Fr. Joseph caught a cold, a group of Fujieda female parishioners gathered to sew a warm set of bedding for their pastor.

After a lifetime of prayer and sacrifice, the Lord brought Fr. Joseph his final cross. Word reached Fujieda in late 1990 that

Fr. Joseph developed cancer and faced imminent death. He was hospitalized on December 11, 1990, for blood transfusions. Perhaps the greatest example of his parishioners' love for him was demonstrated when the parishioners of St. Ann's Church sent him a "spiritual bouquet" — a list of thousands of promises of prayers; sacrifices; Mass attendances, receptions of holy communions, Rosaries, etc.

This hearty spiritual bouquet — whose records this author still keeps at hand — consisted of 709 Mass attendances; 855 holy communions offered up for his recovery; 1,733 decades of the Rosary; 1,324 visits to Jesus Christ in the tabernacle; 263 acts of sacrifices as well as thousands of other prayers and personal devotions offered for his recovery. More remarkably, this number is from only one of the four churches he had set up. Sr. Agnes and the nuns of the Akita convent also prayed intently for his cure. Their loving action and prayers call to mind the words of St. Therese of Lisieux, "We have the only one way to respond to the love we have received — by loving back."

Despite the storm of prayer and sacrifice, God had greater plans for this missionary, who died on January 14, 1991. After the example of Jesus and the holy Mother, Fr. Joseph had given himself to thousands of Japanese Christians and non-Christians, and they reciprocated by loving him in return.

Sr. Agnes told me in a follow-up telephone interview on January 29, 1991, that "Fr. Joseph's greatness emanated from the depth of his faith." She related that, "His tenderness and kindness were a result of his deep love for the Holy Eucharist and Holy Mother Mary." The visionary continued, "I have always admired and been fascinated by his deep faith in the Holy Eucharist and the Blessed Mother."

When this author and two other Fujieda parishioners visited the southern French village of Montbeton early in December of 1990 to bid him a final farewell, Fr. Joseph said, "I do not pray for my cure. Rather, I entrust my fate to God." It was in this village at a house for elderly priests of the Paris Foreign Mission Society that I repeatedly heard him say "Deo Gratias" whenever the excruciating pains of the cancer gripped his body.

A few months before his death, he wrote in a letter dated November 12, 1990 to his friends, "When my doctor told me that an incurable cancer had spread throughout my stomach, pancreas, and liver, I immediately felt a deep internal joy. It was the joy of knowing that I will be able to meet Jesus and Mary whom I have lived for, loved so deeply, and tried to have people love."

"In Heaven, I will directly watch the mystery of what used to take place in my hands on the sacred altar during my Masses mornings and evenings," he wrote, referring to the mystery of transubstantiation. Fr. Joseph also wrote in his letter, "When I made a pilgrimage to Fatima in October 1991, I suffered an excruciating pain in my stomach. Then, I perceived it as a 'wink from the Holy Mother Mary.' Fiat... I felt the joy of knowing that I would be able to admire the real tender face of the Holy Mother Mary, with her splendid tender smiles, who has constantly protected me for the sake of Her Son, Jesus." Fr. Joseph died at the age of 67, on January 14, 1991. The Japanese translation of the letter was carried in the monthly bulletin of the Akita convent in March 1991.

In a word, Fr. Joseph lived the Gospel to the letter. Until early December of that year, he continued to take care of and nurse the elderly priests of his order despite his own deteriorating health.

Until the hospitalization, in keeping with the practices he set since his arrival back in France, he would get up at 2:00 a.m. every day and celebrate a two hour long midnight Mass. During each Mass, he offered up intensive wholehearted prayers to God on behalf of each of the people who needed his prayers.

On December 10, 1990, I returned to Japan via New York, where I visited St. Thomas Aquinas Church. After I heard the news of Fr. Joseph's death on January 14, I telephoned Fr. Yasuda, a good friend of Fr. Joseph, and spoke of the latter's last days back in France. Fr.

Yasuda, with tears in his voice, replied, "Fr. Joseph's soul will go straight up to Heaven, because he loved people so strongly and did such great penance."

The first time Fr. Joseph witnessed the weeping of the statue was on January 24, 1979. It was the statue's 23rd weeping out of the statue's 101 episodes of lachrymations (weeping). By the time he saw it, the weeping had already begun unnoticed. However, it is apparent from various records and testimonies that the statue began shedding tears shortly after Fr. Joseph draped his own Rosary beads around the statue's neck as he was leaving the chapel. Fr. Joseph wrote about why he made the gesture: "So that as an object of piety, a sacramental, it might be enhanced as a vehicle of blessings and graces."

After a nun had noticed the tears and rushed to announce the weeping to those who had gathered in the refectory for supper, Fr. Joseph, Fr. Yasuda and all the other people rushed to the chapel. They began to recite the "Sorrowful Mysteries" of the Rosary together. After the first decade, Fr. Joseph was inspired to take pictures of the tears of the Blessed Mother and did.

For a long time since that occasion, this author felt that God and the Blessed Mother had given Fr. Joseph the privilege of witnessing and photographing the sacred tears of the Holy Mother as consolation to the missionary to reward him for his long years of service to the Catholic Church in Japan and to the Japanese people.

Undoubtedly, the Blessed Mother knows how deeply Fr. Joseph toiled and suffered in helping people and the modern Church. Fr. Joseph has been concerned about the current condition of the Church, whose spirituality has been and continues to be rocked and eroded from both within and without — within by the loss of the true faith by many theologians, clergy and lay people; without by the rampaging forces of egoism, secularism, and the adaptation of materialistic values — all of which have led to the spiritual corruption of many.

Akita: Mother of God as Coredemptrix

As I meditate on how his sacrifices of love increased even more greatly after his 1979 encounter with the holy tears, it appears that Fr. Joseph wisely understood the meaning of His Heavenly Mother's tears as an irresistible appeal to join in Her work of coredemption. It was a voiceless call for him to unite his sufferings, prayers and sacrifices with those of his Blessed Mother. He later wrote, "She weeps to speak a language more eloquent than words."

Holy Mother and Children

On August 22, 1981, the feast day of the Queenship of Our Lady, Fr. Joseph witnessed the weeping of the statue for the second time, together with Bishop Ito, Fr. Yasuda, Fr. Tadami Hayashi, nuns and a group of more than 20 schoolchildren.

The schoolchildren, accompanied by their teachers, Mr. and Mrs. Yoshinaka, had traveled almost fifteen hundred kilometers overnight by train from Wakayama, in order to arrive on time for the six o'clock morning Mass. Eight of the children were baptized by Bishop Ito during their stay.

At around 1:00 p.m. that day, Fr. Joseph noticed a slight, dark spot on the bosom of the statue. Approaching inquisitively, the priest found that, in the folds of her raiment, tears had gathered shining brightly and clearly. Just at this moment, Mr. Yoshinaka entered the room. Fr. Joseph beckoned him, saying, "Please come and see! It looks like the statue is weeping!" Mr. Yoshinaka quickly turned on the electric light.

Fr. Joseph recorded the incident as follows: "In the light, the moist spot on the bosom was most evident. The tears which gathered at the site of the heart of the statue sparkled. We could also see that some tears had dropped onto the globe (beneath the foot of the statue) and then had fallen onto the pedestal. The light also revealed some tears coalescing under the chin." According to the records, when the news reached the children, the boys dashed downstairs in a clatter from their accommodating quarters, crossed the garden, and arrived breathless, falling on their knees, staring at the tears. They said to one another, "She's weeping. She's weeping. Why is She weeping?"

The girls were the next to arrive at the scene, followed by Bishop Ito, Fr. Hayashi, Fr. Yasuda and nuns. Hayashi, who tasted the tears, said the tears not only tasted salty, but contained a human warmth quite different from ordinary water, according to the records. Fr. Hayashi is an active member of the Marian Movement of Priests, founded by Fr. Gobbi.

Fr. Yasuda collected the tears with a cotton ball pinched with a tweezers, and asked Professor Okuhara to send it to the Gifu University's Medical Faculty for the second round of appraisal. The specimen of the tears was forwarded to Professor Kaoru Sagisake of Gifu University, a non-Christian forensic medicine expert.

Professor Okuhara, M.D. of the Medical Faculty of Akita University, with whom Fr. Yasuda had become acquainted, forwarded the fresh specimen of the tears to Processor Sagisaka.

On December 8, feastday of the Immaculate Conception of Mary — after three and a half months — Fr. Yasuda was called over the phone by Dr. Okuhara to come to the university.

Dr. Okuhara handed over a document of medical appraisal to Fr. Yasuda, verifying that the medical appraisal at Gifu University identified the blood type of the tears as Type "O."

The document was issued and signed by Professor Kaoru Sagisaka, M.D. of Gifu University and mailed to Dr. Okuhara of Akita University before being turned over to Fr. Yasuda.

From September 8 to 18, Fr. Joseph was a temporary resident in Akita.

Second Commission and Mary's Tears

On September 12 (from 8:44 a.m.) and September 15 (from 2:00 p.m.), 1981, Fr. Joseph again witnessed the statue weep, together with a total of 78 Christians and non-Christians. The weepings were the statue's 100th and 101st lachrymations.

He described the experience on the morning of September 12th as follows: "(After the morning prayers and Mass had ended) Sr. Therese Kashiwagi came before the statue...and urged me to come to see a large drop plainly visible at the waistband, on the left side of the bosom. As before, another tear fell onto the globe and then onto the pedestal....Some tears also had gathered below the chin and some had also trickled to the neck."

September 12 (Saturday) was the second day of the final two-day meeting of the second commission of inquiry, which had been set up by Bishop Ito on the strength of the local bishop's canonical authority by advice of the Holy See. On the very morning of the 100th weeping, the commission was on the brink of handing down a ruling on the issue of the supernatural authenticity of the apparition at the chancery of the See of Niigata — about four hundred kilometers south of Akita.

The community of nuns fasted during the two days of the meeting of the commission so that God would illuminate the minds of commissioners so they might make a fair judgment guided by the Holy Spirit. Many other Catholics, even some children such as the group shepherded by the Yoshinakas in the previous month, also fasted and prayed intensely for the same intention.

Sr. Kashiwagi, Mother Superior, confirmed in a recent telephone interview with me that she had telephoned Bishop Ito, head of the seven member commission, on the morning of September 12, 1981, to inform him of the 100th weeping. The news was immediately conveyed to the commission. She also said that she had entreated the Bishop to be steadfast in the defense of the cause of the Blessed Mother.

The eloquent tears of the Heavenly Mother appear to have altered the disposition of the commission in favor of the apparitions in Akita. The commission voted to approve its supernatural authenticity in a 4-to-3 ruling. Fr. Joseph strongly felt that the prayers, sacrifices and fasting, particularly those of the children, all contributed to the leverage against doubt and negation.

Fr. Joseph's records show that on September 15, the feast day of Our Lady of Seven Sorrows, the statue wept for the 101st and last time. Fr. Joseph witnessed the tears, along with 65 other witnesses. His records state, "Tears dotted much of the statue above the waistband. The eyes, the cheeks, the lips, the mouth, the chin, the bosom, and later even the waistband, were wet with tears."

The priest's records further stated, "Even the non-Christians joined in prayer during the Sorrowful Mysteries of the Rosary. Among these, a young girl of fifteen years, named Junko, prayed with all her heart. Later, I would instruct her in the first lesson of the catechism. How gently does Our Lady introduce unbelievers to the reality of God's love! How readily does God draw the humble and guileless of heart to Himself, through the invitation of the Divine Mother!"

Humble Support for Bishop Ito

It is crucial to describe one more important part played by Fr. Joseph Marie Jacq in the history of the Marian apparitions in Akita. On March 13, 1982 — six months after the 101st weeping of the statue — Bishop Ito forwarded a very important letter describing the bishop's own eyewitness account of the statue's weeping and theological analysis, as well as several crucial documents to Cardinal Joseph Ratzinger, Prefect of the Sacred Congregation for the Doctrine of the Faith.

These documents included the French translations of (1) the messages of the Holy Mother Mary of Akita, (2) the spiritual diary of Sr.

Agnes Katsuko Sasagawa, (3) Fr. Yasuda's 43-page theological appraisal of the apparition and his refutation of the ectoplasmic theory, (4) photographs of the weeping statue of Mary, and (5) the eyewitnesses' accounts of the weeping of the statue.

Fr. Joseph and Bishop Ito.

Bishop Ito asked Fr. Joseph to translate and type out his long letter — even more detailed than his 1984 pastoral letter authorizing the veneration of Our Lady of Akita — as well as all these Japanese-language documents. They were translated precisely and this author was given the copies of most of both the French and Japanese original texts of these documents.

The Bishop thanked Fr. Joseph for the time-consuming translation of the work and then forwarded the whole set of documents together with his own letter to the Holy See through the Apostolic Nunciature in Tokyo.

A French Missionary

His 1984 pastoral letter which was issued on the strength of the bishop's canonical authority and based on the Congregation of the Doctrine of Faith's guidelines for judgments on apparitions, was structured according to his 1982 letter to Cardinal Ratzinger. Just as the visionaries came under slander at Fatima, Bishop Ito also suffered from some misunderstandings that emanated from some Japanese Church officials as a result of misinformation. According to several of the Bishop's remaining letters and the testimonies of those who were close to both of these men, Fr. Joseph assisted Bishop Ito greatly through the repeated encouragement he gave to the Bishop. Bishop Ito trusted Fr. Joseph and confided to him the internal suffering he felt in the face of such adversity. In these letters which reached Fr. Joseph in France, the bishop often asked for Fr. Joseph's prayers. They also reported the latest developments in Akita, and inquired about the degree of acceptance of the apparitions in Akita among grass-root Catholics in Europe.

As Akita lies within the diocese of the then local ordinary Bishop Ito, the congregation's canonical guidelines gave the responsibility and power of intervention and judgment upon the supernatural authenticity to Bishop Ito.

During his daily Masses and Rosary, Fr. Joseph prayed hard for the intention that Divine grace would encourage the Bishop to approve of the supernatural character of the Marian apparition and messages in Akita. It seems to me that both his and the nuns' fervent prayers moved the Sacred Heart of Jesus. For after 11 years of his own investigation into the Akita apparitions and after his own experiences as an eye-witness, the bishop issued the pastoral letter on April 22 (Easter Sunday), 1984, declaring the supernatural authenticity of the apparition of the Holy Mother Mary in Akita and authorizing the veneration of the Holy Mother of Akita.

Akita: Mother of God as Coredemptrix

Chapter 7

How God Tried to Revive People's
Faith in Real Presence of
Jesus in Holy Eucharist

WHAT IS THE MEANING of the mysterious happenings in Akita? Why did God do this? The apparitions in Akita stem from God's deep love for all mankind, and especially for His Catholic Church which Jesus instituted 2000 years ago on the rock of Peter as an instrument of His salvation. However, what specific lessons did God plan to convey in Akita from His Sacred Heart all on fire with infinite Divine Love for mankind?

To answer these crucial questions, I will quote from the visionary, from theologians, from the words of Popes John Paul II, and Paul VI as well as from the guardian angel of Sr. Agnes in explaining the meaning of the Divine events in Akita.

Sr. Agnes' Testimony on Communion on Her Tongue

Fr. Joseph said there are two key lessons of grave importance God planned to convey to the whole Catholic Church through the Marian apparitions in Akita.

Akita: Mother of God as Coredemptrix

Fr. Joseph said one of the two lessons is the instruction regarding how to revive the Catholic people's dwindling spiritual ability to recognize the real presence of Jesus in the Holy Eucharist. The second is the clarification of the role of the Blessed Mother as "Coredemptrix," he said.

Fr. Joseph said, "There is a profound meaning in both the bleeding of the left hand of Sr. Agnes and the right hand of the statue of the Blessed Mother of Akita." He drew attention to the crucial testimony of Sr. Agnes, who described the outcome of her stigmata on July 26, 1973 as follows:

"Mass started a little after 5 p.m. Just as Sister Ishikawa was renewing her vows, my hand started to ache almost unbearably. I almost screamed. It was bleeding and ached just as if someone had pierced my palm all the way to the back with a nail. I tried with my whole strength to bear it. My forehead was in a greasy sweat. At that moment, clinging to our Lady's medal, I prayed, " Mary, help me!" I tried to endure the pain by thinking of the sufferings of Jesus on the Cross. This all took place in just a short time, but when I was bearing the pain, it seemed like a very long time. I still cannot forget it. At Holy Communion, everyone received in their hands, but since I could not open my palm because of the pain, I received in my mouth."

When Sr. Agnes was asked to describe the bleeding wound on her hand as compared to that of the statue, the nun gave the following description:

"The two wounds were exactly the same in that both of them had the shape of a cross, from whose center blood flowed." However, since the statue had a hand much smaller, its cross was smaller. Its central opening was about as large as the hole of a sewing needle. Mine was much larger, like the thickness of a nail."

"In the most painful moments, I felt as if someone was driving a large nail into the palm of my hand, piercing it from one side to the other. It was then that the blood began to flow from the central opening of the wound, but it caused so much pain that I did not have the strength to dry it. All I could do was to try to force a piece of gauze into the small opening of my clenched hand in order to sponge up the blood.

Regarding this occurrence, Fr. Joseph said, "The episode on July 26 shows us that God wants lay people and nuns to receive Communion on the tongue, because Communion by their unconsecrated hands carries with it the potential danger of hurting and undermining their faith in the real presence."

In backing up this argument, he quoted the pontifical pastoral instruction, *Memoriale Domini* issued by Pope Paul VI on May 29, 1969, which tells us that the faithful should receive Communion on the tongue *in order to protect their "sensibility and spiritual worship" towards the true presence of Jesus in the Eucharist.*

This pastoral instruction *"Memoriale Domini"* first explains — historically — why the universal Catholic Church introduced and mandated the custom of receiving communion on the tongue, in early centuries.

Just as Pope John Paul II also stressed in his 1980 pastoral letter *"Dominicae Cenae,"* the custom was introduced for the spiritual "common good" of lay communicants and nuns, whose hands are not consecrated, with sacrament of priestly ordination, by a bishop through whom the Holy Spirit works to sanctify the hands of new priests.

By anointing the hands of a new priest during an ordination rite, a bishop, with the invisible intervention of the Holy Spirit into the rite, gives the priest a privilege of touching and administering the Holy Eucharist to a communicant, according to the Pope.

Pope John Paul II said with his doctrinal infallibility in the pastoral letter, "A special grace and power is necessary precisely for priests' hands."

Now, let's see Pope Paul VI's pastoral instructions *"Memoriale Domini"* (translated from the original Latin text) states unequivocally as follows;

"...In the following period, after the true meaning of the Eucharistic mystery, its effect, and the presence of Christ in it had been profoundly investigated, the Church introduced the custom by which the priest himself would place the piece of consecrated bread on the tongue of the communicants from a deeper sense of reverence toward this holy sacrament and of the humility which its reception demands."

"In view of the state of the Church as a whole today, this manner of distributing Holy Communion therefore should be observed, not only because it rests upon a tradition of many centuries but especially because it is a sign of reverence by the faithful toward the Eucharist."

The practice of placing Holy Communion on the tongue of the communicants in no way detracts from their personal dignity."

"It is a part of the preparation needed for the most fruitful reception of the Lord's body."

"This traditional manner of administering Holy Communion gives more effective assurance that the Holy Eucharist will be given to the faithful with the due reverence, decorum and dignity."

"This manner would enable the faithful to avoid any danger of profaning the Holy Eucharist, in which the whole and entire Christ, God and man, is substantially contained and permanently present in a unique way."

"Finally, the traditional manner would make sure that priests maintain the diligent care which the Church has always requested for the very fragments of the consecrated bread."

"If a particle or fragment of the Holy Eucharist is dropped or lost, perceive it as a lessening of a part of your own body."

"The usage of placing the consecrated bread in the hand of the communicant also includes the following dangers."

"The new manner of administering Holy Communion in the hand of the communicant, then, leads to a lessening of reverence toward the holy sacrament of the altar. The new manner leads to profanation of this blessed sacrament. It also leads to the adulteration of the correct doctrine (of the real presence of Jesus in the Holy Eucharist)."

"Three questions were therefore proposed to the bishops of the entire Latin Church. By March 12, 1968, the following responses had been received."

1) Do you believe the rite of administering Holy Communion in the hand of the faithful should be permitted?
   Yes: 567
   No: 1,233
   Yes, with reservations: 315
   Invalid votes: 20

2) Should experiments with this new rite first be conducted in small communities, with the assent of the local ordinary?
   Yes: 751
   No: 1,215
   Invalid votes: 70

3) Do you think the faithful would accept this new rite willingly, after a well-planned catechetical preparation?
   Yes: 835
   No: 1,185
   Invalid votes: 128

"From these responses received, it is thus clear that by far the greater number of bishops felt that the rule of placing communion on the tongue should not be changed at all. If it were changed, this would offend the sensibilities and spiritual worship (of the Holy Eucharist) on the part of the bishops and most of the faithful."

"The Supreme Pontiff judged that the traditional manner of administering the Holy Eucharist should not be changed, after he considered the observations and the counsel of the bishops whom the Holy Spirit has placed as overseers to feed the Church of God in view of the seriousness of the matter and the importance of the arguments made."

Note to readers: The following are the original Latin texts of Pope Paul VI's pastoral instruction *"Memoriale Domini,"* which correspond with the above English translation of the quoted paragraphs of the Pontifical instruction. The words in the brackets in the English texts are the author's own words to make the meaning more clear.

Insequenti tempore, postquam eucharistici mysterii veritas, eius virtus ac praesentia Christi in eo altius explorata sunt, urgente sensu sive reverentiae erga hoc Sanctissimum Sacramentum sive humilitatis qua illud sumatur oportet, consuetudo inducta est, ut per se minister panis consecrati particulam in lingua Communionem suscipientium deponeret.

Ilic sanctam Communionem distribuendi modus, bodierno Ecclesiae statu in universum considerato, servari debet, non solum quia in tradito plurium saeculorum more innititur, sed praesertim quia Christifidelium reverentiam erga Eucharistiam significat. Huiusmodi autem usus nihil de dignitate personae detrahit iis, qui ad tantum Sacramentum accedunt, atque ad eam praeparationem pertinet, quae requiritur, ut Corpus Domini modo maxime frugifero percipiature,

Haec reverentia non «panis et potus communis», sed Corporis et Sanguinis Domini communionem significat, vi cuins «populus Dei bona sacrificii paschalis participat, renovat novum foedus semel in sanguine Christi a Deo cum hominibus factum, ac in fide et spe convivium eschatologicum in regno Patris praefigurat et praevenit».

Praeterea hac agendi ratione, quae translaticia iam censenda est, efficacius cavetur, ut sacra Communio qua par est reverntia, decore atque dignitate distribuatur, ut quodvis periculum arceatur species eucharisticas profanandi, in quibue «modo singulari, adest totus et integer Christus, Deus et homo, substantialiter et continenter», ut denique diligenter cura servetur, quam de ipsis panis consecrati fragmentis Ecclesia semper commendavit: «Quod enim intercidere patieris, id tibi tamquam ex propriis membris deminutum puta».

Quapropter, cum paucae quaedam Conferentiae Episcopales atque nonnulli singulares Episcopi postulassent, ut in suis territoriis usus admitteretur consecratum panem in christifidelium manibus ponendi, Summus Pontifex statuit ut singuli universi Ecclesiae latinae Episcopi rogarentur quid censerent de opportunitate huiusmodi ritum introducendi. Mutatio enim iu re tanti momenti, quae antiquissima et veneranda traditione innititur, praeterquam quod disciplinam pertingit, pericula etiam secumferre potest, quae timentur forte oritura ex novo modo sacram Communionem misistrandi, ne scilicet perveniatur sive ad minorem erga Augustum altaris Sacramentum reverentiam, sive ad eiusdem Sacramenti profanationem, sive ad rectae doctrinae adultera eiusdem Sacramenti profanationem, sive ad rectae doctrinae adulterationem.

Quam ob rem Episcopis tres quaestiones propositae sunt, quibus usque ad diem 12 superioris mensis Martii hoc, qui sequitur, modo responsum est:

1. Videturne exaudiendum votum, ut praeter modum traditum, etiam ritus recipiendi sacram Communionem in manu permittatur?
   Placet: 567
   Non placet: 1,233
   Pl. iuxta modum: 315
   Suffragia invalida: 20

2. Placetne ut experimenta huius novi ritus in parvis communitatibus prius fiant, assentiente Ordinario loci?
   Placet: 751
   Non placet: 1,215
   Suffragia invalida: 70

3. Putasne fideles, post praeparationem catecheticam bene ordinatam, hunc novum ritum libenter esse accepturos?
   Placet: 835
   Non placet: 1,185
   Suffragia invalida: 128

Ex redditis igitur responsis patet Episcopos longe plurimos censere hodiernam disciplinam haudquaquam esse immutandam; quae immo si immutetur, id tum sensui tum spirituali cultui eorundem Episcoporum plurimormque fidelium offensioni fore.

Itaque, attentis animadversionibus consillisque eorum, quos «Spiritus Sanctus posuit Episcopos Regere» Ecclesias, pro rei gravitate et allatorum argumentorum momento, Summo Pontifici non est visum modum iamdiu receptum sacrae Communionis fidelibus ministrandae immutare.

Fr. Gerard McGinnity from Ireland, said: "If spiritual sensibility towards the presence of Jesus in the Eucharist is offended by the practice of Communion by hand, then, the decline in the communicants' ability to love their neighbors will follow inevitably, because such weakened sensibility reduces the influx of God's graces into the souls of the communicants."

"The message of Akita tells us of the importance of receiving Communion with the thoughtfulness and sufficient awareness for the enormous gift of the Eucharist, *in which Jesus is truly present.*" Fr. McGinnity said.

Teaching of Pope John Paul II

Fr. Joseph also said all bishops and priests have to listen humbly to the profound teachings of Pope John Paul II in one of the Pope's pastoral letters, *"On the Mystery and Worship of the Holy Eucharist (Dominicae Cenae) — Latin name for the pastoral letter,"* which was issued to all bishops of the world on February 24, 1980.

Pope John Paul II said in the pastoral letter, in his intimate and solemn appeal to all of his fellow priests around the world, as follows;

"Our greatest glory consists in exercising this mysterious power over the Body of the Redeemer, over and above our compliance with the evangelical mission."

"All that is within us should be decisively ordered to this (glorious mission). We should always remember that we have been sacramentally consecrated to this ministerial power and that we have been chosen from among men 'for the good of the people.'"

"We, the priests of the Latin-Roman Catholic Church, should especially think about the fact that our ordination rite added the custom of anointing the priests' hands in the course of many centuries..."

"One must not forget the primary obligation of priests, who have been consecrated by their ordination to represent Christ the Priest; for this reason their hands, like their words and their will, have become the direct instruments of Christ..."

"How eloquently the rite of the anointing of priests' hands in our Latin ordination tells that a special grace and power of the Holy Spirit is necessary precisely for priests' hands!"

"To touch the Holy Eucharist and to distribute them with their own hands is a privilege of the ordained."

Mother Teresa of Calcutta, founder of the Missionaries of Charity, once said she and other nuns of her convent would not be able to continue their activities of love of neighbors, unless they drew the spiritual strength of love from Holy Communion they receive into their souls during their daily morning Masses.

Over the past decade, Mother Teresa frequently visited Japan to establish two branches of her Missionaries of Charity there. The specific mission with which she charged her missionaries was to save the lives of babies threatened by abortion, especially by unwed mothers in this predominantly non-Christian land.

During her Mass attendances in Japan, Mother Teresa, probably unwittingly, demonstrated her deep reverence and keen spiritual sensibility toward the real presence of Jesus in the Holy Eucharist by receiving Holy Communion on her tongue.

Concerning the Akita nuns' method of reception of communion, Sr. Agnes told me, "In those days, (before the nuns in Akita changed their method of communion to that on the tongue) I felt that to receive communion in our hands was an act lacking respect for the Holy Eucharist."

Fr. Joseph said that the angel's statement to Sr. Agnes, *"The wound in the palm of the Blessed Mother is deeper and more painful than yours,"* means that the Blessed Mother, as the Heavenly Mother especially of all Catholic priests, is suffering in view of her sons' (priests') practice of distributing Holy Communion upon the hands of laymen and non-priest clergy.

Fr. Joseph appealed to Catholics to ponder the meaning of the "double coincidences."

He said, "The cross-shaped wound formed in the *right* hand of the statue of the Heavenly Mother, as **Priests (Her sons) distribute Communion with their right hands. The recipient usually receives communion in his or her left hand. It was Sr. Agnes' left hand that developed the painful stigmata which forced her to receive her communion on the tongue.**"

Fr. Joseph said "I believe this Divine coincidence was arranged by God to give Catholics a key lesson to urge them to receive the Holy

Eucharist on the tongue to defend their spiritual sensibility to the real presence of Jesus in the Holy Eucharist." He said this sensibility would grow through reviving the practice of communion on the tongue if the practice had been replaced by communion by hand in a certain diocese.

Fr. Joseph said one of his fellow priests confessed to him that he had suffered from a guilty conscience, as he is forced by a bishop to distribute communion onto laymen's hands against his conscience.

Following the mysterious phenomenon of the bleeding palms of Sr. Agnes and the Statue and a subsequent mysterious event, all the nuns at the convent stopped receiving holy communion in their hands and resumed the practice of communion on the tongue.

The event which led to this favorable change was what observers call a "Divinely-arranged summons" by Our Lord of Fr. Thomas Teiji Yasuda, S.V.D. to this convent in February 1974, about four months after Mary delivered her third and last message to Sr. Agnes.

Fr. Thomas Teiji Yasuda, Priest Prepared by God

Fr. Yasuda first visited the convent on February 14, 1974 to comply with a request to say a Mass for the nuns of the convent of the Handmaids of the Holy Eucharist. The convent had lost its chaplain, Fr. Mochizuki, on June 5, 1973. So, nuns had prayed to God for more than 9 months, so that God may vouchsafe to give the convent a good pastor to guide it spiritually, until Fr. Yasuda moved there as a Divine gift. He had come back to his hometown of Akita on a temporary stay, when heavy snowfall paralyzed all transporation means for 2 days. Although he asked a truck driver to drive him to the convent on the hill, the snow prevented the truck from approaching the convent. Fr. Yasuda had to ask a bulldozer that happened to pass to tow the truck along the steep slope path leading up to the convent. Not long after this visit, he felt a divine urge to resettle from his Parish in Tokyo's Kichijochi Church to this holy place of Marian apparitions.

After his superior of the Society of Divine Word recommended Fr. Yasuda be appointed as the chaplain of the Akita convent in a message to Bishop Ito, Fr. Yasuda moved to the community of nuns in Yuzawadai, Akita, on March 10, 1974, — about two months after his initial visit. After he was officially appointed by Bishop Ito as the chaplain of the convent, he assumed his duties as the spiritual director of this community of nuns.

In an interview with me, Fr. Yasuda said that he gave the following suggestions to the nuns:

"I believe communion on the tongue would be of greater benefit to your souls. Although I will not force you to do so, I ask you to choose, in accordance with your consciences, whether you would receive holy communion on your tongue or in your hands."

Fr. Yasuda said in the interview, "I told the nuns communion on the tongue would be a better method to ensure that they receive the Body of Christ with reverence and faith."

"From my experiences as a parish priest at Tokyo's Kichijochi Church, I know communion by the hands of non-priest Catholics could damage their reverence and faith in the real presence of Jesus in the Holy Eucharist," the priest said.

The nuns meditated upon this suggestion for the time being. Finally, the nuns came to Fr. Yasuda, saying, "Father, we thought about the issue of how to receive communion in view of your suggestion. We have decided to receive communion on our tongues from now on because of the decision we made on the basis of the dictates of our own consciences."

After Bishop Ito, noticed that the nuns changed the method of communion, he asked the nuns whether the priest had ordered them to do so. The nuns replied, "No. He did not order us to do so. We chose to adopt the practice of communion on the tongue by our own consciences." The bishop decided to respect the nuns' decision and has continued to distribute communion on their tongues ever since.

Guardian Angel's Message on Fr. Thomas Teiji Yasuda's Mission as Spiritual Director

Here, we must pay attention to the crucial fact that a guardian angel of Sr. Agnes told her in one of the angel's messages that Fr. Thomas Teiji Yasuda, S.V.D. is a priest whose spirit had been especially prepared and enriched by God for the mission of giving spiritual guidance to the community of the Handmaids of the Holy Eucharist.

The angel gave this message on June 28, 1974, on the eve of the feast day of Saints Peter and Paul during the nuns' adoration of the Holy Eucharist displayed in a monstrance. The angel urged greater respect for this priest's Divine mission by clarifying the holy mission given by God to this priest of the Society of Divine Word.

The following is the English translation of the complete message to Sr. Agnes by her guardian angel on June 28, 1974, concerning the Divine mission of Fr. Yasuda as the spiritual director of the Convent of the Handmaids of the Holy Eucharist.

The angel said, *"The Catholic priest (Fr. Yasuda), who has been prepared in advance by God for this Convent, has made a firm decision to stay and work with you as a result of your prayers."*

"The priest plans to guide you spiritually, while obeying your superior (the Ordinary of the Niigata diocese — then Bishop Ito, now Bishop Sato) with the same intentions as those of the superior's. The priest made this decision, believing that your superior will be pleased with his decision."

"Why has the superior (Bishop John Shojiro Ito) refrained from quickly announcing to everyone, with joy, the fact that this priest was given by God

as the spiritual director of this convent, although I have made it clear that this priest was given in response to your prayers?"

"This convent is not the possession of your superior alone."

"The priest, who plans to guide you, is determined to give himself entirely to the service of the convent, while obeying your superior."

"It is not right (for the superior) to try to avoid requesting this God-prepared priest to provide all the spiritual guidance you will need, despite this message, while trying to avoid entrusting the priest with the total spiritual guidance of the community."

"Your superior and this convent loved by God, who dispatched me here, has been guided well until today in the light of all the messages which I was ordered by God to deliver here."

"You must tell your superior to announce to all people, with joy and trust, this message which I was ordered to deliver here. Tell the superior to ask the priest presented, to provide all spiritual guidance to the convent and entrust this priest with the work of guidance."

"Why are you hesitating to comply with my instructions? Without hesitancy, convey this message with trust in God."

*"Otherwise, divine graces and guidance, which have been given to your superior, **will be taken away**."*

"With courage, convey this message to your superior."

Sr. Agnes also wrote down the following note on June 28, 1974, — the very day she received the messages — "When I received this message, I prostrated myself and started to weep. I felt as though I was hit on the head with a strong blow."

"After a while, my guardian angel assumed its usual tender expression she had shown to me whenever she recited the prayers of the Rosary together with me."

"The angel told me (Sr. Agnes), *'You need not worry. Pray with confidence. No matter what difficulties and obstructions you and this community may face in the future, God will defend and guide this community and you, because you have faithfully conveyed the messages which I was ordered by God to bring here.'"*

"'Pray very, very much with trust in God. Pray for many people, for this community and for your superior.'"

"The angel vanished after leaving these messages. Now, when I (Sr. Agnes) am writing this down, it has revived the fear which I felt at that time (in the face of the angel's stearn attitude.)"

Sr. Agnes immediately reported the above messages to the bishop, who was staying at the convent at the same time the messages were delivered to Sr. Agnes. His response to the message was to weep.

Sr. Agnes said in a telephone interview in 1994, "Until Fr. Yasuda arrived as the new chaplain, all of us, the nuns of the convent, used to pray hard to God, asking Him to give us, as our spiritual director, a Catholic priest who could please His Divine Heart."

"We prayed to God with this intention (of seeking a good pastor) from the time our former chaplain, Fr. Nozumu Mochizuki, left the convent until March 10th, 1974, when Fr. Yasuda arrived here as the new chaplain," she said.

We should note that this holy priest gave this crucial guidance regarding the appropriate method of receiving Holy Communion to the nuns.

Three Angels Surround Fr. Yasuda
God's Revelation on Fr. Thomas Teiji Yasuda's Mission

About five weeks later, on August 8 of the same year, Fr. Yasuda abruptly fell into a serious illness during a Mass he was celebrating. He was taken by an ambulance to the Akita City Hospital in downtown Akita run by the city government. Doctors diagnosed that his colon had burst open and was bleeding. They found that Fr. Yasuda was on the verge of death and in the urgent need of surgery to repair the burst colon. Strangely, none of the surgeons had the moral courage to conduct the urgently-needed, but difficult, surgery. They did not want the responsibility for this high-rate-of-failure surgery.

They did not want to be held responsible for his possible death, even though they were sure that, without such surgery, Fr. Yasuda would not survive the breakup of his colon.

At the very moment these surgeons were showing their reluctance to perform the surgery, Sr. Agnes was given a "vision" by God, while staying in her room at the convent, which is located a few kilometers from the hospital. It seems as though God sometimes tells her the crucial spiritual meaning of an occurrence by means of such mysterious visions or dreams. This time, Sr. Agnes saw a surgery room at the hospital in her vision, along with these hesitant surgeons. In the center of the hospital room was a surgery table. Fr. Yasuda was lying upon it. The color of the skin of his hands had turned purple due to the worsening of his physical condition and, most probably, because of the loss of a large amount of blood from the vein in the burst colon.

Sr. Agnes simultaneously "saw" the developments and heard the conversations between the surgeons and noticed that the weak kneed hesitation was scaring them away from conducting the necessary surgery. Then, she saw a group of three solemn angels surrounding Fr. Yasuda and his surgery bed. While reciting prayers, the three angels were heard saying, "Sanctus, Sanctus, Sanctus (Holy, Holy. Holy)" towards Fr. Yasuda.

Then, she saw an elder brother and nephew of Fr. Yasuda (both excellent doctors practicing medicine in Akita) rush into the hospital room after being alerted of the news of his brother's sudden illness. (Their hasty arrivals were also physically occurring at this instant.) Fr. Yasuda's brother and nephew strongly urged the hesitant surgeons to conduct the surgery, saying, "We will take all the responsibility, even if he should die. So, please do not worry. Please perform the surgery." The surgeons then agreed to conduct the surgery, which took about five to six hours. The operation proved successful.

Sr. Agnes, still in her second-floor convent room, after watching the actual developments in her vision came down the staircase to another room on the first floor, where her sister nuns gathered anxiously.

She told the nuns, "Now, you no longer have to worry about Fr. Yasuda's condition. The doctors finally agreed to perform the surgery on Fr. Yasuda, so he will be cured." At that time, the nuns did not take Sr. Agnes' words at face value, because they sounded too optimistic at that serious life-or-death moment. Later, however, when news of the successful operation reached the convent, the nuns realized that what Sr. Agnes saw in one of her mysterious visions had come true.

Fr. Yasuda said in an interview in 1994, "The expression 'the real presence of Jesus in the Holy Eucharist' does **not** mean that if you examined a small particle of the Holy Eucharist with a microscope, you could recognize the face of Jesus in the particle."

"The real presence means the **mystical, sacramental presence** of Jesus in the Holy Eucharist, rather than His physical presence in the Holy Eucharist," the priest said. "Because it is the **mystical** presence, it means **even more real and stronger presence** of Jesus Christ in the Holy Eucharist, than the mere physical presence of Jesus," he said.

Holy Father's Example Regarding Communion on the Tongue

Pope John Paul II visited Japan in February 1981, celebrating Mass at the huge Korakuen Stadium in Tokyo in front of tens of thousands of Japanese Catholics. Fr. Joseph Marie-Jacq, M.E.P., told me in an interview that during this occasion, he went to observe how the Pontiff would distribute Holy Communion to Japanese Catholics. Fr. Joseph said he has been suffering very much from a great deal of pressure from a diocesan bishop to change his Parish's practice of Communion on the tongue into that on the hands. Fr. Joseph said he was determined to follow any example the Pontiff should show on the matter. "I was determined that if the Pope distributed Communion onto laymen's hands, then I would follow suit due to my avowed loyalty to the Holy Father," he said.

During the solemn Mass at the stadium, Fr. Joseph was happy to confirm, with his own eyes, that the Pontiff distributed Holy Communion onto Communicants' tongues ONLY, even when Catholics thrust their hands towards the Pontiff, seeking to receive in their hands. The Pontiff showed exactly the same example as in this case, when he visited France and other countries in Europe, Africa, Oceania and Asia.

At one of the Masses he celebrated in France, the wife of then French President Giscard D'estaing was present. On the occasion, Madame Giscard D'estaing was determined to receive Holy Communion in her hands from the Pontiff, despite her awareness of the reputation that the Pontiff never distributes Communion onto laymen's hands. Therefore, when the moment of Communion arrived during the Mass, Madame Discard D'estaing walked towards the Pontiff with her both arms and hands stretched straight forward in front of her body. John Paul II, however, placed the Holy Eucharist on her tongue, as he did for every other Communicant who attended the Mass. The Pontiff's refusal to place the Host in her hand, despite her apparent demand to receive in her hand, became the talk among many French Catholics.

There took place another moving episode when the Pontiff celebrated Mass at the Tokyo stadium. Fr. Joseph noticed that there was a middle-aged man standing at the rear of the queue lining in front of the Pontiff. When his turn to receive Holy Communion came, the man knelt in front of the Pontiff and opened his mouth to receive the Host on his tongue. In response, the Pontiff tenderly smiled to this man and placed the Host on his tongue in a graceful manner, according to the testimony of Fr. Joseph.

How God Tried to Revive People's Faith

A few years later, this author had a "chance" encounter with this middle-aged man — probably by Divine arrangement. Over the dining table at a condominium of one of my acquaintances, I spoke with him about Fr. Joseph's experiences and observation of the Pontiff's Mass at the stadium. To my surprise, the man replied, "I am the man who fell on my knees before the Pope at the stadium." It turns out that he was a Mexican Catholic priest, Rev. Fr. Jesus Pantoja, who came to Japan as a missionary.

Meanwhile, Fr. Joseph said he discussed the issue of appropriate reception of Holy Communion with Bishop Stefano Minoru Hamao of the Yokohama diocese, the one who was pressuring him to Communion upon laymen's hands. At that occasion, Bishop Hamao pointed to an exceptional case that took place in Germany. The Bishop told Fr. Joseph that the Pope did distribute Holy Communion onto German laymen's hands on one occasion.

Fr. Joseph replied when an Episcopal Conference ignores the Pontiff's teachings on this issue and pressures the Pontiff to distribute Holy Communion in a layman's hand, the Pontiff has no other way but to comply with the demand. The Pontiff was forced to comply, because he did not want to risk antagonizing the Episcopal Conference in question and thereby triggering a possible schism.

The Pontiff does such things to prevent a schism from undermining the spiritual benefit of the flock of Catholics who are placed under the influence of such a disobedient Episcopal Conference.

A German Catholic magazine, "The Defender (Editor, Rev. G. Walker)," carried an article describing another significant moment, at which Pope John Paul II answered some Catholic pilgrims' questions about "Communion in the hand." The publishers in Germany kept minutes of the meeting. A pilgrim asked, "Holy Father, what is your opinion of Communion in the hand?" The magazine quoted from the minutes, in which the Pontiff replied, "... I tell you, that I am not in favor of it, neither will I recommend it."

On another occasion, the Pope said during an Angelus message on January 10, 1982, that, "To exert violent pressure on others' conscience — in a sense — would constitute a greater mortal sin than murdering a man." Fr. Joseph quoted a colleague missionary priest as telling him, "I want to work as an assistant priest at your church. I suffer every day whenever I am forced to suppress my conscience by distributing Holy Communion onto the hands of the lay communicants."

During the liturgically turbulent '70's, some bishops of the Japanese Episcopal Conference strongly recommended and demanded that communion in the hands be introduced throughout Japan. This was an attempt to follow the lead of the French Episcopal Conference. Conscientious resistance to this forced change came from various parts of Japan, especially from the Nagasaki diocese. (Nagasaki is the holy land protected by Japan's numerous Martyrs, who were executed for their refusal to renounce their Catholic faith during the 250 years of persecution that started in the late 16th century.) Still today, in Nagasaki, about 90 to 95 percent of Catholics receive communions on their tongues.

Cardinal Who Encouraged Saint Maxmillian Kolbe to Come to Japan

Cardinal Joseph Asajiro Satowaki of Nagasaki called a few years ago a meeting of Catholic priests working in his diocese and instructed them NEVER to break away from the universal Catholic Church's centuries-old practice of distributing communion on the tongue.

Cardinal Satowaki said in his letter to Mr. Masahiro Tominari, a parishioner in Fujieda, "I have been recommending that lay Catholics in Nagasaki receive the Holy Eucharist on their tongues. I am aware that Pope John Paul II also wants lay Catholics throughout the world to receive the Holy Eucharist on their tongues."

The sole Japanese cardinal's letter, whose copy I obtained from Mr. Tominari, also says, "Communion on the hand appears to be hampering the influx of God's blessings into souls. This has, in turn, triggered a sharp decline in the number of priestly vocations and ordinations to the Catholic priesthood in Japan — just as it has in Germany, which has also introduced the practice of communion on the hand extensively." This is the very cardinal who advised Fr. Maxmillian Kolbe in 1928 to come to Japan as a missionary when the cardinal was a seminarian studying theology in Rome.

After receiving a Divine call to rethink the appropriate method of communion in March, 1974, in the form of a suggestion from a Catholic priest sent by God to the convent as its spiritual director, the nuns at the Akita convent began receiving holy communion on their tongues.

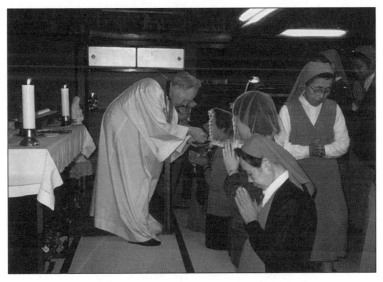

Holy Communion during a Mass at the Akita convent

Not only do the nuns receive the Holy Eucharist on their tongues, but their sensibilities move them to receive on their knees in deep reverence and love for God. Our God who is Love called us to, and still calls us to use this method of receiving Him on our tongues to protect and nurture our spiritual ability to recognize His real presence in the Holy Eucharist.

Inestimable Gift (Pastoral Instruction)

Fr. Joseph, the French missionary priest and the translator into Japanese of Pope John Paul II's pastoral instruction, *Inaestimabile Donum* (Inestimable Gift), said the pontiff articulated his intentions and spiritual guidance on this key question throughout the publication of this pastoral instruction. The pastoral letter was issued Holy Thursday on April 3, 1980, with Pontifical confirmation from the Congregation for the Sacraments and Divine Worship.

Fr. Joseph said, although this pastoral instruction was widely ignored and opposed by the Episcopal Conferences of various nations, individual clergy should have the moral courage to pass these Pontifical teachings on to the faithful of the world. He reminds us that faithful Roman Catholics cannot scrap their belief in the doctrinal infallibility of the Holy Father, and that they should listen to these key Pontifical lessons with greater humility.

Article 9 of the Pastoral letter states, "The Holy Eucharist is the gift of the Lord, which should be distributed to laymen THROUGH the INTERMEDIATION of Catholic PRIESTS who are ordained especially for this work. Laymen are neither permitted to take the Sacred Host by themselves nor the Consecrated Chalice."

The following are the original texts of this pastoral letter in both Latin and French, respectively:

9. "Communio Eucharistica. Communio donum est Domini, quod fidelibus a ministro traditur ad eiusmodi officium destinato. Non licet ipsis fidelibus panem consecratum sumere

neque calicem sacrum tantoque minus de manu in manum inter se ea transmittere."

9. "La Communion Eucharistique. La communion est un don du Seigneur, qui est donne aux fideles par l'intermediaire du ministre qui a ete deleque pour cela. Il n'est pas permis aux fideles de prendre eux-memes le pain consacre et le calice; et encore moins de se les transmettre les uns aux autres."

In one of the eight books he authored, Fr. Joseph writes, "The events in Akita have imparted an understanding that Christ suffers most intensely from the coldness, the indifference and the profanations dealt by His consecrated ones toward the sublime sacrament of His love." As the translator into Japanese of *Inaestimabile Donum,* Fr. Joseph spoke up in defense of the Holy Father's teachings on the liturgy and Holy Communion.

Not surprisingly, he suffered a terrible backlash from some Church officials who have tried to write off the Holy Father and those who defend the Holy Father as conservative.

Fr. Joseph has tried, humbly and courageously, to guide back to the genuine Catholic dogma these people who have been disgruntled with the Pontiff's teachings. Fr. Joseph also defended the Holy Father's infallibility on doctrinal affairs in Japanese Catholic communities that had been negatively affected by some influential theologians whose theological opinion had broken with the constant teaching of the Church.

When I (this writer) appeared on the "Family Night" live show of Mother Angelica's Eternal Word Television Network, March 8, 1994, she pointed out that communion in the hand could lead to unconscious sacrilegious acts by reducing lay Catholics' reverence towards the Holy Eucharist.

"I think it's important that we know... it is preferable to receive Communion on the tongue to keep Our Lord from being blasphemed and to keep particles of the Host from being just everywhere," she said.

"We find them (Holy Eucharists) in missalettes, we find the Host under pews under chewing gum, we find terrible things. We find particles on the floor and it all comes down to a lack of faith that it is the real Body and Blood, Soul and Divinity of Jesus."

"That irreverence brings other kind of irreverences to the Eucharist," she warned.

During the live show, the reverend mother and I discussed what God planned to teach to Roman Catholics by inflicting the painful, cross-shaped stigmata onto Sr. Agnes' left hand and the bleeding wound to the palm of the statue of the Holy Mother Mary.

Mother Angelica said, "If you remember Francis telling us that Sr. Anges' stigmata was in her left hand. The stigmata on the statue (of the Holy Mother Mary) was in the right hand. The significance, I think, is very important."

"What Francis was telling me today was when Sr. Agnes' hand (fingers) was pulled in for the pain (of the stigmata), she was unable to receive Communion in her hand," she said.

"It seemingly could be implied that she was making reparation for many, many sacrileges that have been committed by receiving Communion in the hand," she said.

"The one in Our Lady's right hand may be in reparation for priests who insist on giving Communion in the hand (of lay Catholics.) Their (priest's) hands have been blessed and anointed to handle, to touch and to give, to you and I, the Holy Eucharist."

Later in the live show, Mother Angelica went, as usual, for telephone calls from the audience.

When a man from New Jersey, with a serious voice, telephoned her seeking her advice on this critical issue on behalf of, probably, millions of TV viewers with the same inquiry, Mother Angelica gave him a really thoughtful, heart-warming advice.

She said, "If you look at what has happened with communion in the hand... when you take communion in the hand, let's look at the fruits of it."

"If anybody — Bishops, priests, religious, lay people, — look at the fruits... I have seen a 9 year-old girl go to communion and pop it like an M&M, I have seen people put it into their sleeves, put it in their pockets, leave it on the pew."

"If we understood that this is the Real Body, Blood, Soul and Divinity of Jesus... if we had *not lost our faith*... I have seen a Host drop on the floor and the priest did not bother about it."

"Once you lose that weapon as Our Lady said, once you lose the reality (of Jesus' presence in the Eucharist), then you have no weapon to fight the enemy (Satan) with, and that is what has happened with the communion in the hand."

Mother Angelica said, "Now I am asking and Our Lady is asking in Akita to re-examine why you began communion in the hand. Be honest... Be honest. Do you really believe in the Real body of Jesus? If you do, can you say, at this point, twenty years later (since the

Mother Angelica and this author on "Family Night"

introduction of communion in the hand), it has done good that our dear Lord has been lifted up? ... No...NO."

"Very few children I have met have ever been taught that He is really, truly, present in the Holy Eucharist."

Mother Angelica went on to say, "I am only asking and I think Our Lady is saying, "Please rethink... rethink having communion in the hand."

"Look at the fruits. You can't say particles don't fall all over the floor... We have lost truth. We have been deceived too long — too long."

When Mother Angelica and I were discussing Our Lady's call to Christians to offer up prayers, sufferings, penance and sacrifices in connection with the Holy Eucharist, she told the television audience, "Now, what we are hearing Our Lady say to us is that we should offer up to God reparation for our Lord so insulted especially in the Holy Eucharist, so blasphemied... so much indifference towards the Holy Eucharist."

"She (Our Lady) is saying to us... everyone who wants to do something for the Lord... make reparations with your own pain, your own weakness, your own difficulties."

"Whatever difficulties, whatever cross you carry, give that to the Lord, especially for Bishops, priests and, I would add, religious — all those who have been chosen by God to lead us in the path of salvation," the reverend mother said.

Fatima's Prophesy on "Outrages and Sacrileges" towards Holy Eucharist

Fr. Joseph pointed out that, just as in the apparitions at Akita, the Angel of Peace, in the Prophetic 1916 message at Fatima, also appealed to all Catholics, through the three shepherd children, to make reparation for the sins of profanation and sacrileges that would be committed against the Holy Eucharist.

How God Tried to Revive People's Faith

To understand why Fr. Joseph underscores the theological importance of the Angel's prayer at Fatima, which reveals the most serious of Divine messages there — a message of profound consequence that affects the fate of the world - the Angel's third apparition at Fatima is represented here:

When the Angel appeared for the third and last time in Cabeco of Fatima in late September, 1916, the three children saw the angel, resplendent, dazzling and hovering in the air before them. The Angel was holding a chalice, over which a Host was suspended in mid-air.

The awestruck children noticed that drops of blood were falling from the Host into the chalice. The Angel then left the Host and Chalice suspended in the air, while he prostrated himself on the ground and saying the following prayer of most profound meaning:

"Most Holy Trinity, Father, Son, Holy Spirit, I adore you profoundly, and offer you the most Precious Body, Blood, Soul and Divinity of Jesus Christ, present in all the tabernacles of the world, in reparation for the OUTRAGES, SACRILEGES, and INDIFFERENCES which HE is offended.

"And through the infinite merits of His Most Sacred Heart and of the Immaculate Heart of Mary, I beg of You the conversion of poor sinners."

This the Angel said three times. Then raising himself back up, he took the chalice and the Host, then knelt on a flat rock, held the white Host in front of him and told the shepherd children:

"Receive this and drink the Body and the Blood of Jesus Christ, HORRIBLY OUTRAGED by ungrateful men. Make reparations for their sins and console your God."

The Angel then placed the Host on the tongue of Lucia. To Jacinta and Francisco, who had not yet received First Communion, the Angel gave the Blood of Christ from the chalice. They drank of it. After this, he once more prostrated himself on the ground repeating the same prayer three times.

The children repeated it with the angel. Then, for the last time, the angel faded away into the shimmering sunlight.

Of this episode, Fr. Joseph remarked that, "The essence of all the messages delivered at Fatima is contained in this prayer." Perhaps our Holy Father is aware of the profound meaning of this DIVINE PLEA, in view of the fact the Pontiff declared the following in his February 24, 1980 pastoral letter *Dominicae Cenae* (Divine Food):

"How eloquently the rite of the anointing of priests' hands in our Latin ordination tells that a special grace and power of the Holy Spirit is necessary precisely for priests' hands!"

"To touch and distribute the Holy Eucharist (to laymen) with their consecrated hands is the privilege an ordained priest."

Encounter with Marthe Robin

In 1974, a year after the apparitions started in Akita, Fr. Joseph visited France to meet and talk with Marthe Robin, a victim soul, who died on February 6, 1981, after having lived for 52 years with no other nourishment than the Blessed Sacrament of Love. Marthe shed blood from her stigmata every Friday during an agony similar to that of Sr. Agnes'. Fr. Joseph not only met with Marthe Robin, but gave the Holy Eucharist to her. He described the remarkable experiences he had on this occasion to me. He said, "When I began to bring the Host toward Marthe's mouth, I could not. The Communion itself flew toward her mouth and placed itself onto her tongue."

Making a gesture with his forefinger and thumb of his right hand as in the way he usually pinches the Host, Fr. Joseph said, "I could not carry communion to her mouth with my fingers any closer than 'this' (showing me a distance of some 30 centimeters with another gesture of his hands), as the communion leapt onto her tongue by itself."

God appears to have used both women — Marthe Robin and Sr. Agnes — to revive Catholics' dwindling spiritual ability to recognize the real presence of Jesus in the Holy Eucharist. How encouraging Marthe's presence had been to many Catholic priests — whose spiritual sensibilities faced the erosive pressure of today's theological confusion regarding the Holy Eucharist — is seen in the attendance of her funeral at which 250 priests and five bishops assisted.

Marthe Robin, founder of the world-wide *Foyer de Charite* (Fireplace of Love of Neighbor) movement, was born a daughter of a farmer, March 13th, 1902, in the borough of Chateauneuf-de-Galaure, southern France.

Marthe was felled by a severe physical illness and became bed-ridden for more than 50 years. Marthe lived a life of prayer, day and night, and offered up her sufferings and sacrifices, especially for the intention of sanctification of priests.

Even with her haunting physical pains, Marthe — just as Sr. Agnes does — maintained her cheerful disposition and carried the Cross with her burning love for Jesus, who told all Christians to "take up your cross every day and follow me." It is the same Jesus who told us, "Shoulder my yoke and learn from me, for I am gentle and humble in heart, and you will find rest for your souls."

People, seeking spiritual advices, came to Marthe from around the world, to whom she spoke in plain language.

When Fr. Joseph paid a visit to Marthe Robin in 1974 in Chateauneuf, the pair spoke about the mystery of the Holy Eucharist, from which that *inexplicable sweetness of God's love, true inner peace and rest* would fill the souls of its *humble* communicants.

Akita: Mother of God as Coredemptrix

Fr. Joseph Marie-Jacq, M.E.P. saw a Holy Communion, which he had held with his fingers, leap into her mouth on its own accord, when he was slowly and carefully carrying it to her after the Consecration at Mass.

In March, 1994, prior to my appearance on Mother Angelica's live show on March 8, I stayed with a Christian family in Atlanta, Georgia.

When the wife of my friend read Fr. Joseph's descriptions of his mysterious Eucharistic experiences in the home of Marthe, she exclaimed, "This is clear evidence that God wants lay communicants to receive His Body on their tongues!"

She continued, "I believe communion in the hands of lay communicants carries the dangers that it erodes belief in the *Divine Mystery* of the Holy Eucharist and this in turn causes a lessening of sanctifying grace, placing the One, Holy, Catholic and Apostolic Church in great danger."

When this writer, one of former parishioners of St. Ann's Church of Fr. Joseph, was meditating upon the meaning of the Eucharistic miracle in Chateauneuf, I thought God might have given an "answer" to guide Fr. Joseph, who was then suffering so much after he complied with a strong outside order to intoduce communion in the hands in his church in the early 1970s.

Eight years after his return from France, Fr. Joseph wrote a beautiful printed pamphlet "Defense for Communion on the Tongue" of September 21, 1982, in which he theologically explained why communion on the tongue has to be maintained to protect and nurture lay Catholics' spiritual ability to recognize the real sacramental presence of Jesus Christ in the Holy Eucharist.

Fr. Joseph, author of several theological books, wrote on the first page of the pamphlet, — both in French and Japanese — "I myself used to feel that my heart told me that communion on the tongue should be preserved." even before his 1974 encounter with Marthe

Robin and his pilgrimage to Rome, where he came to know the true intention of Paul VI on this crucial matter.

This author believes these words of his implies that he was then under a constant inner urge from the Holy Spirit and his pastoral intuition to maintain communion on the tongue for the good of his flock of parishioners.

In view of his agony that emanated from his deep genuine love for God and his flock, God might have arranged for this Eucharistic miracle to take place at the home of Marthe Robin as a powerful encouragement and guidance concerning what the missionary should do for the Catholic Church.

This miracle — combined with his witnessings of four out of the 101 episodes of weepings of the statue of the Holy Mother Mary of Akita — encouraged him to speak up in his books and sermons to defend the Holy Father's pastoral teachings concerning communion on the tongue.

In the early 1970s, Fr. Joseph used to follow strong recommendations from the Japanese Episcopal Conference that urged priests to administer the Holy Eucharist onto the hands of lay communicants in documents delivered to parish churches. However, he realized that the Pope wants to maintain the custom of communion on the tongue in 1974, when he made pilgrimags to Rome and Jerusalem, alongside his visit to Marthe Robin. When Fr. Joseph visited the Basilica of St. Peter, he heard Vatican officials tell visiting foreign Catholic priests, by means of "electronic loud speakers" at the basilica, that the Catholic Church bans communion on the hands and that priests should distribute the Holy Eucharist onto the tongue of lay communicants. The broadcast used to be made continuously throughout the days.

During his visit to Jerusalem, Fr. Joseph read instructions which told Catholic priests to administer communion onto the tongue of lay communicants "at all sacristan rooms" which he visited to prepare for a Mass. He also studied Pontifical documents.

After he returned from Europe to his parish church, St. Ann's Church in Fujieda, Fr. Joseph told his parishioners, humbly, "My parishioners, I earlier recommended that lay communicants receive communion in your hands. It was a wrong recommendation. Now, let's return to the custom of receiving the Holy Eucharist on your tongues." Then, he explained the reasons why communion on the tongue is necessary to protect people's reverence and faith in the real presence of Jesus in the Holy Eucharist. His parishioners understood the Pontifical teachings on this crucial matter after hearing his explanations and followed the suggestion to return to the traditional custom in accordance with their consciences and free will, as well as these parishioners' deep devotion to the Holy Eucharist.

Ms. Gemma Chie Masuda, mentioned in the preceding chapters, said, "The Blessed Virgin knew of the faith and courage of Fr. Joseph who lived a life of profound martyrdom in defending the Holy Eucharist from sacrileges and insults. I believe the Blessed Mother shed tears in Akita, because so many Catholics neglect efforts to draw spiritual nourishment from the Holy Eucharist despite their easy access to daily Mass. In this neglectfulness, they waste the redeeming Blood shed by Jesus on the Cross at Calvary."

Author's Reflections on Apparitions in Akita

Christian love of neighbor means the giving of oneself to others. Such genuine love creates the goodness — the energy of love — in souls who receive the love. Love creates the strength to love others in the heart of the recipient of the love.

For example, perhaps you have some memories of having been helped by others, when you were suffering or were in great need of material or spiritual help. When a person receives another's selfless Christian love, the recipient is gradually transformed into a better person every time he or she receives that type of love. Because love creates goodness in the recipient's heart, the recipient is altered to become a better and more warm-hearted person than before.

Even if a person is morally very weak or even cold-hearted, the streaming of a really powerful selfless love into his or her soul could transform even that type of person into a warm-hearted, compassionate person.

This is the mystery of love of neighbors.

Now, the crucial question comes up — where can we find a selfless love powerful enough to transform us and this callous-hearted world?

Take Mother Teresa as an example for our consideration. Who transformed her into such a powerful apostle of love? Where did she acquire that powerful energy of selfless love?

When she was born in what is now the war torn Yugoslavia from her Albanian parents on August 27, 1910, she was just an ordinary baby girl crying for her mother's milk and for care by her family. Agnes was her given name.

The infant had to be cared for by her family. Then, she had the only potential of growing up to become such a charitable, compassionate soul. That high level of spiritual maturity and her highly charitable soul — by which we distinguish Mother Teresa — was merely potential at this stage of her life.

Then, Divine and human love continued to stream into the soul of the infant, Agnes — first from her devout Catholic family and then from the Holy Communion she received regularly after her First Communion.

Think of just one particle of the Holy Eucharist. Pope John Paul II once said, if a Catholic has a strong enough conviction in the real presence of Jesus in the Holy Eucharist, and if he or she is humble enough to recognize his or her spiritual poverty (the insufficiency or lack of love in his or her soul), then humility and spiritual sensibility towards the Eucharist will bolster the efficacy of even one reception of Holy Communion in helping that person make genuine progress toward a noble goal of becoming an even more compassionate and warm-hearted person.

However, even God's love can face greater obstacles when it tries to enter into the soul of the arrogant, because such a soul is already filled with impure and corrupt ideas. If a soul is humble enough to recognize his or her spiritual poverty and the need to receive spiritual strength from God, then this condition of the heart makes it much easier for Divine love to stream into it. It is because God's love seeks to fill such humble vacuum of a soul.

Like the Host which leapt onto the tongue of Marthe Robin, Divine love can immediately flood a humble soul's vacuum through Holy Communion. A Roman Catholic should not allow secular desires to replace his or her spiritual hunger and thirst for the Lord in the Holy Eucharist.

This is the reason why Jesus said, "How happy are the poor in spirit: Theirs is the kingdom of heaven." When a humble soul receives the body of Christ into its soul, the soul receives the energy of love — energy of goodness — and becomes a person capable of loving others in action. Through this process of loving others, this soul creates goodness in the souls it loves.

The more frequent a humble soul receives Holy Communions, the more quickly that soul matures in charity.

This is the basis that provides the basis for true Christian hope. This chain cycle of continual creation of goodness in human souls will continue to the end of time. In order to trigger this chain reaction of continual creation of goodness in human souls in the most powerful manner, Jesus instituted the Eucharist in the upper room in Jerusalem, where the Last Supper took place about 2,000 years ago.

It appears to me that the Holy Mother of Akita wept partly because She was saddened at the near-collapse or the serious decline in the spiritual ability of so many Roman Catholics to recognize and love the real presence of Jesus in the Holy Eucharist.

The Holy Mother is apparently aware of the seriousness of the consequences of the weakened spiritual sensibility in the real presence — such faltering sensibility makes it more difficult for Divine graces to stream into human souls.

The Holy Mother appears to have come to Akita — among other major purposes — to revive Catholics' love for the Eucharist and to transform us into apostles of love — like Mother Teresa — so that we can be witnesses of Jesus' love in this cold-hearted, lonely modern society, where so many have gone astray.

Mary, the Heavenly Mother of Love, came to Akita to change us into human beings who can more powerfully love others.

Once we become powerful prayerful Christians in this way, we will be able to console the Sacred Heart of Jesus, so offended by today's egocentric world.

Because God is Love, He wants us to share in His overflowing goodness and warmth. It is for this reason that He instituted the Supreme Sacrament of Love — The Eucharist — with which He planned to nourish our souls since the time of His Creation of the Universe. This appears to be His Plan of Love He has been implementing from the beginning of the Universe.

Today, so many Catholics refuse to accept or seek this inestimable gift of Divine Love, even on the Lord's day. Sunday Massgoers often neglect to seek this gift on weekdays, even when they have daily access to it in nearby parish churches.

Others put the watching of sports or other entertainment programs on television above their worship of God on Sunday. The person has time for TV but no time for God. Where is the genuine spiritual thirst for Jesus in the Holy Eucharist?

It appears to me that, in this sense, many Catholics — in Japan and other countries — daily practice a greater waste than a billionaire who would throw away millions of dollars overnight at a Las Vegas casino.

Such waste — daily practiced by so many Catholics — is not a recoverable material loss. It is a permanent loss. It is the waste of Divine Love.

Satan certainly has intervened and continues still to intervene in this world, offending and undermining Catholics' spiritual sensibility and faith in the real Presence of Jesus in the Holy Eucharist.

Fortunately, the Mother of God, the "Woman" of Genesis 3:15 — entrusted by God with the Divine Mission of crushing Satan's head — also intervenes in this confused world.

In Akita, God Himself seems to have taught the Catholic Church how to revive its damaged spiritual sensibility towards the Body of Christ by causing the cross-shaped stigmata to form in the left hand of Sr. Agnes and by leading her to receive holy communion on her tongue under His Divine pressure from the painful stigmata.

In Akita, the Blessed Mother appealed to Roman Catholics to cooperate with Her work of Coredemption and reconstruction of the spiritually-damaged Catholic Church by uniting their sacrifices, prayers and sufferings with those of Her Immaculate Heart.

Our stony hearts seem only to melt away and begin to repent when we are loved by those who have a genuine powerful Christian love in their hearts or when we learn to receive love from the Holy Eucharist.

This is the reason Catholic souls must be touched by the ineffable Divine Love contained in the Holy Eucharist in order to become such prayerful persons capable of helping others.

If floundering spiritual sensibility in the real presence prevents Catholics from drawing the strength to love their neighbors from Holy Communion, then who else will be able to satisfy the spiritual hunger of people in today's modern world?

However, people whose hearts are filled with Divine Love, can easily summon the courage to go out of their way to assist their

neighbors in need and destitution. Such people strive to meet their neighbors' material and spiritual needs — as do Mother Teresa, Mother Angelica, their Sisters and the nuns of the Institute of the Handmaids of the Holy Eucharist. They are the witnesses of Christ's love in this oft-egotistical world.

How tragic it is when Catholics cannot find the strength to love others in a world where so many thirst so desperately for the love of God in the hearts of other human beings!

This is why the profound meaning of the bleeding of Sr. Agnes' stigmata must be urgently conveyed to as many Catholics as possible, on top of the Holy Father's most profound teachings on the Holy Eucharist.

Akita: Mother of God as Coredemptrix

Chapter 8

The "Fourth and Most Important Message of Akita,"
Holy Mother's Role as Coredemptrix who will crush Satan's Head

F R. T H O M A S T E I J I Y A S U D A, s.v.d., said that the Marian events in Akita point most importantly to the Virgin Mary's role as Coredemptrix, which She has played thoughout the history of salvation of mankind, ever since Her Immaculate Conception.

He said, "It is crucial to note that, when the persona of the Words of God incarnated in the womb of the Holy Mother Mary by the intervention of the Holy Spirit, the Holy Mother shared Her blood and flesh to Her Divine Son."

"Therefore, the blood of Jesus which was shed in Calvary to redeem mankind was given to Jesus from His Mother Mary. As a result, there emerged the profound, inseparable bond between Jesus and the Holy Mother Mary in accordance with God's plan of salvation."

Fr. Yasuda stated that, "The most important message among the various Divine messages in Akita is the one imparted by the invisible angel to Sr. Agnes on the 28th of September of 1981. Even the previous three Marian messages were a precursor to this last manifestation which occurred 13 days after the final weeping of the statue."

The figure "13" indicates the profound connection between Akita and Fatima, Fr. Yasuda said.

"This Divine message has a deep relationship to what Pope John Paul II said in his encyclical letter *The Mother of Redeemer," (Redemptoris Mater)* issued March 25th, 1987, the Marian Year.

On the 28th of September 1981, 13 days after a group of 65 parishioners, pilgrims and nuns observed the 101st and final weeping of the statue of the Blessed Mother, Sr. Agnes suddenly felt the presence of her guardian angel at her side during adoration of the Most Blessed Sacrament. She saw the vision of a large, majestic Bible appear before her eyes, and then the guardian angel instructed her to read a passage.

She recognized the reference — verse 15 of chapter 3 of Genesis.

Then, the guardian angel explained the meaning of the number 101 of the 101 episodes of the weepings of the Blessed Mother of Akita. The angel said:

"There is a meaning to the figure one hundred and one. This signifies that sin came into the world by a woman and it is also by a woman that salvation came to the world. The zero between the two signifies the Eternal God who is from all eternity until eternity. The first one represents Eve, and the last, the Virgin Mary."

The sister was then again invited to reread the passage of Genesis, then the angel left. At the same time the vision of the Bible disappeared.

After adoration, Sr. Agnes came at once to the office of Father Yasuda, asking him to read Genesis 3: 15, saying that she had just received instructions from her guardian angel to read that Genesis passage. She asked Fr. Yasuda to verify the passage before she herself would open a Bible. He took out the modern Japanese translation by noted theologian, Fr. Barbaro, and read the following passage carrying God's prophetic announcement that he would send the Holy Mother to deal a crushing blow to Satan:

"I will place enmity between thee (Satan) and the woman (Mary), between thy seed and hers. She will crush thy head and thou shalt lie in wait for her heel."

Then, Sr. Agnes recounted to Father Yasuda the explanation of the angel concerning the meaning of the number 101, the precise number of times the statue wept. Fr. Yasuda recalled this in an interview with me as follows:

"The passage from the Scripture elucidated the profound meaning of the angel's message regarding the 101 weepings. Here in Akita, God Himself sent the angel to reveal the profound meaning of the message 'by the authority of the Bible'... the words of God. In NO *other place of Marian apparitions in the world throughout the history of mankind, has the meaning of the message been explained by the authority of Scripture!*

Fr. Yasuda gave the following theological interpretations regarding this passage of Scripture and the angel's words in Akita:

"In Genesis, chapter 3, verse 15, the Sovereign God, the Absolute Being, makes the prophetic announcement to Satan of the combat, in which the Blessed Virgin Mary and Her seed will oppose and confront Satan throughout the ages. It is evident that 'the Seed of the Woman' is Jesus, who came into the world through the Virgin Mary, and all those who will believe in Him. The 'seed of the Woman' means the Mystical Body of Christ, (the Church) which is the community of believers of all generations of whom Christ is the Head."

"It is in union with the Church, the Mystical Body of Christ, that the Virgin Mary has received, from the Eternal Father, the mission of fighting against and crushing Satan and his cohorts until the end of the world."

"This passage of Genesis is called 'protoevangelium' and is considered the first promise of a Savior for mankind made by God. It is also the first verse in the Bible which alludes to the Immaculate Conception of Mary, preserved from original sin and thus never under the dominion of Satan."

Fr. Yasuda said, "The miracles of the bleeding and weeping of the statue of the Blessed Mother in Akita were brought about by God in order to illustrate the truth of Mary's role as 'Coredemptrix.'" He described the coredemptrix as the holy person who cooperated with Jesus' work of redemption during His Passion on the Cross on Calvary by offering up the suffering of Her Immaculate Heart's 'spiritual bleeding' to God."

He said, "When the Roman soldier pierced Jesus' side with a lance, Jesus was already dead. At that moment, the lance spiritually pierced, as well, the heart of Mary, who, suffering terribly, observed the cruel act."

"It was then that the prophesy of Simeon in the Temple — where the infant Jesus was presented to God — was fulfilled. Simeon told the Mother of Jesus:...'This child is destined to be a sign that will be rejected — and your soul, too, will be pierced by a sword.'"

Fr. Yasuda went on to say, "The fact that the profound meaning of the apparitions in Akita were explained by the reference to the Words of the Bible (Genesis 3:15) also tells us that the events in Akita is the Divine revelation. The fact also convinces us of the supernatural character of the apparitions and messages here. "

"For Roman Catholics, the Bible is the most powerful authority by which the truthfulness of a certain teaching or dogma is proved and God arranged for Sr. Agnes to see it in a vision in Akita to prove that Mary is the coredemptrix," he said.

"The 101 weepings of the statue of the Holy Mother is the only hard evidence of an ongoing fighting between the Holy Mother and Satan," he said.

During the "Family Night" live show on March 8, 1994, Mother Angelica said, "Our Lady was coredemptrix. What does that mean? That She (the Holy Mother) suffered with the Lord through his entire life."

"She knew what was coming, when She heard the angel say She would be the Mother of the Son of the Most High God. So all of Our Lady's life, She united and suffered with the same pains (as those of our Lord) and suffered with our Lord, especially during His Passion," the mother said.

"So She united Her tears with His Blood that was falling down from the Cross and She became at that moment not equal to, not instead of, but with Jesus. She became Coredemptrix."

Saint Paul said, "This is a wicked generation and your lives should redeem it."

"We know there is only one Redeemer and only one Jesus and only Jesus saves. So we can't add anything finite to anything that is infinite," she said.

However, as Our Lady said in Akita, "Whatever I offer up to the (Heavenly) Father in union with Our dear Lord, goes up to the Father with infinite value," she said.

"What I added on my own is nothing... (but) *when I add* (my suffering) *to their* (Jesus' and Mary's) *pain and sufferings, it becomes very powerful*," Mother Angelica said.

"Now, we are in a time, I believe, when the messages of Akita seem to signify that we are in a very serious time in history when another dogma should hopefully be proclaimed. This is the dogma of Our Lady as the Coredemptrix and Mediatrix of All Graces. What does that mean? It means that this Mother of such a wonderful Son — Son of God — that this Mother of God suffered profusely and intensely with Her Son."

Mother Angelica on the show "Family Night"

"The second is that She (the Holy Mother Mary) is the Mediatrix. She mediates for you and I. She prays for you and I to receive grace upon grace. When She appeared to Catherine Laboure — Miraculous Medal — She appeared like this and from Her hand came beautiful rays in various colors. Catherine Laboure asked what those rays meant. Our Lady said, 'They are the graces that I have to give from the Lord.' She is a channel, not the source of God, only God is the source of grace, a channel through whom these graces flow to the world and She said these are the graces no one ever asked for."

Mother Angelica said, "One day, I pray... and hope you pray... that the dogma of Coredemptrix and Mediatrix of All Graces will become dogma. And I think once it (this truth) is explained, the whole world will embrace our Mother in a way they never embraced her before."

Fr. Thomas Yasuda said, "This Divine elucidation about the role of the Holy Mother in salvation of the mankind corresponds in its profundity to Saint Paul's theological explanation about Christ, as the new Adam, in his apostolic letter to Romans."

The chapter 5 of Saint Paul's letter to Romans says, "Well then, sin entered the world through one man, and through sin death, and thus death has spread through the whole human race, because everyone has sinned. — Adam prefigured the One to come, but the gift itself considerably outweighed the fall. If it is certain that divine grace, coming though the one man, Jesus Christ, came to so many as an abundant free gift. The results of the gift also outweigh the results of one man's sins." (From verses 12, 15 and 16)

Fr. Yasuda said, "It is surprising that God clearly revealed the role of the Holy Mother Mary as the new Eve in inviting the graces of salvation of the mankind through apparitions in Akita, just as God revealed Jesus Christ's mission in the salvation as the new Adam."

"Because the persona of Words of God incarnated in the womb of the Holy Mother Mary by the intervention of the Holy Spirit, the Holy Mother shared and transferred Her flesh and blood to the Son of God. This incarnation resulted in the profound bond between the Holy Mother and Jesus," he said.

"The 101 weepings of the statue of the Holy Mother show us that, just as the old Eve tempted Adam to commit a sin, the new Eve, Holy Mother Mary, with her sufferings, became the channel and cause for which the graces of salvation of the mankind by Jesus Christ reached this world," he said.

Fr. Yasuda said, "It seems to me that the elucidation of the Holy Mother's role in the Salvation is a chief purpose for which the Holy Mother conveyed Her messages in Akita. This leads us to think that both the faithful and clergy should recognize the Holy Mother's mission as the Mediatrix who has continued to channel abundant graces to mankind until today."

His explanation calls to mind the most profound words and insights expressed by the Pontiff in the encyclical letter, *Redemptoris Mater,* of 1987 which states:

"At the foot of the Cross, Mary participated through faith in the mystery of this 'self-emptying.' This is the deepest 'kenosis' (self-emptying: total giving of oneself to live up to God's will) of faith in human history. Through faith the Mother participated in the death of her Son, which redeemed mankind."

"This motherhood, in the order of grace, flows from her Divine Motherhood. She was, by the design of Divine Providence, the mother who nourished the Divine Redeemer, Mary became 'an associate of unique nobility, and the Lord's humble handmaid,' who cooperated by Her obedience, faith, hope and burning charity in the Savior's work of restoring supernatural life to souls. And this maternity of Mary, in the order of grace, will last without interruption until the eternal fulfillment of all the elect," the Holy Father said in the encyclical letter.

The Pope also said in the encyclical letter, "Thus we find ourselves at the very center of the fulfillment of the promise contained in the Protogospel: 'She (Mary) will crush the head of the serpent (Satan)'... How can one doubt that, especially now, on Golgotha (Calvary), this expression goes to the very heart of the mystery of Mary, and indicates the unique place which Mary occupies in the whole providence of salvation?"

He also noted in the encyclical letter, "Genesis 3:15 and Revelation 1:12 elucidates the role of the Blessed Mother in the history of salvation of mankind."

The Holy Father also says, "Her motherhood is particularly noted and experienced by the Christian people at the Sacred Mass... the liturgical celebration of the mystery of the Redemption... at which Christ, his true body born of the Virgin Mary, becomes really present."

"The Christian people has always very rightly sensed a profound link between devotion to the Blessed Virgin and worship of the Holy Eucharist... Mary guides the faithful to the Eucharist," the Holy Father said in the encyclical letter.

Holy Mother's Cooperation with Jesus for Redemption of Mankind

Fr. Yasuda said: "Jesus offered up His Mother's terrible sufferings to God by mingling the offering of her sufferings with that of His own redemptive suffering on Calvary. In this way, Mary cooperated with Her Son's work of redemption, completely,"

The priest went on to say, "The reason why the statue of the Blessed Virgin wept and bled in Akita is to manifest the Blessed Virgin's cooperation with the Divine work of salvation in which She shed Her spiritual blood on Calvary, as prophesied by Simeon."

He said, "The Pontiff's pastoral letter, *Redemptoris Mater,* and the bleeding of the statue of the Blessed Mother in Akita have the same objective: to teach Catholics the importance of the mission and role which the Blessed Mother plays, especially **now**, in the history of salvation of mankind."

"Their aim is to teach Catholics the importance of the prayer of the Rosary — the weapon against Satan — and the need for reviving and strengthening our Catholic faith and thereby loving both God and neighbors," the priest said.

Fr. Yasuda said, "Because the Blessed Mother is the Coredemptrix and is immaculately conceived — preserved free from original sin and the influence of Satan — she is endowed by God with the power to crush Satan's head. Presently, she continues to fight against Satan. The combat will become more and more intense, but the Blessed Mother will crush and defeat Satan."

Fr. Yasuda's explanations appear to correspond with the Holy Father's teachings of *Redemptoris Mater* which states:

"Thanks to this special bond linking the Mother of Christ with the Church, there is further clarified the mystery of that 'Woman' who, from the first chapters of the Book of Genesis until the Book of Revelation, accompanies the revelation of God's salvific plan for humanity."

Akita: Mother of God as Coredemptrix

Pope John Paul II said in the *Redemporis Mater,* "For Mary, present in the Church as the Mother of the Redeemer, takes part, as a mother, in the 'monumental struggle against the powers of darkness,' which continues throughout human history. And, by Her ecclesial identification as the 'Woman clothed with the sun' (Rev. 12:1), it can be said that in the Most Holy Virgin, the Church has already reached that perfection whereby She exists without spot or wrinkle."

Fr. Yasuda stressed that, "The whole Catholic Church must pay attention to, and meditate upon, the meaning of these weepings of the Blessed Virgin in Akita. By *sending the Holy Mother and Sr. Agnes' guardian angel to Akita, God invited official elucidation by the Church of Her role as the Coredemptrix, so that a greater outpouring of Divine graces be brought to mankind."*

Plea for Our Cooperation

Through the Divine messages in Akita, God and the Blessed Virgin appealed to us to cooperate with Our Lord's work of redemption by offering up our own sufferings, sacrifices and prayers, in union with those of the Blessed Mother," he said.

Fr. Yasuda said, "We Christians, especially, have to cooperate with the Divine work of redemption. The salvation of a human being is accomplished in this way."

He went on to say, "Now, let us meditate upon a crucial passage in the third message, which says, 'The only arms which will remain for you will be the Rosary and the sign left by My Son.'"

"The message calls for us to continue offering up the prayers of the Rosary with strong faith and humble obedience. The 'Sign left by My Son' means the Sacrament of the Holy Eucharist, which God gave to believers in exchange for the sacrifice of Jesus on the Cross. This Most Blessed Sacrament is the fruit of the Cross," he said.

Cooperation Between Holy Eucharist and Holy Mother

"Among various mysterious events surrounding the statue of the Blessed Mother of Akita, the miraculous cures of Sr. Agnes' deafness were accomplished by the blessings of the Holy Eucharist elevated with the ostensorium, which followed the joint recitation of the Rosary," Fr. Yasuda said.

"This key episode gives us an important lesson that the Holy Eucharist is the most Sacred sacrament which we should accept with faith in the real presence of Jesus in it, while worshiping this very Sacrament with all our souls and hearts, rather than conducting its mere physical acceptance and consumption," he said.

"Another objective proof of the supernatural character of the weeping of the Holy Mother of Akita came from the miraculous healing of a South Korean woman named Mrs. Teresa Chun Sun Ho."

"Mrs. Chun, who had collapsed and remained bedridden in a coma for 32 days due to her brain cancer, was cured on August 4, 1981, after the Mother of Akita appeared to her in her hospital bedroom in Seoul."

"After her healing, Mrs. Chun testified to a Korean church commission as follows: 'The Blessed Mother Mary of Akita who appeared to me in hospital bed held in Her arms a lamb as white as snow. She breathed three times on my forehead and I could see the fur of the lamb flutter as the Blessed Mother breathed on me.'"

Fr. Yasuda said, "Her testimony also shows that the grace of her cure was given by the sacrament of the Holy Eucharist who is Jesus Christ Himself, the Lamb of God."

"The abundant flows of tears in the 101 weepings of the statue of the Holy Mother symbolizes the flows of God's infinite graces, which are given to believers who cooperate with the Holy Mother in assisting with Her fight against Satan," he said.

Akita: Mother of God as Coredemptrix

"Her tears also mean that the Immaculately conceived Holy Mother has cooperated with the Redeemer Jesus Christ, really present in the Holy Eucharist," he said.

"God, in his salvific plan for the mankind, arranged for the Holy Mother's tears to continue to flow throughout the history of mankind in an invisible way and thereby get mingled with blood of Jesus in accomplishing the salvation of many people," he said.

His statement revived the memory of a profound passage in Blaise Pascal's Pansees that the agony of Christ will continue until the end of the world.

Supernatural Sufferings and Tears of Holy Mother

"The supernatural tears and sufferings of the Holy Mother is still continuing invisibly at this very moment and working together with the blood of Jesus to accomplish the salvation of many people," Fr. Yasuda said.

He said, "The 101 weepings of the statue of the Holy Mother in Akita prove that the Holy Mother, with Her supernatural sufferings and tears, has cooperated with Jesus who shed blood of redemption."

"Just as Jesus gave up his life on the Cross to accomplish the redemption, the Holy Mother also spiritually gave up her life by her selfless love for mankind. Her Immaculate Heart was pierced spiritually by a lance of a Roman soldier as prophesized by Simeon," he said.

"In consecrating bread and wine into His own Body and Blood in the upper room in Jerusalem, Jesus said, 'This cup which is poured out for you is the new covenant in my blood', " he noted.

"Jesus' blood was the blood of the covenant between God and the Savior that is valid forever," he said.

"The Holy Mother participated in Her Son's work of redemption by shedding Her spiritual blood and offering up Her sufferings, thereby fulfilling Simeon's prophesy at the Jerusalem Temple that Her heart will be pierced by a lance," he said.

"God wanted the Holy Mother to participate in the work of redemption by Jesus Christ," he said

"Because sin came into the world through collaboration of Adam and Eve, God arranged for salvation to enter the world through the cooperation of the new Adam and new Eve, who is Jesus and Mary," he said.

Fr. Yasuda said, "God, who is almighty, could have single-handedly defeated Satan who defied God."

"However, because God is Love, He planned to give the graces of salvation to mankind by calling the Holy Mother and believers to cooperate by their free will with Jesus' work of redemption by loving God and neighbors and by offering up their sufferings."

"God, who is Love, rejoices at sacrifices of love offered by human beings," the priest said.

"Now that the Holy Mother taught us in Akita that the Rosary and the Holy Eucharist are the only arms to fight against Satan with, we Catholics should worship and venerate the Most Holy Sacrament with strong faith, while stepping up efforts to draw spiritual strength from the two 'weapons,'" the priest said.

"To realize that the cooperative relationship between the Holy Mother and the Holy Eucharist would encourage Catholics to step up their efforts to draw spiritual strength from the Rosary and the Eucharist in their attempts to live as good warm-hearted Christians," he said.

Fr. Yasuda told me in an interview in 1993: "Both of the miraculous healings of Sr. Agnes' deafness in 1974 and 1982 were accomplished during the Benedictions, when people prayed the Rosary in front of the Eucharist exposed in the ostensorium." The two healings demonstrate the cooperation of the Holy Mother and Jesus in the Holy Eucharist. This cooperative relationship continues to bring about Divine blessings for the mankind."

During the interview, this author asked Fr. Yasuda the following question: "Why would a recognition by Catholics of the holy mission of Mary as Coredemptrix help bring about a revival of the dwindling faith of Catholics around the world?"

Fr. Yasuda answered, "Because that knowledge would encourage people to live up to the truth of salvation — namely, the need to follow the command of Jesus Christ, who taught us, "If anyone wants to be a follower of mine, let him renounce himself and take up his cross and follow me. For anyone who wants to save his life will lose it; but anyone who loses his life for my sake will find it."

"Nowadays, so many Catholics abandoned this truth of salvation which is the necessary condition for their respective salvation, although they know this truth of salvation which was conveyed by Jesus' words," Fr. Yasuda said.

This refusal of a cross resulted from the huge theological confusion, which has left so many Catholics astray. So many people seek to obtain only comforts, an easy life, joys and pleasure in their lives. "Even numerous Catholics seek to enjoy materialistic affluence and comforts, while forgetting the importance of taking up their respective crosses and following Christ," he said.

"Salvation without taking up one's cross is an impossibility. The Holy Mother Mary reminded Catholics of this truth in Akita through Her apparitions," Fr. Yasuda said.

Weapons for Salvation; Eucharist, Rosary and the Readiness to Offer up Sufferings to God

When Catholics realize the Holy Mother's teachings and start trying to draw spiritual strength from the Holy Eucharist and the Rosary, God will give them the capacity and actual strength to live as good warm-hearted Catholics, along with deep inner peace, which only God can give. For this reason, the Holy Mother taught in Akita:

"The only arms which will remain for you will be the Rosary and the Sign left by my Son. (The Eucharist)"

"Sufferings and crosses are necessary for one's salvation. In Akita, the Holy Mother Mary tried to help Catholics learn the importance of accepting and offering up one's sufferings for God," Fr. Yasuda said.

"Realizing the mystery of Coredemptrix would help modern Catholics accept and offer up their sufferings and sacrifices in order to cooperate with Jesus' work of redemption after the example of the Holy Mother who suffered for God as the Co-redemptrix," he said.

"Offering up sufferings and sacrifices for others is the profound form of genuine Christian love, just as the Holy Mother taught three shepherd children in 1917 in Fatima — and then in Akita in 1973," he said.

Cardinal Edouard Gagnon said in an after-dinner speech on September 17, 1993, in New York: "When God gives the duty to love, He also gives the capacity."

When the Holy Mother tried to revive the profound Christian practice of offering up sacrifices and sufferings for neighbors and God in Akita, the Holy Mother taught Catholics how to obtain "the capacity" to do so — counting on two arms of Christians — the Eucharist and Rosary.

Cardinal Gagnon, now president of the Pontifical Committee for International Eucharistic Congresses, also told the audience of some 450: "Where is Christ? He is in the Eucharist. Christ is in the Mass. He is in our churches. As we see our duty to react against the pagan attitudes in our times, we have to come back to Christ and put the Eucharist back in our lives."

Yes, Jesus said: "This is my body which will be given for you." If a Catholic refused to take up a cross and sufferings in his or her life, the Catholic would, unwittingly, be squandering the Divine graces contained in the precious Eucharist.

Akita: Mother of God as Coredemptrix

Such refusal of a cross would undermine the effectiveness of a Holy Eucharist in pouring Divine graces into the refuser's soul.

The Catholic Church has long called the Eucharist "food of travelers of life." We, the travelers who trek in our journeys of life — often through a difficult and burdensome path — would be able to find the abundant spiritual strength to love and endure in the Holy Eucharist we receive in a daily Mass, if we keep an attitude of taking up our respective cross and following the example of Jesus and the Holy Mother as the Coredemptrix. Then, after Their holy examples, we would be able to offer up our sacrifices, prayers and sufferings to help and love our neighbors and God courageously.

Fr. Yasuda called the most careful attention to the Holy Mother's messages on August 3, 1973, which stated: "Many men in this world grieve the Lord. I seek souls to console Him. In order to appease the anger of the Heavenly Father, I wish, with my Son, for souls who will make reparation for sinners and the ungrateful by offering up their sufferings and poverty to God on their behalf."

What can a Catholic do to console the Lord?

Fr. Yasuda asked: "Are we not being asked to run to Jesus' help on the road to Calvary and, like Veronica who courageously offered a towel to dry the face of the Lord, to brave the prejudices and the oppositions of the entourage and to approach and participate with all of our being, in the Holy Sacrifice?"

He said: "We must recognize that believers themselves are affected and fooled by current fashion... flight before suffering, frantic searching for pleasure... and ending up by renouncing the Cross. Even many Catholics wish a Christianity without a cross and have developed a false belief that salvation in sweetness and without much effort and sufferings is possible."

"Is it not because of this sad state of things that Our Mother has manifested tears so many times?" he asked.

In closing this chapter, I would like to quote testimonies from Sr. Agnes, that vessel of suffering, about the mysterious relationship between a Christian's efforts to offer up sufferings and true happiness God gives to such a Christian who truly loves Him by taking up the cross.

Sr. Agnes, who has suffered so much due to her physical illness and slanders from the outside world, said on July 4, 1994, in a telephone interview with this author, "Through my years of illness, I realized that when a person offers up his or her pain to God, rather than merely enduring the pain, the very pain is transformed into joy and inner peace."

Sr. Agnes, now 63, who had been bedridden for nearly 10 years since the age of 19, fell again two years ago after working for 29 years as a catechist and then as a nun. Although she is still bedridden, she leads a compassionate, prayerful life for others with a clear sharp intellect.

Sr. Agnes said, "Each moment I receive pains, I offer them up to God and I do so with my Lord Jesus Christ."

"When I receive Jesus Christ present in the Holy Eucharist each day, I embrace Him in my soul and I feel that I am in Heaven while living on this earth."

"If we are with the Lord Jesus in the Holy Eucharist, any place on this earth is transformed into Heaven," she said. "My soul is constantly filled with gratitude for God."

"Everyone has a cross in life. And my expriences tell me that when we accept and offer up crosses as a gift from our Lord Jesus, they are transformed into sources of genuine joy."

"When we suffer, we should not say, 'Oh, I am suffering.' If we complain like that, then, we would end up shutting out incoming Divine graces from our souls," she said.

"If you complain about your pains, you would be plunged into depression, from which you would find it hard to get out," she said.

"When I offered up my sufferings by uniting them with the Passion of my Lord Jesus, the cross became much easier to carry," she said. "In comparison with the Passion of Jesus, my cross is only a light one."

"I am a weak human being, but God has helped me, transforming my pains into joy and gratitude," she said.

Christianity provides the paradox of happiness given to a soul amidst suffering, as Christianity promises to give genuine happiness, peace, and true sweetness felt by souls as something given by God amidst the suffering.

The writer is forced to ask the following question;

Does not Sr. Agnes' precious testimony encourage us to learn from the example of the Holy Mother Mary, who offered up Her sufferings, sacrifices and prayers to cooperate with Her Son's work in the Redemption of mankind and so became for us the Coredemptrix ?

Chapter 9

Scientific Analysis of Tears from the Statue
by Akita University and Gifu University

ON JANUARY 11, 1975, Fr. Thomas Teiji Yasuda asked Professor Eiji Okuhara, M.D., a Catholic physician of the prestigious Akita University's Department of Biochemistry, to analyze the three kinds of liquid (tears, sweat, and blood) which had been collected from the statue.

The collection of the liquid was done with absorbent cotton, gauze and a cotton cloth. The collected samples, separated by the type of the liquid collected, were then placed into three separate vinyl bags and a paulownia box before being brought to the Akita University for analysis . (The samples of blood were put in both a vinyl bag and a small paulownia box.)

On January 24, Dr. Okuhara asked Dr. Kaoru Sagisaka, M.D., a non-Christian specialist of Forensic Medicine, to analyze the three liquids, without informing him beforehand that it had flowed from the wooden statue.

The information on the source of the liquid was withheld from Dr. Sagisaka to ensure that the outcome of his ensuing analysis be free from any prejudice and apriori judgments and to ensure objectivity.

Dr. Okuhara told me on August 15, 1993, "Dr. Sagisaka examined these liquids without any information on its source."

"I myself witnessed the weepings of the statue of the Holy Mother repeatedly," said Dr. Okuhara, who is a former Rockefeller Foundation fellow . This expert on molecular biology studied at Columbia University in New York when Dwight D. Eisenhower was the president of the university.

Medical Scientists Identify Tears as Human Tears

Dr. Sagisaka, an assistant professor of the university at the time, analyzed the liquids and issued a certificate of medical appraisal on January 29, 1975, verifying that the constituents of the liquid were identical to those of human tears.

In the certificate, Dr. Sagisaka also verified that the blood type of the tears was of group AB blood, whereas that of the blood was of Group B.

Dr. Sagisaka, currently a professor of the Tohoku University after his temporary service as professor at Gifu University, explained that human tears and perspiration simulate blood types, because they contain special proteins called antigens.

Antigens are a substance also found in human blood, and are required in examining blood types.

Catholic novelist Shusaku Endo, during his investigative stay in Akita, visited the Akita University to interview Dr. Eiji Okuhara.

Dr. Okuhara said of Mr. Endo, "Mr. Endo took a humble attitude when he first telephoned me and told me he wants to get true information about the reported apparition as he is a Roman Catholic."

Endo, in his investigative report, quoted Dr. Okuhara as saying, "I handed the gauze (and cottons) that absorbed the liquids from the statue of Mary to Dr. Sagisaka of the Faculty of Medicine."

Scientific Analysis of the Tears

"In order to prevent Dr. Sagisaka from being affected by any subjective judgments and prejudice, I did not tell him that the liquids absorbed in them were collected from the wooden statue."

At the request of Dr. Okuhara, Dr. Sagisaka analyzed the blood from the statue and identified it as that of blood-type B. On the other hand, his analysis identified the blood-type of the statue's tears as AB. (See appendix A.)

Fr. Yasuda explained to me, "Although it is impossible to have different blood-types out of tears and blood from a same human being, God, who is almighty, can create different blood types in a wooden statue."

Fr. Yasuda said, "The most important fact is that the scientist proved that the liquid from the statue contain the constituents (such as antigens) which are the exactly same constituents found in human tears and blood. They were not mere waters."

"Because only God can create human tears and human liquid, the fact shows that the weeping of the statue and its bleeding are the outcome of the supernatural intervention by God," he said.

Second Analysis of Tears from the Statue

After Dr. Sagisaka started working as a professor at Gifu University, Fr. Yasuda again asked Dr. Okuhara to ask Dr. Sagisaka to conduct yet another analysis of a new specimen of tears he collected with a tweezer.

Fr. Yasuda said that a new analysis became necessary, because doubts and criticisms were raised by some individuals since the cotton and gauze subjected to the first analysis had been partially contaminated by "a very minute amount of human body fluids" from the fingers of the persons who had wiped away the tears and blood from the statue. This contamination was later proved to be the result of perspiration of the collectors by Dr. Okuhara's analysis.

The certificate of the first medical appraisal clearly stated:

"At the time the specimen was taken, or by the time the examiner (Dr. Sagisaka) received the specimen, it could have been contaminated by a minute amount of body fluid of type A or type AB."

Dr. Sagisaka wrote in the certificate,

"The group-specific double-combination method is a very sensitive one... In conclusion, the blood type of the proved blood stain is type B and that of the body fluid (tears) is type AB."

In the medical appraisal document, Dr. Sagisaka said the fact that a very minute amount of AB-type liquid was detected from the specimen of blood is not a contradiction, because the detection method (group-specific double-combination method) is "very sensitive."

The contamination by a "very minute amount of human body fluids" can be clearly distinguished from the much larger amount of blood he detected in the specimen, which were verified to belong to B-type blood, the scientist said.

Opposition from a Theologian

Fr. Garcia Evangelista, a chief member of the first commission of inquiry, asserted and spread the theory that Sr. Agnes has an ectoplasmic power, which, he alleged, enabled her to "transfer" her own B-type tears and blood onto the statue of Mary.

This "ectoplasmic theory" triggered serious confusion among many faithful and clergy of the Catholic church in Japan, according to the testimonies of Fr. Yasuda and Bishop Ito.

Both Bishop Ito and Fr. Yasuda pointed out that Fr. Evangelista ignored the scientific findings of Dr. Sagisaka, who verified that the blood type of the tears of the statue belongs to the group AB.

The blood type, AB, which Dr. Sagisaka detected from the tears of the statue is different from that of Sr. Agnes, whose blood type is B.

Fr. Evangelista acknowledged this allegation during my interview with him. The priest said, "I did not read the medical appraisal documents issued by Dr. Sagisaka."

Gifu University identifies Blood Type of Tears as O

Concerned about the confusion triggered by the ectoplasmic theory, Fr. Yasuda said he faced the need to seek an entirely new medical appraisal by submitting to a scientist a newly-collected specimen of the statue's tears. Fr. Yasuda said that he was aware that the new specimen must be free from any contamination by the human body fluids of the person who will collect the tears.

Regarding the collection method of the new specimen for the new medical appraisal, Fr. Yasuda wrote, "On August 22, 1981, taking immense precautions, and a new morsel of cotton with tweezers, I made a ball as large as an apricot seed. I then carried it beneath the wooden chin where a drop was clinging and, after absorbing it in the cotton, I put it into a sack of new vinyl."

Three months later, on November 30, 1981, the new analysis conducted by Dr. Sagisaka at the forensic medicine laboratory of Gifu University led to a finding. His medical appraisal certificate reported that, "I certify that human body fluid is adhering to the specimen and that the blood type of the specimen is type O." (See Appendix B.)

Concerning the new and different conclusion, Fr. Yasuda remarked, "It is beyond the capabilities of a human being to create blood, tears and sweats. The pure act of creating is the privilege of God. If the ectoplasmic theory is correct, all of the blood types detected by Dr. Sagisaka's appraisal should logically be identical to that of Sr. Agnes, which is group B."

"Here in Akita, God has manifested His creative power. He first created the blood of type B, then the tears of type AB and finally the tears of type O — three different blood types in the same statue of the Blessed Mother. God Himself placed an absolute refutation to the senseless theory of ectoplasmic powers invented by Fr. Evangelista," he said.

Amid the theological confusion provoked by Fr. Evangelista, many priests and theologians in Japan ignored even the videotaped phenomenon of the weeping of the statue, the many testimonies of the eyewitnesses, the hard evidence of the cotton and gauze soaked with the tears, and, above all, the findings of the scientific analysis by Dr. Sagisaka.

Professor Shoju Itaya of the Tokyo Institute of Technology, an expert in the field of ectoplasmic power, in response to an inquiry by Bishop Ito, testified that exerting any ectoplasmic power would require that the holder of such power use his or her will power deliberately and intentionally to exercise the influence of such power on other objects.

Fr. Evangelista told this author in an interview that, "Sister Agnes can transfer her tears and blood onto the statue, as long as she stands within a 15 meter range from the statue."

Bishop Ito also said, "The ectoplasmic theory must be rejected, because the tears flowed from the statue when Sr. Agnes was asleep, or when she was away visiting her family at a distance of some two hundred and fifty miles (400 Kilometers). Fr. Evangelista came to Akita with a pre-conceived negative conclusion regarding the veracity of the Marian apparition — even before he started his probe. He seems to have invented his ectoplasmic theory in order to justify his negative conclusion."

Dr. Theresa Wei, an American medical doctor, said the ectoplasmic theory of Fr. Evangelist is absurd. She said she herself saw the statue of the Blessed Mother of Akita shed tears when Sr. Agnes was in the kitchen cutting a watermelon to serve to pilgrims. Dr. Wei said it is unthinkable that Sr. Agnes could allegedly concentrate any will power deliberately to influence the statue when she was doing the other things in the kitchen.

The statue, for example, shed tears on October 11, 1978, when Sr. Agnes was far away visiting her family in her hometown of Joetsu in Miigata Prefecture. The weeping on this day was witnessed by 23 persons, including two nuns of the order of Caritas Sisters of Miyazaki, as well as pilgrims from Maebashi City and Aomori City.

Author's Interview with Fr. Evangelista

During my interview with Fr. Evangelista, I asked him to explain these facts and the results of Dr. Sagisaka's new scientific findings, which identified the blood type of tears as group O, because these facts contradict his ectoplasmic theory. The priest defended his theory saying:

"There 'must' be several more nuns who possess an ectoplasmic power in the Akita convent and they 'must' have transferred their tears onto the statue in order to back up Sister Agnes when she is away from the convent. "

He could not explain why the scientific analysis by Akita and Gifu Universities identified the blood type of the tears as types O and AB, which are different from the blood type of Sister Agnes.

Even if his assertion that other nuns can invoke their alleged ectoplasmic power to transfer their tears and blood onto the statue is worthy of attention, the assertion is again contradictory, because there were no nuns with the blood type of AB in the convent at the time of the 1975 scientific analysis.

Our reasons and common sense say that there are no such things as "ectoplasmic power" in this world. If someone have ever encountered some sorts of strange phenomenon that appeared to be the outcome of ectoplasmic power in his or her eyes, it is more logical to attribute such phenomenon to the work of Satan.

Just as Bishop Ito pointed out in his pastoral letter, the apparitions in Akita cannot be the outcome of any Satanic intervention, because it produced such wonderful spiritual fruits as conversions,

miraculous healings and spiritual progress among pilgrims who trek
to this place of the apparition for more than 20 countries.

Fr. Rene Laurentin

The Catholic magazine, 30 *Days — In the Church and In the World,*
quoted noted French Mariologist, Fr. Rene Laurentin, as terming the
negative judgment of the first commission of inquiry (headed by Fr.
Evangelista, and which questioned the supernatural character of the
apparition in Akita) as, "bizarre and lacking in scientific value."

Sr. Theresa Kashiwagi, the mother superior, said in an interview,
"Although we [the Sisters] suffered from the theological confusion
and misunderstandings of the apparition as the result of this ectoplasmic theory, we bear no grudges against Fr. Evangelista. We have
prayed for him."

The mother superior said, "Our deepest wish is that the whole
Catholic Church will come to know about the Marian apparitions
and her messages in Akita, so that souls can receive an abundance
of Divine graces through them."

Chapter 10

History of Christianity in Japan

Why God Sent Holy Mother to Japan

IT IS A WELL-KNOWN FACT that Saint Francis Xavier was the first missionary to come to the Japanese archipelago in 1549. The Jesuit missionary landed on August 15 — the feast day of the Assumption of Mary — and the Japanese people heard the Christian Gospel for the first time. The movement met with both success and persecution.

A lesser known fact is the important role U.S. President, Ulysees Simpson Grant, played in 1872, in persuading the Japanese government to terminate its 250-year bloody persecution of the Christian community in Japan. After all the missionaries had been expelled or tortured to death, Japanese Catholics clandestinely handed on their faith over seven generations throughout the era of persecution.

Grant urged Vice Prime Minister Tomomi Iwakura to renounce its repressive policy against Christians and to allow the return home of 3,349 Japanese Catholics in exile. They had been uprooted and banished to a six-year period of detention at 19 detention camps across western Japan since 1867... about five years before Iwakura visited the White House for trade talks on March 3, 1872. Grant received the reports from U.S. Ambassador De Long in Tokyo who alerted the White House of the exile and ordeals of these Catholics, which included 163 children.

When the Japanese diplomatic mission visited Washington, D.C. in 1872, the information on the jailed Christians motivated President Grant to warn the Japanese Vice Premier against persecuting the Japanese Christians.

Grant told Iwakura at the White House the American people achieved its prosperity and happiness, because it made much of freedom of faith and conscience and tolerated all religious creeds, authorizing, too, freedom of the press. The president also told the Japanese entourage that the happiness and strength of Americans stemmed from the fact that the government did not impose any curbs on freedom of faith or conscience, not only for its own citizens but for all foreigners residing within its borders.

State Secretary Hamilton Fish proposed working out a treaty committing both nations to tolerate and guarantee religious freedom in a follow-up meeting on March 16 of that year with the Japanese diplomatic mission. Iwakura and his mission rejected the proposal, saying, "There is no need to include such provision on religious freedom in the treaty, for the Japanese government has made great progress and because the Japanese people respect each other's human rights."

In response, Fish pointed to the exile-torture incident of Nagasaki Christians as well as the "Imari incident" in which another 67 Catholics were arrested and imprisoned on December 17, 1871, at the prefecture of Imari (currently Saga) — just four months before the bilateral talks.

Cabinet Minister Takayoshi Kido refuted the U.S. criticism, saying, "The incident has nothing to do with foreign countries. A religious situation should not be linked to efforts to expedite trade profits and diplomacy." Fish replied the United States would remain reluctant to initiate more active economic relations with Japan, unless Japan stop its crackdown on Christians. Kido denied any persecutions were underway. Here, Ambassador De Long intervened in the talks, blasting the breakups and exiles of Catholic families to the 19 detention camps across Japan and denouncing the cruelty of Japanese policy.

With the impasse still in place, the despondent Japanese mission left the U.S. for London, then to Paris and Brussels. On November 27th, British Foreign Secretary Granville also urged Iwakura to stop the persecution. Queen Victoria as well pleaded for a policy change for religious tolerance.

Three months later, with the persecution still continuing, an incident occurred in Brussels, Belgium wherein many ordinary citizens, angered by the reported crackdown, surrounded the horse-drawn carriages of the Japanese mission in February 1873, chanting their demands for the release of Nagasaki Christians from jails. The French congress, at this point, also expressed its condemnation of the imprisonment of Japanese Catholics.

Finally, Iwakura gave in. He forwarded a telegram to the Tokyo government in February 1873, which read, "Wherever we went, we were confronted by foreign people demanding the release of exiled Christians and the guarantee of their freedom of faith. Japan will never be able to get friendly concessions from foreign nations (in trade talks), unless we release the Christians from jails and express our intention to give a bit more freedom of faith. " Government leaders in Tokyo were astonished at the telegram and issued a Cabinet order on February 24 of that year, authorizing the release and return of jailed Christians who survived the torture.

The government also ordered the removal from Japanese streets scattered across the nation of thousands of wooden bulletin boards that had warned its people for centuries of the ban on Christianity and reprisals to possible offenders of the ban.

250 years of Persecution

While in hiding, the underground Japanese Catholic community managed to hand down their faith on the strength of their devotion to the Blessed Mother and the daily recitation of the Rosary. There is believed to be a profound relationship between the 250-year history of martyrdom of Japanese Christians and the Marian apparition in Akita.

Since Xavier's arrival in 1549, about 100 missionaries came to Japan over the next 60 years and showed the example of Christian love of God and neighbors. They actively engaged in evangelical activities. Before coming under the relentless persecution of the government crackdown, their selfless love and efforts helped Christianity flourish in Japan. The persecutions took the lives of some 5,000 identified martyrs whose records are documented... and hundreds of thousands more who were unidentified in giving their lives for their faith. At its peak in the 17th century, there were well over 1 million Catholics in Japan, according to a book by the late Bishop Wasaburo Urakawa. The bishop estimated the total number of baptism of both adults and infants between 1549 and 1630 at 2 million.

Angered at the rapid acceptance of Christianity that advocated the supremacy of God as the sole ultimate Ruler and Judge of all mankind (including "Shogun," the secular military ruler of Japan), the martial government established a nationwide network of spies and informants to detect and arrest missionaries and Japanese lay Catholics. The government ordered local authorities to post notifications at numerous places across Japan, encouraging ordinary citizens to betray and hand over their friends or acquaintances in exchange for silver coins paid by the government. This huge reward for information constituted an irresistible temptation for many destitute citizens.

The peak of conversion among Japanese came around the time when the Pilgrim Fathers aboard the Mayflower landed on Plymouth

Rock in 1620 to escape persecution by the Church of England. They sought freedom of faith and conscience in the "new world." In Japan, however, as the government's intolerance grew, the persecution began. In addition to the 5,000 identified martyrs mentioned above, historians say, there were "at least 250,000 more anonymous martyrs" who were executed due to their refusals to renounce the Catholic faith in the face of persecution. Another well-researched estimate says the aggregate number of anonymous martyrs came to almost one million.

Hakuseki Arai, an 18th century non-Christian academic and politician who served the Tokugawa Shogunate government, said in one of his books that, "An estimated 200,000 to 300,000 Japanese Catholics" were executed as a criminal penalty for their refusals to abandon their faith. His writing entitled *Rabajin Shochi Kengi* (Proposals on Treatment of an Italian) contain the records of the grilling of an Italian Jesuit missionary, Fr. Giovanni Sidotti, who was arrested for slipping into Japan in 1708 to help the Christian flocks who had gone underground after Japan had outlawed Christianity.

Fr. Thomas Teiji Yasuda, a priest of the Society of the Divine Word noted, "Throughout this Japanese archipelago, from the northernmost Japanese Island of Hokkaido to the southernmost Island of Okinawa, there are no places which are not soaked with the blood of martyrs. Throughout the history of the Catholic Church worldwide, there are no other countries whose lands absorbed such large quantities of martyrs' blood as has Japan."

How Christians Were Detected for Torture

Historians say successive military governments in Japan outlawed Christianity, as they regarded the Christian teachings of personal dignity and equality among humanity as unacceptable. The basis for these historians' arguments was that Christian teaching denied the ideological base of their feudalistic system of government based on exploitation of farmers by feudal military rulers.

The government went on to impose a legal requirement obligating every Japanese citizen to go to local government offices once a year to undergo a Christian-identification test widely known as "Fumie"... literally translated as "Trampling upon Images." During the tests, people were required to trample upon sacred Christian images and symbols... such as a crucifix, a replica of the Pieta or the Infant Jesus in the bosom of the Blessed Mother... to disclaim his or her suspected affiliation with Christianity in front of government judges. Refusal to tread upon them proved a person's Christian identity, and many chose death, rather than offending God by trampling upon His images and that of Mary, whom they loved so deeply.

When the government intensified its house-to-house searches for Christians, the latter began making ceramic images of Mary that looked like the Buddhist Goddess known as "Kannon." A small cross was placed inside or behind the image. Often these statues of "Maria Kannon" also carried a child in their arms. Kannon's face is always feminine to emphasize her gentleness and all-embracing compassion for the ordeals of human beings in this hard life. When official investigators conducted surprise raids on Christians' homes, and seeing them kneeling before these "Kannon" images, these Christians could defend themselves by claiming they were Buddhist devotees of "Kannon" and that they should not be arrested or tortured.

Government Bans Christianity

Edwin Reishauer, a former U.S. Ambassador to Japan in the administration of President John F. Kennedy and a noted Japanologist, wrote in his book, *Japan, The Story of a Nation* that in the 17th century the successors of Dictator Ieyasu Tokugawa started to close Japan to virtually all foreign trade, because of their fears that over seas Japanese and traders traveling to foreign ports might bring back Christianity or dangerous foreign ideas. The Tokugawa government prohibited all Japanese from going abroad. Since then, no Japanese resident abroad was allowed to return to Japan.

The church in Japan went underground in the early 17th century and established a secretive system of baptism and catechetical instruction. It was designed to hand down the Catholic faith, especially its doctrine, to future generations... even without receiving pastoral care by some 100 foreign missionaries and a total of 38 Japanese Catholic priests. Of the 38 ordained Japanese priests, 25 were Jesuits, Franciscans, Augustinians and Dominicans, while the remaining 13 were diocesan priests.

These 38 Japanese priests were ordained either by studying at a seminary set up in Arima, north of Nagasaki, or in foreign countries such as the Philippines, Macao, or Malaysia. Twenty-three of these priestly candidates were exiled by the government while they were still seminarians. Most of the exiled 23 priests defied the anti-Christianity laws and slipped back into Japan, where they were later detected, arrested and tortured to death after engaging in priestly activities. The foreign missionaries who slipped into Japan to replace the ones who were executed were quickly apprehended, betrayed by their obvious Western facial features and accents.

Faith and Travel of Fr. Kasui Kibe

Four seminarians traveled as far as Rome by land and sea. A Japanese Jesuit seminarian, Peter Kasui Kibe, was expelled to Macao in 1614, together with other Catholic religious. In 1618, Kibe headed for Rome on a long dangerous trip via Goa in India. After landing at Goa, he WALKED through countries which are currently Iran, Iraq and the Persian Desert (Syria). After departing from Baghdad, Kibe walked to Jerusalem by crossing the Persian Desert. Fr. Hubert Cieslik, a Jesuit of Sophia University in Tokyo, wrote of this trip after probing Kibe's marvelous life that he "probably... joined a caravan to cross the desert)."

Akita: Mother of God as Coredemptrix

After arriving in Rome by sailing across the Mediterranean Sea from Jerusalem, he was ordained a priest by Bishop Raphael on November 15, 1620 at the Basilica of Laterano at the age of 32 by the special permission of the Holy See. A man of excellent intellect and deep faith, Fr. Kibe proved to have a command of the Latin language which he learned while a seminarian. Today, his handwritten registry, in Latin, of his family background is still preserved in the headquarters of the Society of Jesus in Rome. The registry says, "My name is Peter Kasui. I am a son of Romano Kibe and Mary Hata. I am 33 years old. I am from Urabe, province of Bungo, Japan." Rev. Fr. Kibe returned to Japan despite warnings from his priestly colleagues not to go back to Japan where brutal persecution would be awaiting him. Undaunted, he did return to administer the sacraments, especially the Holy Eucharist, to Japanese Christians who were hungry and thirsty for this Supreme Sacrament. Fr. Kibe followed the example of our Lord Jesus who gave His life in love on a Cross at Calvary for the sake of the redemption of mankind.

Dr. Yakichi Kataoka said in his 700-page book, *The History of Martyrdom of Japanese Christians,* that, "Christians in Japan who faced persecution and died the death of martyrs year after year, desperately needed the spiritual help of a Catholic priest who could sanctify their spirits and bolster their faith."

"From the beginning, it was Peter Kibe's intention to become a priest in Rome and then to return to his home country in order to strengthen his fellow Christians' spirits. He foresaw what his fate would be ... that of a martyr, and he was ready to shed his own blood and give up his physical life for that purpose," Dr. Kataoka wrote.

In 1630, Fr. Peter Kibe slipped back into a southern Japanese coast, Kagushima Prefecture, after a hurricane capsized his ship near the coast. After nine years of priestly activities and of helping Christians under persecution, he was arrested by the authorities who were tipped by an informant. Fr. Kibe and two other Catholics were soon subjected to one of the then widely-used tortures of "anazuri," by which victims were hung upside-down in a dark hole for several days, while blood dripped from small wounds bored into one's ears. The wound delayed the arrival of death and prolonged sufferings of victims by relieving blood from the congested veins in the brain of the victim.

Instead of giving in to the torture, Fr. Kibe continued to utter encouragement to the groaning fellow Christians put in the same hole, not to renounce their faith. This attitude angered interrogators, who then dragged Fr. Kibe out of the hole and beheaded him. It was on July 4, 1639.

In those days, there were numerous Christians who risked their lives by giving shelter to escaping missionaries like Fr. Kibe. By placing the priests under their wings, these Christians called "yadonushi"... literally translated as "accommodating hosts"... risked incurring capital punishment in challenging the cruel authorities. There are several interesting cases of documented evidence of these courageous providers of sanctuary from the repressive dragnet.

The Society of Jesus' (i.e., the Jesuits') annual bulletin, published in 1615, reads, "This town (Nagasaki) would give us shelter, whatever persecution we may suffer from the authorities who are under the influence of Satan. At present, seven Jesuit priests are in hiding. So are diocesan priests and clergy of other orders. Every lay Christian here is proud of giving refuge to them."

This author interviewed one of today's foremost authorities on the history of martyrdom, Sr. Chizuko Kataoka, the president of the Immaculate Heart of Mary Women's College and the daughter of Dr. Kataoka. She said, "The fact that thousands of lay Christians sheltered escaping Catholic priests shows how deeply these Christians loved the sacraments and respected the holy mission of the priests."

"These Catholic priests went into hiding... in some cases, even into a narrow space inside a moist wall during daytime... in order to survive the anti-Christian dragnet, even if for only one more day, so as to carry out their holy mission as priests. After darkness, they used to come out of their hiding places and visit lay Christians to celebrate Masses and give sacraments. One priest is known to have died of rheumatism which gripped his whole body as a result of lurking in this moist place."

The Crucification of the 26 Martyrs

Dictator Hideyoshi Toyotomi grew apprehensive at the swiftly increasing number of Christians. He noticed these converts' absolutely, hearty loyalty to their beloved Lord... a somewhat different attitude from the forced loyalty the people showed to Hideyoshi... a "loyalty" which stemmed from the fear of reprisals meted out to the disloyal.

In a government decree of July 24, 1587, he banned Christianity, and to emphasize his point, he ordered twenty-six Christians to be arrested in the then-capital city of Kyoto. Following their arrest, he force-marched them through the depths of winter to Nagasaki, a thirty-day journey by foot. They were to be executed by crucifixion upon arrival.

Dictator Hideyoshi thought that a public witness of blood-letting would quickly convince the Christians to renounce their faith. To this end, he ordered the executions to be slow public spectacles. The city of Nagasaki was told of the hour of arrival of the condemned and a great throng of Christians turned up to cheer them and to shout encouragement.

On February 5, 1597, the twenty-six travel worn, barefoot victims limped into the city and were marched to Nishizaka Hill. The youngest of the twenty-six was Louis Ibaraki, a son of a Samurai (warrior) family baptized by the Jesuits. He was then 12 years old. According to an account written by Fr. Francisco Blanco, as young Ibaraki force marched, a samurai warrior offered to adopt him if

Ibaraki agreed to abandon his Christian faith. The boy answered, "It is better for you to accept baptism and come to the Paradise where I am going soon."

When he and the other 25 condemned reached Nishizaka, he asked Hanzaburo Terasawa, a commander in charge of overseeing the executions, on which cross he would be crucified. When Terasawa pointed his finger to the smallest cross lying on the ground of the hill, Louis smiled and ran to the cross, embracing it with his both arms, kissing it.

After the twenty-six sang "Benedictus" together while on their knees, they were fastened to the crosses by iron rings and straw ropes. No nails were used. After they were tied to the crosses, all twenty-six were lifted almost simultaneously. A sudden thump dropped them into the waiting holes, sending a shock of pain through the victims' bodies.

All of a sudden, the Hill of Nishizaka had grown a new forest, a long row of 26 trees spanning at intervals of two or three yards. Far away one could see the Jesuit college, where Bishop Peter Martins was ordered to stay at the time with most of the Jesuit missionaries.

Along with the non-believers, an estimated 4,000 Christians were crying and praying, mesmerized by the crosses, their eyes tense with anxiety. Rev. Fr. Martin of the Assumption, OFM, delivered a short sermon to the throng from, atop his cross, saying that the martyrdom the 26 would soon undergo is an inestimable grace from God. The victims sang "Te Deum" together from the lines of crosses.

Terasawa ordered his men to put up a board with a notice that read, "These men came from the Philippines under the guise of ambassadors, and chose to stay in Miyako (the capital city) preaching the Christian doctrine, which the government has severely forbidden all these years. The government has, therefore, decided to decree that they be put to death, together with the Japanese who have accepted that doctrine." Four samurai executioners stood beneath the crosses with unsheathed bamboo lances, waiting to run their weapons up under the rib cages of the prisoners.

Then, a Jesuit brother, Paul Miki, 33, delivered a sermon with his vigorous voice from atop his cross. He straightened himself on the cross and his voice thundered. His sermon at this time was recorded by Fr. Luis Frois, a Jesuit missionary from Portugal, who came to Japan in 1563.

Miki, 33, son of a samurai warrior, was an accomplished preacher and catechist who was near his ordination date to the priesthood. As he was very knowledgeable in Buddhist doctrine, he used to compare the teachings of Christianity and Buddhism when he preached to a Japanese audience with traditional Buddhist background. He used to lead his audience to ponder upon which doctrine was truly worth following.

Miki said from the cross, "I did not come from the Philippines. I am a Japanese by birth and a brother of the Society of Jesus. I have committed no crimes. The only reason I am condemned to die is that I have taught the holy teaching of Our Lord Jesus Christ. Yes, I have preached my Lord Jesus Christ's truth. Yes, I am going to tell you the truth. I have only one last request: that you believe and ask for Christ's help for your salvation. At this crucial period, I want to stress and make it unmistakably clear that man can find no way to salvation other than the Christian way."

He went on to say, "The Christian law commands that we forgive our enemies and those who have wronged us. I must therefore say here that I forgive Taikosama (Dictator Hideyoshi) and all who took a part in my death. I do not hate Taikosama. I would rather have him and all the Japanese become Christians.

"I pray to God that God will send His merciful graces to all. I hope that the blood which I will soon spill will invite a tender shower of Divine blessings upon you, my brethren Japanese," he preached.

Terasawa, apprehensive that the execution was turning into a display of Christian strength, signaled to the executioners to move in with their long steel-tipped, sword-like, bamboo lances. A guttural yell, a sudden thrust, and the two spears crossed each other into the chest of each martyr. Sometimes, the blades came through the body at the shoulders. The death was almost immediate. Bishop Martin in the Jesuit college said at the time, "I heard the uproar from the crowds when the martyrs were being executed."

The twenty-six were canonized by Pope Pius IX in 1862 after canonical investigation... 265 years after their executions on February 5, 1597. When Pope John Paul II visited the hill of execution in Nagasaki, on February 26, 1981, the Pontiff told the audience as follows;

"Like Christ, they were brought to a place where common criminals were executed. Like Christ, they gave their lives so that we might all believe in the love of the Heavenly Father, in the saving mission of the Son, and in the never-failing guidance of the Holy Spirit. On Nishizaka, on February 5, 1597, twenty-six martyrs testified to the *power of the cross.* They were the first of the rich harvest of martyrs to follow, for many more would subsequently hallow this ground with their suffering and death."

Consecration of Japan to Mary's Immaculate Heart

Seven generations of Japanese Christians pinned their hopes on a prophecy by a Japanese Catholic brother by the name of Sebastien. Sebastien prophesied that, "After seven generations pass, missionaries will come back to this country aboard black ships (steel-made ships) to listen to our confessions and reconcile us with God through the sacrament of confession." This "Sebastien dictum" was handed on for some 250 years, along with his accurate "Catholic calendar of feast days" and the precise formula for the "Latin-worded prayer" of baptism for new-born babies — a Latin version of "I baptize you in the name of the Father, the Son and the Holy Spirit."

Akita: Mother of God as Coredemptrix

In 1858, Japan was forced to scrap its isolationist policy and open itself to the outside world. The arrival of U.S. Navy Commodore Perry's gunboats upset Feudal rulers. Perry came to demand the inauguration of trade relations. Japan reluctantly opened two ports to U.S. ships.

Then Fr. Bernard Petitjean of the Paris Foreign Mission Society, came to Japan and discovered the clandestine community of "hidden Christians" on March 18, 1865. He was astonished by the accuracy of the Latin baptismal prayer and the Christians' precise knowledge of the liturgical calendar (e.g., Advent, Christmas on December 25, the 40-day Lent and Easter). One tradition which attested to this was the extra hay the Christians gave the cattle on December 25. Anti-Christian regulations were still in place, however, forcing Fr. Petitjean to disguise himself as a farmer and to wait until after dark to go to their village to celebrate Mass at a village cowshed.

Archbishop Francisco Xavier Kaname Shimamoto of the Nagasaki diocese, a descendant of hidden Christians, told me in an interview in July 16, 1990, that, "There is a profound and close relationship between the history of the Church in Japan and the Blessed Mother. The Blessed Mother is always present and intervenes at decisive turning points of Japanese political and spiritual history. For example, St. Francis Xavier landed in Japan as the first missionary on August 15, 1549 — the very feast day of the Assumption of the Blessed Mother."

The Archbishop went on to say, "Clandestine Christians who endured and survived bloody persecutions were discovered by Fr. Petitjean by the medium of the statue of the Blessed Mother, in front of which a Christian woman uttered Her holy name, "Santa Maria," to the priest."

"Japan declared war against the U.S. on the feast day of Immaculate Conception of Mary on December 8, 1941, (the war that finally liberated Japan from fanatic militarists' rule) and Japan accepted the unconditional surrender to the Allied Forces on August 15 — again, the feast day of Assumption. In this sense, the Blessed Mother has strongly linked Herself with the Church in Japan and this country itself," the archbishop said. He is now the president of the Japanese Episcopal Conference.

Several noted missionaries consecrated the Japanese Archipelago to the Immaculate Heart of Mary during the era of persecution. It was again consecrated by Japanese bishops after World War II at some key turning points of Japanese history.

Among these consecrations was one accomplished by Fr. Augustine Forcade, a missionary from the Paris Foreign Mission Society, on May 1,1844. He performed this consecration to the Immaculate Heart of Mary during a Mass he celebrated on a French warship that brought him to the southern Japanese Island of Okinawa. Fr. Forcade suffered two years of continual surveillance and harassment by Japanese authorities, who placed severe restrictions on his missionary activities on the island. He could only say Mass and Rosary in a Buddhist temple designated by the authorities as his residence. Our Lady eventually rewarded him, in turn, obtaining for him the consecration to bishop. Later, the Holy See approved this consecration and formally decided to place the Catholic Church in Japan under the protection of the Blessed Mother's Immaculate Heart. Later, Fr. Forcade was appointed to the bishop of the French diocese of Nevers.

In September 27, 1863, Bishop Forcade encouraged Bernadette Soubirous of Lourdes to become a nun of the "Sisters of Charity and Christian Instructions of Nevers" in his diocese. In those days, Bernadette was suffering from refusals by various convents to accept her as a novice. Bishop Forcade told Bernadette, "Leave everything to me." Then, Bishop Forcade persuaded the superior of the convent of the "Sisters of Charity and Christian Instructions of Nevers" to accept Bernadette as a nun.

Fr. Teiji Yasuda of the Society of Divine Word wrote in one of his books, "When Saint Francis Xavier set foot on this corner of the

Akita: Mother of God as Coredemptrix

Japanese archipelago (Kagoshima) on August 15, 1549, Xavier certainly did not fail to show his love and devotion to the Blessed Mother who had preserved him from dangers through a most perilous crossing. Beyond doubt, he consecrated Japan to the Virgin Mary's Immaculate Heart and prayed for its conversion without losing sight of the fact that he landed in Japan on Her most glorious feast day — Her Assumption."

I wish, here, to point out two historical episodes mentioned in Xavier's two letters to the Society of Jesus in Goa, India, and to his benefactor in Malacca, Malaysia, both dated November 5, 1549 — about 10 weeks after his landing.

Soon after his landing, Xavier arranged for his Japanese assistant Paul Anjiro to show a painting of the Blessed Mother with Jesus to Takahisa Shimazu, a warlord ruler of Kagoshima province, and to the mother of the warlord. It was the first Christian painting brought to Japan. The letter says, "When the warlord watched the painting of the Blessed Mother, he was deeply moved and fell on his knees in front of the painting. He expressed deep reverence and instructed his men to follow his manner."

"A few days later, the mother of the warlord dispatched an official to our lodging and asked how she could obtain a painting similar to the one that moved their hearts. At that time in Japan, there were no tools to copy the drawing to comply with her request. So, the woman then asked us to translate and write down the Christian teachings and doctrine for her study," according to Xavier's letters.

Xavier's other letter, addressed to Pedro da Silva da Gama, then the top administrator of the Portuguese colony of Malacca, states, "Within two years, we hope to inform you of a completion of a church dedicated to our Blessed Mother Mary in the Japanese capital of Miyako (Kyoto). Its aim is to help everyone sailing to Japan to count on the protection of the Our Lady of Miyako even in the face of heavy seas."

These letters show Xavier's deep devotion to the Blessed Mother and suggest Her intervention in the leading of a Japanese warlord to give initial authorization for missionary activities in Japan. The letters were translated from Spanish into Japanese by Rev. Fr. Pedro Allupe, former superior of the Society of Jesus, who was acting as a missionary at the western Japanese city of Hiroshima, when the atomic bomb was dropped. Fr. Allupe aided Japanese citizens exposed to radiation, who were suffering from its after-effects.

Mary Helps in the Discovery of Underground Christians

Fr. Bernard Petitjean's discovery of the clandestine Christians is a remarkable story in itself. He came to Japan in 1863 with strong expectations that he would like to discover the descendants of the Christians, who chose death, rather than renounce their faith. He completed a beautiful Gothic-style church in Oura in December 29, 1864, in the southern part of Nagasaki, and dedicated it to the 26 martyr saints crucified in 1597 at Nagasaki.

While still a seminarian in Paris, the headquarters of the Paris Foreign Mission Society, Rue du Bac, Fr. Petitjean was fascinated by books depicting the courageous faith of the Japanese Christians. However, his initial experiences in Japan after his arrival in Nagasaki in 1863, might have been bitter and even frustrating for him, as Fr. Petitjean found only hostility to the Christian faith in Japan. Only Westerners were allowed to express their Christianity in this country of martyrs.

On March 17, 1865, around half past noon, Fr. Petitjean was on his knees before Our Lord present in the Holy Eucharist reserved in the tabernacle at the central altar of the church. He was aware that a group of some 15 roughly-clad Japanese men and women had entered the chapel and surrounded him.

Fr. Petitjean later said in a letter to his superior that he prayed to Our Lord present in the tabernacle for Divine blessings upon these

Japanese. "I fervently pleaded with God to place upon my lips inspirational words capable of winning some of them over as believers who would worship God." Then, a middle-aged woman named Yuri, which translates as "Lily," came up to him holding her hand over her heart and said, "Our faith is the same as yours."

The priest's heart was moved with joy. Scarcely believing it and in utter amazement he asked, "Is it true? Where are you from?" She answered, "We are from the Urakami Village (Urakami is a farming region in Nagasaki.) Nearly all Urakami villagers embrace the same faith as ours." Then she asked, "Santa Maria no go zo wa doko? (Where is the statue of Santa Maria?)"

Fr. Petitjean wrote in the letter, "When I heard her words blessed by Santa Maria, all remaining doubts were dispelled. I was convinced that I was looking at descendants of Japanese Christians. I thanked God for this consolation."

He led them to the side altar against the eastern wall where the statue was kept. Excited to see it, one of them exclaimed, "Look! It's Santa Maria! She's holding the Holy Child Jesus in her arms!" As the season was Lent, another said they were presently observing the Lenten fast and asked Fr. Petitjean if he also was. The priest replied, "yes."

These Christians had to summon great courage to disclose their Christian identity to this stranger in missionary garb. The government had posted a fierce warning outside the church which stated that any Japanese found inside the church would be prosecuted to the fullest extent of the law. Mary opened the way.

In reflecting upon this incident in light of the tears of the Akita statue of Mary, Fr. Yasuda remarked that, "Had it not been for the statue of the Blessed Mother at the chapel, Fr. Petitjean would never have discovered the hidden Christians. Just as this statue of Mary in Nagasaki opened the way for a fresh outpouring of Divine blessings into the Catholic community in Japan, the statue of Mary in the Akita convent is a harbinger of God's plan to shower abundant Divine graces unto, the universal Catholic Church."

He also said, "I presume the reason the Blessed Mother appeared in Japan is that the blood of nearly one million Japanese martyrs have been appealing to God over the past 400 years to bring conversions and salvation to Japan. These martyrs in heaven have also been beseeching Mary to pray for sinners in Japan. This, I think, is the reason for Her apparition in Akita."

"Hidden Christians and their descendants have treasured their faith as a precious heritage from their ancestors. They have maintained a pure faith in which they have regarded the salvation of souls as the ultimate goal above and over other values."

From out of this genuine faith flowed the Japanese Christians' warm-hearted love of neighbors as demonstrated by their great charity throughout centuries. For example, during World War II, poor Nagasaki Christians forwarded great assistance by way of aid materials to poverty-stricken civilians in China, which Japanese troops had invaded. In the process, they risked the full wrath of military government leaders.

Dr. Takashi Nagai

After the atomic bomb snuffed out the lives of 74,000 citizens leaving hundreds of thousands more gripped by the after-effects of radiation, on August 9, 1945, Dr. Takashi Nagai, a Catholic radiologist of Nagasaki University, threw his medical skills into the service of the victims, despite his own leukemia and personal suffering of the after-effects.

Following days of selfless service to the heavily injured, he returned to his own bomb-devastated home near ground zero, only to find the charred skeleton of his wife Midori, a devout Christian, among the broken roof tiles and white ash.

Looking upon her remains, his eye caught a dull glint among the powdered bones of her right hand. Though the beads were melted into a blob, the chain and cross identified it as the Rosary he had seen slipping through her fingers so often. He bowed his head and sobbed.

Dr. Nagai later wrote, "I have heard that the atom bomb... was destined for another city (Kokura). Heavy clouds rendered that target impossible and the American crew headed for the secondary target, Nagasaki. Then, a mechanical problem developed and the bomb was dropped further north than was planned and burst right above the Cathedral. It was not the American crew, I believe, who chose our suburb. God's providence chose Urakami and carried the bomb right above our homes. Is there not a profound relationship between the annihilation of Nagasaki and the end of the war? Was not Nagasaki the chosen victim, the lamb without blemish, slain as a whole-burnt offering on an altar of sacrifice, atoning for the sins of all the nations during World War II?"

Fr. Diego Yuki, S.J., a pastor of the Church of the 26 Holy Martyrs, told me in an interview, "Even today, there are many charitable Christians in Nagasaki who are active in offering up sacrifices of love and contributing to the good of society and churches. The history of these martyrs gives us a lesson that God grants abundant blessings to Christians with a pure humble faith in the Holy Eucharist, rather than to intellectuals with frail faith."

Around the mid 19-century, most Christians in the village of Urakami used to trample upon the sacred Christian symbols at the annual Christian-identification tests in front of government judges, to avoid being killed.

When Fr. Petitjean told the hidden Christians it is the sin of denying God to trample upon sacred Christian symbols, just as Peter committed the sin of disowning Christ three times at the courtyard of the high priest, he dealt a heart-wrenching shock to these Christian descendants.

History of Christianity in Japan

This realization led these humble Christians to deep repentance and to develop a fervent eagerness to make reparation for both their own and their ancestors' sins of denying God, by offering up sufferings and sacrifices for God. It was this humble abandonment to God's will that brought so many Catholics to accept the government's decision in 1867 to uproot and expel them to detention camps nationwide. Rather than complaining, staging demonstrations, or giving into despair, these heroic Christians saw a profound opportunity to make reparation for their sins and the sins of the denial of Christ by their ancestors.

These Christians would see starvation and severe torture in the camps. They were subjected to beatings or thrown naked into deep icy ponds. Sometimes the cruel officials would strip a woman naked and bury her in freezing snow. All told, some 660, one-fifth of those exiled since 1867, were martyred.

In a camp in Tsuwano city in the prefecture of Shimane, where a group of 125 were detained, starvation was severe and lasted for years. One day, a local farmer kindly threw in some living cicadas (large insects which resemble locusts) as toys for some children who were detained in a large bamboo cage. The children pounced on the cicadas and ate them immediately to ease their hunger.

On a more inspiring occasion, a tiny little boy was summoned to a hearing by an interrogator. The official displayed some delicious-looking confectioneries and told the boy to renounce his faith in exchange for the sweets.

"I will give you all these confectioneries if only you stop being a Christian," the official said, trying to coax the boy into apostasy. The boy replied "No." The official asked, "Why?" The boy answered, "My mother taught me I could go to heaven if I refuse to renounce my faith. She told me once I entered heaven, I could enjoy much much sweeter things than such confectioneries."

Sr. Chizuko Kataoka, president of The Immaculate Heart of Mary Women's College in Nagasaki, an authority on the history of martyrdom, told me in an interview, "Nagasaki Christians endured persecutions with inner joy, as they saw, in their oppression, opportunities to prove their love for God. They offered up their plight as gifts to God. Nagasaki Christians risked their lives to follow their faith-filled consciences, rather than submitting to the official orders of the powerful government to apostasize. These people chose faith, rather than to live in comfort."

Her own paternal great grandparents were among the Urakami Christians who were uprooted and dispersed. Nonetheless, they maintained the faith, according to her writing.

In Sr. Chizuko's home, there are two objects which help to hand down the "Tale of Journey" — a euphemism for the experiences of the harsh life in exile. One is a round chip box shaped like a soldier's mess tin, and the other is a scroll of rough paper on which her great grandmother Sada wrote down her experiences of the "Journey." The former was used by her great grandfather to hold the tiny portion of watery porridge distributed once a day to him while he was imprisoned in Kochi Prefecture. Sada's scroll is a journal of her experiences from the day of departure through the period of imprisonment in Wakayama Prefecture — several hundred kilometers distant from Kochi, where her husband was jailed.

It was on December 6, 1869, that Sada was uprooted and expelled, along with her four daughters, among whom was her two-year-old baby, Naka. Sada departed with Naka fastened to her back with a belt, while holding the hands of her other two daughters. The eldest daughter, Shika, 12, followed Sada's footsteps. They walked through heavy snow-covered, village roads, while reciting the Rosary aloud. They were forced to board a ship bound for Wakayama.

As a child, Sr. Kataoka's father, Yakichi, often listened to his grandparents' stories about the life of exile. With philosophical indifference, they related gruesome ordeals such as having to eat maggots to stave off hunger or being thrown into icy ponds in mid-winter as torture. To her father, Yakichi, the stories of these "noble deeds of endurance for the sake of God" had all the mystery and beauty of fairy tales.

Yakichi grew up and eventually became a leading historian. Dr. Yakichi Kataoka also became an exemplary Christian full of heartfelt love inspiring him to write many books on the history of martyrdom in Japan — spiritual treasures among Japanese Catholics, and a powerful source of encouragement in difficult times of trouble or agony.

Dr. Kataoka wrote, in his Japanese masterpiece, *History of Martyrdom of Japanese Christians,* about how various exiled Catholics responded to their interrogators and how they dealt with the tenacious efforts of bureaucrats to persuade these Catholics to apostatize. Among the many episodes is one about Senuemon Takagi, an uneducated farmer who was thrown naked into an ice-covered pond on November 26, 1868.

Senuemon told the interrogators, "I know that, since Dictator Taiko (Toyotomi Hideyoshi) outlawed Christianity, successive governments have banned Christianity. However, I believe in the Creator of this universe. This is the way to serve God, the Creator. The Christian faith has been handed on from my ancestors over generations. If I had complied with the order by the governor of Nagasaki to renounce my faith, I would have been given as much land and properties as I wished. However, because I would rather secure everlasting happiness in heaven, I will not renounce my faith, despite whatever torture I am exposed to. I have endured the torture so far. So, I will never abandon my faith, whatever treatments I may have to undergo."

Holy Mother Mary Helps Christians
Overcome Persecution

As you read the preceding chapters about the 1973 apparitions of the Blessed Mother in the northern city of Akita, you are already aware of the fact that the spirit of the martyrs and their willingness to offer their sufferings for the genuine love of God is still alive in some Japanese Catholics. This attitude still survives in our secular modern age. You can find it in the examples of genuine Christian love, endurance and prayer of Fr. Thomas Yasuda, the visionary nun, Sr. Agnes Sasagawa, and her sister nuns at the convent in Akita.

What lessons did God plan to convey to the Catholic Church in allowing these terrible ordeals to strike Japanese Christians? What mystery lies behind the survival of the Christian faith through 250 years of bloody persecution?

This bloody history and the ultimate victory of faith over persecution tells us of the awesome power God has given to the Blessed Virgin Mary with which to crush the head of Satan. Faith survived centuries of repression, because these weak people drew true strength from their devotion to the Mother of God and the prayers of the Rosary, even after the feudal government expelled and/or executed all the missionaries in Japan.

This history of martyrdom is a testimony to the "Power of the Cross" wherein evils and Satan are crushed when people offer up their sufferings to God based on a genuine love of Him. When Christians love and honor His Mother through devotion to Her rosary, She gives them in return the spiritual strength to love God, even at the risk of death.

This seems to be what the Japanese martyrs taught us by their blood.

Appendix A

First Official Analysis of Blood, Tears and Perspiration From Statue of the Holy Mother of Akita

On Jan. 24, 1975, Dr. Eiji Okuhara, M.D., of the Department of Biochemistry, Akita University School of Medicine, requested the Department of Forensic Medicine of the same school to make a scientific test of:

(a) a piece of cotton cloth wrapped in vinylbag.
(b) two cotton balls wrapped in two separate vinyl bags.
(c) a piece of gauze in a paulownia (a kind of precious tree) box.

Dr. Okuhara asked the department to answer the following questions:

(1) Is the material adhering to the above objects blood, tears and sweat?
(2) If so, is it of human origin?
(3) If it is of human origin, what is the blood type?

I. Description of Items Investigated:

There were three items in three separate envelope-size vinyl bags and a fourth in a paulownia box.

The three items in the three vinyl bags were labeled respectively: Blood (A), Sweat (B) and Tears (C).
(From here on, each item is referred to as A, B, C, and the item in the paulownia box as D.)

The item "A" is bleached white cotton cloth, the center of which appears slightly brownish.

The items "B" and "C" are white cotton balls without pigmentation.

Each item measures about 5 x 5 x 0.5 cm. Item A is folded. Item D is a piece of gauze in a paulownia box, 7.3 x 4.6 x 1.7 cm.

When the piece of gauze (Item D) was unfolded, it was found that there were two light brown areas, one of which had a small dark brown dot.

II. Results of Investigation:

1) Test to determine whether each specimen contains blood or not.

Miliar-sized specimens were taken from each item: A, B, C, and D, and a leucomalachite-green test was made. The results were as follows:

Specimens from the brown parts of A and D reacted positively, while specimens from B and C as well as the non-colored areas of A and D did not react.

2) Test to determine whether the contained material is of human origin or not

Using antihuman rabbit hemoglobin (homemade No. 3 — antigen value 1: 64,000) and antihuman rabbit serum (homemade No. 1 — antigen value 1: 32,000), antiserum agarplates were made. Each specimen was added to these antiserum agarplates and kept overnight at 4 degree Celsius.

The results were as follows:

The brown parts of A and D reacted positively to the anti-human rabbit hemoglobin test, but the others did not react.

Appendix A

In addition, the brown parts of A and D, as well as C reacted positively to the antihuman rabbit serum, while B did not.
A human blood stain, a human serum stain and a piece of clean gauze were used as controls, and they all showed the expected results.

3) Tests for blood type:

A test was made on each specimen, using the group-specific double combination method. This method is an improved version of the mixed agglutination method.
The results are shown in the table below.(Three parts of non-colored areas of D were also examined.)

Specimen	Anti A - A type erythrocyte system	Anti B - B type erythrocyte system
A. brown part	–	+++
non-colored part	+	+
B.	–	–
C.	+	+
D. brown part	–	+++
non-colored part 1	–	–
non-colored part 2	–	–
non-colored part 3	+	+

(Note on how to read the table:)
The cross mark (+) in the table shows the occurrence of a positive reaction. The triple cross (+++) shows a strong positive reaction. The Minus Mark (-) shows the failure of a reaction to take place.

When a certain specimen reacts positively to anti-B system, It shows the specimen contains B-type human liquid. If it reacts to anti-A system positively, that shows the presence of A-type human liquid. If a specimen reacts positively to both anti-A and anti-B system, it means the specimen contains AB-type human liquid.

Discussion

The first leucomalachite-green test showed that the brownish parts of A and D contain blood. The second test using anti-human rabbit hemoglobin and anti-human rabbit serum showed that the blood is definitely human blood.

By the third group-specific double combination method, this blood detected from the items A and D was identified as type B.

As there was positive reaction against anti-human rabbit serum, the material adhering to C was identified as human-body fluid, and the blood type of this fluid was identified as type AB.

The non-colored areas of A and D showed no reaction to the anti-human hemoglobin or antihuman serum. Therefore, it can be considered that these parts are not adhered to by human blood or human fluid.

However, when the group specific double combination-method tests were conducted, the non-colored areas of A showed type AB, and the non-colored areas of D showed type B and AB.

The group-specific double combination method is more sensitive than the agglutination method using the anti-human serum, so this kind of results are not rare.

The above results showed blood type B from some parts of the specimens A and D, and blood type AB from other parts of the same specimens.

This may seem to be a contradictionat a glance. But as stated above, the group-specific double combination method is a very sensitive one. It can sometimes identify blood types of cases of contamination with even a very minute amount of body fluid, which would show no reaction to anti-human serum.

Therefore it is not a contradiction.

If specimens A, B, C, and D were all taken from the same person, the blood type B detected from the brown parts of A and D, which were clearly identified as bloodstains, is the blood type of the examinee.

At the time when the specimens were taken, or by the time the examiner received the specimen, it could have been contaminated by a minute amount of body fluid of type A or type AB.

Therefore the above results are considered reasonable.

Conclusion

From the tests and the reason mentioned above, the following conclusions were reached:

1. Is the material adhering to the above mentioned objects blood, tears or sweat?

Answer: Blood was detected from the brown part of the bleached cloth in the vinyl bag described as "Holy Blood" and from the brown part of the gauze in the paulownia box.

Also human body fluid was detected from the cotton in the vinyl bag labeled "tears."

2. If the material is blood, tears or sweat, is it of human origin?

Answer: The blood detected from the specimen is human blood and the detected body fluid is human body fluid.

3. What is the blood type?

Answer: The blood type of the blood stain is type B and that of the body fluid is type AB.

Meanwhile, a type A and a type AB material, which are considered to be the results of body fluid contamination by someone other than the examinee, were also detected from specimen, except for the cotton piece in the bag labeled as sweat.

> Jan. 29, 1975
> (signed) Kaoru Sagisaka, M. D.
> Associate Professor of Forensic Medicine
> Akita University School of Medicine
> 1 - 1 Hondo, Akita, Japan (and sealed).

Appendix B

Second Official Analysis of Tears
From Statue of the Holy Mother of Akita

Document of Appraisal

The person who requested this appraisal:
Professor Eiji Okuhara
University of Akita, School of Medicine,
Department of Biochemistry.

The date of request: Aug. 22, 1981.

The object for appraisal: A small cotton piece placed in a small vinyl
bag

Items of Appraisal:

Is the material absorbed in the above mentioned cotton piece the
tears of human origin?

Results:

1. General appearance:

A pea sized cotton piece placed in a vinyl bag. Almost white except for a tiny black spot which is present in the cotton.

2. Tests by anti-human rabbit serum:

The specimen for this appraisal is described as "tears." However, it is serologically difficult to distinguish tears from other clear body fluids by the current technique of forensic medicine.

Therefore, I conducted tests to determine whether it is human body fluid, by using antihuman serum.

Before conducting the tests, I confirmed that the anti-human serum became no longer capable of reacting with monkey serum by taking away its constituents (antibodies) capable of reacting with monkey serum. After this process, the anti-human serum became capable of reacting only with human body fluid.

After this process, I examined the specimen by the method of precipitation electrophoresis. As you can see on the attached photograph, this specimen showed a clear precipitation-line. The human serum used as a control also reacted positively. The monkey serum stain showed a negative reaction.

3. Tests for blood typing:

Following heat fixation of one part of the specimen, the group-specific double combination test was performed. The specimen portion showed a negative reaction to both anti-A-A type erythrocytes system and anti-B-B type erythrocytes system.

It was examined anew by an elution test using an (Ulex europaens) anti-H system.

The specimen showed a negative reaction to both the anti-A and anti-B system.

However, the specimen showed a mild positive reaction to the anti-H system.

Explanation:

1. Results using anti-human rabbit serum:

The anti-human serum used in this test not only reacts with human serum, but also reacts with human saliva, semen, tears or sweat. Therefore, the anti-human serum does not have any ability for organ distinction. However, it never reacts with monkey serum.

This also means that the anti-human serum will not react with the serum of mammals whose evolution levels are lower than that of monkeys.

This means that the anti-human serum provides high accuracy for species distinction. Therefore, this result revealed that human body fluid exists in the specimen.

2. Tests for blood typing:

When the group-specific double combination method test was performed, it showed that the specimen did neither react with anti-A nor anti-B system.

However, it showed a mild positive reaction against anti-H system when an elution test was conducted by using anti-A, anti-B, and anti-H system.

Therefore, I conclude that there is O type material in this specimen.

Appraisal:

By the reasoning stated in the explanation, I hereby conclude as follows:

I certify that human body fluid is adhering to the specimen, and that the blood type of the specimen is type 0.

Nov. 30, 1981.

Examiner for appraisal:

Kaoru Sagisaka, M.D. (signed and sealed)
Department of Forensic Medicine,
School of Medicine,
University of Gifu
Gifu City, Japan.

Appendix C

*Pastoral Letter of the Bishop of Niigata on the
Subject of the Statue of the Virgin of Akita*

John Shojiro Ito, Bishop of Niigata, 1984

I

To all members of the diocese, my blessing and very best wishes for this Feast of Easter. Twenty-two years have elapsed since His Holiness John XXIII appointed me bishop of the diocese of Niigata, in 1962. In conformity with the legislation of the Church I have reached the age of retirement and now I must retire as the local ordinary of the diocese. My thanksgiving goes to each one of you for prayer and cooperation which have permitted me, despite many difficulties, to fill my task up to the present day.

Before leaving you, I must confide to you a preoccupation. It has to do with the series of mysterious events concerning a wooden statue of the Virgin Mary in the Institute of the Handmaids of the Sacred Heart of Jesus in the Holy Eucharist. (The request for ecclesial recognition of this secular institute has been introduced in Rome.) This institute is found in Yuzawadai, Soegawa, Akita, in this diocese of Niigata (Japan). You are without doubt aware of these events through magazines, books, television, and so on.

Akita: Mother of God as Coredemptrix

When the first commission of inquiry was named in 1976, I publicly announced that it was necessary to abstain from all official pilgrimage and all particular veneration of this statue while the inquiry was underway. From that day I have made no declaration on this subject. Indeed, being a question of important events concerning the Church, one cannot treat them lightly. However, to keep silence at the time of leaving my function as bishop, since I have been at the heart of the events, would be a negligence with regard to my episcopal duties. For that reason I have decided to make a new declaration in the form of this pastoral letter.

Since 1973, when the events began, eleven years have passed. As that was the first time I was a witness of the rather extraordinary events, I went to Rome to the Sacred Congregation for the Doctrine of the Faith in 1975 where I consulted Archbishop Hamer, deputy secretary of this Congregation, and whom I already knew. He explained to me that judgement regarding such a matter falls under the jurisdiction of the local Ordinary (bishop) of the diocese in question.

In 1976, I asked the archbishop of Tokyo for the creation of a commission of inquiry. This first commission declared that it was not in a position to prove the supernatural events of Akita. In 1979, I presented to the Congregation a request for the formation of a second commission of inquiry. This second commission permitted us to examine the facts still more in detail.

In 1981, a letter of the Congregation, unfavorable to the events, ws sent to the nunciature in Tokyo. But this letter contained some misunderstandings. Esteeming it my duty to restore the exactitude of the facts, I re-examined all the facts in 1982 at the time that the mysterious events, seemingly, came to an end. Through the intermediary of the Apostolic Nuncio in Tokyo, I sent the complete dossier, augmented with the new facts, to Rome.

Appendix C

At the time of my trip to Rome in the month of October last year (1983) I was able to meet with three officials charged with the matter in the Congregation for the Doctrine of the Faith. At the end of this meeting we had decided that the dossier should remain under examination.

II

The series of events relative to the statue of the Virgin Mary include the flowing of blood from the right hand of the statue, also a *perspiration* spreading a sweet perfume, perspiration so abundant that it was necessary to wipe it away from the statue. However, the most remarkable fact, in our opinion, and the most evident, is the overflowing of an aqueous liquid, similar to human tears, from the eyes of the statue of Our Holy Mother.

This began on the 4th of January, 1975 (Holy Year) and some *tears* flowed 101 times, until the 15th of September, 1981, Feast of Our Lady of the Seven Dolors. I was able myself to witness four lachrymations. About 500 persons have also been eyewitnesses. I twice tasted this liquid. It was salty and seemed to me truly human tears. The scientific examination of Professor Sagisaka, specialist in legal medicine in the faculty of medicine at the University of Akita, has proved that this liquid is indeed identical to human tears.

It is beyond human powers to produce water where there is none, and I believe that to do this the Intervention of a non-human force is necessary. Moreover, it is not the question of pure water, but of a liquid identical to liquid secreted by a human body. It flowed only from the eyes of the statue, as tears flow, and that more than 100 times over a period of several years and before many numerous witnesses. It has been established that it could not have been by trickery or human maneuvers.

If these events are not natural one can envisage three causes. They would be due to:

1. Ectoplasmic power of a human being;
2. Machinations of the devil;
3. A supernatural intervention.

I do not know well what could be ectoplasmic power. However, certain individuals say that Agnes Katsuko Sasagawa, member of the Handmaids of the Sacred Heart of Jesus in the Holy Eucharist, and who was the one linked most especially to the events of Akita, might possess such powers permitting her to transfer her own tears to the statue. For that however, it would be necessary, according to Professor Itaya of the Tokyo Institute of Technology (specialist in this field) that the interested person use his or her will power in order to cause such powers to exert any influence. Now the tears have flowed from the statue when Agnes Sasagawa was sleeping and even when she was not aware of weepings of the statue of the Holy Mother, because she was at home with her family 400 kilometers from Akita. I think therefore that the hypothesis of ectoplasmic power must be rejected.

There are also persons who suppose that it is a question of a machination of the devil. If that is the case it should lead to evil effects relating to the faith of the people. Not only have there not been such effects, but quite to the contrary there have been favorable effects. For example, Mr. Yoichi Imatani, whose Catholic wife had for a long time recommended conversion, decided to receive baptism after witnessing the tears flow from the statue.

In another case, a former believer, separated from the Church for several decades, returned to the regular practice of our religion after seeing the tears. And again, following a visit to the place, yet another believer resolved to work in evangelization. Alone she created two circuit churches by offering up her financial resources and has continued this work to the present day.

Furthermore, there are numerous reports of miraculous cures of diseases such as cancer, thanks to the mediation of the Virgin of Akita. I am going to mention two, the most proving.

One is the sudden cure of a South Korean woman, Mrs. Teresa Chun Sun Ho. Following cancer of the brain, she was reduced to a vegetative existence from July, 1981. The Virgin of Akita appeared to her and told her to get up. Almost at once she was able to get up, having entirely recovered her health. This healing took place while priests and Korean women prayed to the Virgin of Akita for her cure and asked for a miracle in view of the canonization of the Korean martyrs. There are X-ray photographs of this person taken during the sickness and after the complete cure. The X-ray photographs show her cure even to the eyes of nonprofessionals. The authenticity of the X-rays is attested to by Dr. M.D. Tong-Woo-Kim, of the Hospital of Saint Paul in Seoul who took these X-rays, and also by Father Roman Theisen, STD, president of the ecclesiastical tribunal of the archdiocese of Seoul.

All of the records have been sent to Rome. I went myself to Seoul (South Korea) last year and was able to interview the cured woman involved; I could thus assure myself of the truth of the facts of her miraculous cure. For her part the person came to Akita to thank Our Holy Mother.

The second case is the complete cure of the total deafness of Sr. Agnes Sasagawa. I will speak in detail of this later.

Such facts propitious to the faith and to physical health exclude that the events of Akita could be of diabolical origin. There remains therefore only the possibility of a supernatural intervention. It is in any event difficult to hold that this is not a question of supernatural phenomena.

III

But why have such phenomena taken place? I ask if they are not with regard to the messages coming from the statue of the Virgin and perceived by the deaf ears of Agnes Sasagawa.
The first message was given to her on the morning of July 6th, 1973, first Friday of the month. A voice coming from the statue of Mary, always splendid, saying:

"My daughter, my novice, you have obeyed me well, abandoning all to follow me. Do you suffer much because of the handicap which deafness causes you? You will be assuredly healed. Be patient, It is the last trial. Does the wound in your hand give you pain? Pray in reparation for the sins of humanity. Each person in this community is my irreplaceable daughter."

"Do you say well the prayer of the Handmaids of the Eucharist? Then, let us pray it together:"

"Most Sacred Heart of Jesus, truly present in the Holy Eucharist, I consecrate my body and soul to be entirely one with Your Heart being sacrificed at every instant on all the altars of the world and giving praise to the Father, pleading for the coming of His Kingdom."

"Please receive this humble offering of myself. Use me as You will for the glory of the Father and the salvation of souls."

"Most Holy Mother of God, never let me be separated from your Divine Son. Please defend and protect me as Your special child. Amen."

"Pray very much for the pope, bishops, and priests. Since your baptism you have always prayed faithfully for them. Continue to pray very much... very much. Tell your superior all that passed today and obey him in everything that he will tell you. Your superior is wholeheartedly seeking prayers now."

Agnes Sasagawa lost her hearing when she was working as a catechist in the church of Myoko-kogen. Because of this deafness she was for a time in the hospital of Rosai in the city of Joetsu. Dr.

Sawada diagnosed her total deafness as incurable and issued the documents permitting, for this reason, state subsidy. No longer being able to work as a catechist, she came to the Institute of the Handmaids of the Sacred Heart of Jesus in the Holy Eucharist at Akita, where she began to live a life of prayer.

The second message, like the first time, was given by the voice coming from the statue of the Holy Virgin:

"My daughter, my novice, do you love the Lord? If you love the Lord, listen to what I have to say to you.

"It is very important. Convey it to your superior.

"Many men in this world grieve the Lord. I seek souls to console Him. In order to appease the anger of the Heavenly Father, I wish, with my Son, for souls who will make reparation for sinners and the ungrateful by offering up their sufferings and poverty to God on their behalf:

"In order that the world might know the wrath of the Heavenly Father toward today's world, He is preparing to inflict a great chastisement on all mankind. With my son, many times I have tried to appease the wrath of the Heavenly Father. I have prevented the coming of the chastisement by offering Him the sufferings of His Son on the Cross, His Precious Blood, and the compassionate souls who console the Heavenly Father... a cohort of victim souls overflowing with love.

"Prayer, penance, honest poverty, and courageous acts of sacrifices can soften the anger of the Heavenly Father. I desire this also from your community: please make much of poverty, deepen repentance, and pray amid your poverty in reparation for the ingratitude and insults toward the Lord by so many men. Recite the prayer of the Handmaids of the Sacred Heart of Jesus in the Holy Eucharist with awareness of its meaning; put it into practice; over your life to God in reparation for sins. Let each one endeavor by making much of one's ability and position, to offer oneself entirely to the Lord.

"Even in a secular community, prayer is necessary. Already souls who wish to pray are on the way to being gathered in this community. Without

attaching too much attention to the form, pray fervently and steadfastly to console the Lord."

After a moment of silence She continued:

"Is what you think in your heart true? Are you truly prepared to become the rejected stone: My novice, you who wish to become the pure bride of the Lord. In order that you, the bride, become the spouse worthy of the Holy Bridegroom, make your vows with the hearty readiness to be fastened to the Cross with three nails. These three nails are honest poverty, chastity and obedience. Of the three obedience is the foundation. With total obedience follow your superior. Your superior will understand you well and guide you.

The third and last message was given also by the voice coming from the statue of the Holy Virgin on the 13th of October in the same year:

"My dear daughter, listen well to what I have to say to you. And relay my messages to your superior."

After a moment's silence:

"As I told you, if men do not repent and better themselves, the Heavenly Father will inflict a great punishment on all humanity. It will definitely be a punishment greater than the Deluge, such as has never been seen before.
"Fire will plunge from the sky and a large part of humanity will perish. . . The good as well as the bad will perish, sparing neither priests nor the faithful. The survivors will find themselves plunged into such terrible hardships that they will envy the dead. The only arms which will remain for you will be the Rosary and the sign left by My Son (Eucharist).
"Each day recite the prayers of the Rosary. With the Rosary pray for the bishops and priests. The work of the devil will infiltrate even into the Church.

One will see cardinals opposing other cardinals... and bishops confronting other bishops.

"The priests who venerate me will be scorned and condemned by their confreres; churches and altars will be sacked; the Church will be full of those who accept compromises and the demon will tempt many priests and religious to leave the service of the Lord.

"The demon is trying hard to influence souls consecrated to God. The thought of the perdition of so many souls is the cause of My sadness. If sins continue to be committed further, there will no longer be pardon for them.

"With courage, convey these messages to your superior. He will tell each one of you to continue prayers and acts of reparations for sins steadfastly, while ordering all of you to pray fervently. Pray very much the prayers of the Rosary. I alone am able still to help help you from the calamities which approach. Those who place their total confidence in Me will be given necessary help."

This message is based on the condition *if men do not repent and better themselves ... I* think that it is a serious warning, although one feels here the maternal love of Our Heavenly Mother in the words: "The thought of the perdition of so many souls is the cause of My sadness." If the promise contained in the first message of 1973 was not realized *Do you suffer much because of the handicap which deafness causes you? You will be assuredly healed.* one would be able to doubt the veracity of these messages. But this promise was kept nine years after the beginning of the sickness.

Before this happened, an angel announced to Sr. Agnes Sasagawa (the 25th of March, and the 1st of May, 1982): *"Your deafness causes you to suffer doesn't it? The moment of the promised cure approaches. By the intercession of the Holy and Immaculate Virgin, exactly as the last time, before Him Who is truly present in the Eucharist, your ears will be definitely cured in order that the work of the Most High may be accomplished. There will still be many sufferings and obstacles coming from outside. You have nothing to fear. "*

Effectively on the last Sunday of the month of Mary, the 30th of May, 1982, Feast of Pentecost, at the moment of Benediction of the Blessed Sacrament her ears were cured completely and instantly.

That same evening she telephoned to me and we conversed normally. On the following 14 of June, I visited Doctor Arai of the Eye and Ear Division of the Hospital of the Red Cross of Akita who had verified the complete deafness of Sr. Agnes Sasagawa at the moment she arrived in Akita nine years before. I asked his impression. He expressed his amazement at this complete cure. Doctor Sawada of the Rosai Hospital of Joetsu who had been the first to examine her when she became deaf, has now issued a medical certificate dated June 3rd, 1982, attesting that following minute examinations of her auditive capacities, he certifies that there is no further anomaly in the two ears of Sr. Agnes Sasagawa.

I have known Sr. Agnes Sasagawa for more than ten years. She is a woman sound in spirit, frank and without problems; she has always impressed me as a balanced person. Consequently the messages she says that she has received did not appear to me to be in any way the result of imagination or hallucination.

As for the content of the messages received, there is nothing contrary to Catholic doctrine or morals, and when one thinks of the actual state of the world, the warning seems to correspond to it in many points.

Having set down here my experiences and my reflections with regard to the events relative to the statue of the Holy Virgin of Akita, I esteem it my duty, as Ordinary of the diocese, to respond to the requests of the faithful to give pastoral directives on this subject. It is only the bishop of the diocese in question who has the power of recognizing a fact of this kind. The Congregation of the Doctrine of the Faith has given me directives in this regard.

I have been in close and constant communication with the Institute of the Handmaids of the Sacred Heart of Jesus in the Holy Eucharist since its foundation. I know precisely the situation concerning this Institute and its members. In studying the history of the apparitions of the Virgin Mary up to this day, I am aware that it is always the local ordinary of the diocese who has authorized the veneration of the Virgin Mary when She has manifested Herself in their dioceses.

After long prayer and mature reflection, I hand down the following conclusions in my position as Bishop of Niigata:

1. After the investigation conducted up to the present day, I recognize the supernatural character of a series of mysterious events concerning the statue of the Holy Mother Mary which is found in the convent of the Institute of the Handmaids of the Sacred Heart of Jesus in the Holy Eucharist at Yuzawadai, Soegawa, Akita.

    I do not find in these events any elements which are contrary to Catholic faith and morals.

2. Consequently, I authorize, throughout the entire diocese, the veneration of the Holy Mother of Akita, while awaiting that the Holy See publishes definitive judgment on this matter.

    And I ask that it be remembered that even if the Holy See later publishes a favorable judgment with regard to the events of Akita, it is a question only of a private Divine revelation. Christians are bound to believe only content of public Divine revelation (closed after the death of the last Apostle) which contains all that is necessary for salvation.

Nevertheless, the Church, until now, has equally made much of private Divine revelations as they fortify the faith. For reference, I cite the following texts of the document on Catholic Doctrine:

"The saints and the angels, having been conformed to the Will of God, receive from Him grace and glory in abundance and it is right to venerate them because this amounts to offering praise and thanksgiving to God Himself. Among the saints the Virgin Mary deserves a special veneration. Indeed, She is not only the Mother of Our Savior who is God, but also the Mother of us all, and it is as Mother that She intercedes for us, full of Divine grace greater than those received by all the saints and angels." (Article 72)

"One venerates the statues and images of Christ and of the saints to sustain the faith, to adore Christ, to venerate the saints. This act thus becomes praise to God." (Article 170)

Finally, I beg God that He accord to you all abundant graces, and I send my Apostolic blessings.

Niigata, Feast of Easter, April 22, 1984
Signed, John .Shojiro Ito, Bishop

Appendix D

Brief Biography of the Author

ALBERT FRANCIS FORBES MUTSUO FUKUSHIMA was born in Fuji City, Shizuoka Prefecture, central Japan, on January 17, 1958.

Albert Francis Forbes is the Christian name he adopted in accepting baptism into the Catholic Church on October 19, 1980. Mutsuo Fukushima are his given and family names. As of this writing in 1994, he is 36, and serving as a journalist for a Japanese news organization.

He served until 1992 as vice-president of the International Federation of Catholic Journalists, an arm of the International Catholic Union of the Press (UCIP) in Geneva.

Mr. Fukushima studied at the Foreign Language Faculty of the Jesuit-run Sophia University from 1976-1980, and obtained a Bachelor of Arts in 1980.

He studied the novels of Graham Greene, a British Catholic novelist, and based his graduation thesis, "Philosophy of Love in Graham Greene's Power and Glory," on them. Keeping the future in mind, he also studied international politics at the University, working towards the goal of becoming a conscientious journalist.

Mr. Fukushima's education by the Jesuits at Sophia University instilled within him unwavering ideals defending the dignity of human life and values that strive for the actualization of social justice in a corrupt modern world, the conveyance of truth in a deceitful society, and the importance of fostering Christian love in an egocentric world through charity (love in action), rather than ostentatious preaching about love.

Though he was brought up in a poor Buddhist family, he became quite knowledgeable in the field of Western literature and Christian values contained therein. His mother, who possesses a rich intellectual background, bought him a set of 50 volumes of beautiful Japanese translations of literature from China, America, and various European countries during his elementary school days.

Regarding his intellectual conversion, the author states, "I have to admit that, in my pre-university days, I had grown up to be a fairly cynical senior high school student. The mindnarrowing influence of the intensive competition-oriented Japanese society, whose education program fosters the notorious 'examination hell phenomenon,' drives the nation's youth to excessive lonely rivalry in a heated race to pass the entrance examinations for the 'first-rate' universities which are supposedly capable of guaranteeing materialistically promising professional careers."

"In those days, I doubted whether a human being really had a 'conscience,' an inner noble voice which, according to Catholic philosophers, suggested that, for example, a person carry an injured stranger victimized by a burglar to a hospital. I questioned myself as to whether a human being is capable being of such a noble existence. I was puzzled by the significant question of whether in one's soul every human being shares a compassionate capability to be a good Samaritan. I was searching for an answer."

"The good moral education at the Jesuit-run Sophia University, whose many bilingual graduates had won high reputation in Japan's powerful business community, brought about a revolution of conscience in my soul and a reversal of my cynical values."

"Encounters with several warm-hearted American and Spanish Jesuit missionary professors at the university provided me with irrefutable evidence that the human soul is capable of genuine compassion and sacrifice,' contrary to the prevailing belief in this predominantly non-Christian Japanese society that human beings are essentially egoistic animals with intelligence sharp enough to have created their civilization, and that human beings are motivated chiefly by materialistic and carnal desires and love of power, never sharing the image or true love of the God of Mercy."

In the Sophia University of those days, Mr. Fukushima had an encounter with several missionary professors, such as Fr. John Nissel, Fr. William Everett and Fr. Robert Forbes, who, following the model of Fr. Pedro Arrupe, the now-deceased head of the Society of Jesus and a survivor of the Hiroshima atomic-bombing, would pump all of their physical and spiritual energy into the moral education and evangelization of Japanese youth to produce a "man for others" who would bring Christian values into the Japanese society.

In most cases, these missionary professors won the genuine respect from some Sophia students. However, by the time most of the students were admitted into the university, their hearts had been hardened by the Japanese education system and its materialistic society. Hence, many of them remained indifferent to the respectable efforts of the devoted missionaries to instill Christian values and teachings in them. Mr. Fukushima was among the few students who decided to accept baptism, moved by the powerful witness of Christ's love through these missionaries who worked hard for their students.

He also had to accept the truthfulness of a hypothesis that in the hearts of all human beings there remains a potential for a genuine love of neighbor. He observed an heroic love of neighbor on the part of some Jesuit missionaries who readily abandoned their secular desires, to become the witnesses of Christ according to their love for God and resultant apostolic zeal.

Then, the hypothesis remained no longer a hypothesis for him, but became a reality as he witnessed American missionaries giving all of their time, energy and themselves wholeheartedly to educating the Japanese youth — even cutting short their sleep to prepare for next day's classes or catechism courses.

He states, "If I had seen only one such warmhearted missionary, I would have brushed his example aside as that of an 'exceptional case,' but I found many Jesuit missionaries who heartily concerned themselves with producing youth who would carry within them a strong thirst for justice and the ability to demonstrate love and compassion in action."

He continues, "Gradually, questions crept into my heart. What is the common source of the tenderheartedness demonstrated by these missionary professors? What or Who gives these missionaries the strength of will to serve alien Japanese students in a land located far away from their native countries? Why are the eyes of this tall American missionary named Fr. Forbes so tender and sparkling with kindhearted light behind his broken glasses?"

Logically and intrinsically, he could find only one answer. The Supreme Presence behind the universe, whom these missionaries call "God," must exist and that very God must be the common source of the energy behind their love. He deduced further that the white round bread distributed at Masses — which Catholics call the "Holy Eucharist" — may be the very source of the energy behind their love and that something Divine may be present in the Eucharist.

His cynicism was completely defeated and crushed by the example of love he saw in the missionaries. He began attending catechism courses taught by Fr. Robert Forbes, from whom he took part of his Christian name. He wept terribly at the death of this priest.

Fr. Forbes often said he "would like to die while teaching my class or when celebrating Mass." As a sign of God's favor upon this priest, he actually did pass away while teaching in class. God heard his prayer.

Mr. Fukushima accepted baptism on October 19, 1980, by an American Jesuit, Fr. William Everett from West Virginia. He was influenced by the goodness of this priest and Fr. John Nissel from Baltimore, as well. These living witnesses of Christ's love enabled him to confirm the veracity of a statement by the American Christian novelist, William Faulkner, who said:

"A human being has a soul capable of compassion, sacrifice and endurance."

He adopted the name Albert for part of his Christian name, from his long-cherished and deep respect for Dr. Albert Schweitzer, a French medical doctor and Protestant missionary, who interrupted his successful career as an organist to put his medical skills into service of the African people plagued by various diseases and epidemics.

Mr. Fukushima also took the name, Francis, for part of his Christian name, in respect for the uncompromising courage of Mr. Francis Kim Gi Ha, the long-imprisoned South Korean Catholic dissident poet, who came under persecution for standing up to the dictatorial rule of now deceased President Park Jung Hee.

Mr. Fukushima's conversion was also aided by his reading of the works of many Christian novelists and philosophers, such as Feodor Dostoevsky; Shakespeare; Leo Tolstoy; and Simone Weil, a Jewish philosopher who worked for the French resistance under General Charles De Gaulle against the Nazis during World War 11. The philosophy classes of Fr. Francisco Perez, whose profound thinking was apparently influenced by St. Augustine and St. Thomas Aquinas, also stimulated Mr. Fukushima's conversion.

In March 1985, Mr. Fukushima became a professional journalist in charge of economic and general news by joining a Japanese news organization. Now, he writes about Japanese politics and foreign policy. In the same year, he obtained membership in the prestigious Catholic Journalist Club (CJC) of Japan. Later, he accepted the office of the executive secretary of the club under the chairmanship of CJC chairman, Kazuo Yokokawa.

Mr. Fukushima is concurrently a member of the International Catholic Union of the Press (UCIP) based in Geneva, Switzerland, which is an international body composed of thousands of Catholic journalists and mass media professionals in both the Western and ex-Communist bloc. At a UCIP triennial meeting in Rupolding, Germany in October, 1989, he was elected as one of the two vice-presidents of the International Federation of Catholic Journalists, an important arm of UCIP. It was a post of three-year tenure.

He states, "My deepest wish is that the whole Catholic Church will come to know about the Marian apparitions and her messages in Akita, so that many Catholics can become the powerful warm-hearted witnesses of Christ capable of living up to *Christ's command* to 'take up a cross and follow after me.' Such Catholics would be able to present edifying examples of offering noble sacrifices of love of neighbors, so that they could help others receive the graces of conversion and salvation."

Appendix E

Detailed Instructions on How to Go to Akita

UPON ARRIVAL at Narita International Airport, the chief gateway to Tokyo, you have to transfer to Japanese Railways (JR) train or a limousine bus to go to Haneda Airport, as it is from Haneda that all flights leave for Akita airport. All Nippon Airways (ANA), Japan Airline (JAL) and Japan Air System (JAS) serve Akita from Haneda.

If you arrive at Narita late in the afternoon or even at night, you would have to accomodate yourself at a hotel in Tokyo.

To get to Haneda airport from Narita Airport, walk to the Narita Airport Train Station, located on the "B- 1 " basement floor beneath the airport terminal building. Use the elevators. This will take only a few minutes.

Then, I recommend the pilgrim take the railway service called, "The Narita Express. " It's rapid and comfortable. The train platforms are located on the "B-2" basement floor. So take the elevator again.

The Narita Express train is the fastest and most convenient transportation between the airport and Tokyo. It links the two places in 53 minutes for the fare of 2,890 yen (about 22 dollars as of this writing time). A taxi fare could be astronomical, so please be cautious.

Akita: Mother of God as Coredemptrix

After arriving at the Tokyo Station, pilgrims are advised to take another train to "Hamamatsucho Station" on the "Yamanote Line" for the fare of about one dollar. Hamamatsucho is the third stop from Tokyo Station.

From Hamamatsucho, transfer to the enjoyable "Monorail" train to go to the Haneda Airport (domestic flight airport). It takes only 10 minutes to go from Hamamatsucho to Haneda.

Upon arrival at the Haneda airport, go to the counters of airline companies and buy an air ticket for about 28,800 yen (approximately 288 dollars). It only takes about an hour to fly from the Haneda to the Akita airports.

The Institute of the Handmaids of the Eucharist, the convent where the Marian apparition took place, is called "Seitai Hoshikai" in Japanese.

It takes some 55 minutes by bus and taxi to go to the convent from the Akita Airport.

Frequent services of inexpensive "limousine bus" transportation are available between the airport and the Akita station. I recommend using this service.

Once you arrive at the bus terminal in front of the Akita Station, transfer from bus to a taxi cab. Taking a limousine bus from the airport to Akita Station, and then a taxi from Akita Station to the convent, costs only 2,300 yen (about $17)

Those wishing to save travel expenses have to take the limousine bus from the airport **before** transferring to taxis at Akita Station.

All taxi drivers know the location of the convent due to the growing number of pilgrims. I tested the depth and spread of information on the convent among taxi drivers. I gave an instruction to a taxi driver in Japanese, "Maria sama no Shudoin e itte," (Please bring me to the convent of St. Mary). This brief statement was enough. The driver immediately understood my destination!

But, if English-speaking persons feel like visiting there, you need utter only two Japanese words for assuring your arrival at the convent — **"Yuzawadai"** (for the name of the place) and **"Seitai Hoshikai"** (for the name of the convent).

It is not difficult to reach the convent. Additionally, many of the Japanese citizens that you will see on any street (especially the youth and middle-aged) understand and speak enough English — thanks to Japan's official foreign language education.

Two inexpensive hotels with hot spas are located rather close to the convent. One is Akita Onsen Plaza with the telephone number of 0188-33-1919 and the other is Satomi Onsen Hotel with telephone number of 0188-33-7171.

Both hotels are located within a distance of 10-minute taxi drive from the convent. The address of the convent is: 1 Yazawadai, Soegawa, Akita City, (postal code 010)

Akita: Mother of God as Coredemptrix

Akita Notes

Anti-Akita criticism and logical refutation against the criticism

1. **Critics of Akita alleged Akita created confusion within the Church in Japan because Holy Mother predicted difficult times for the Church.**

   Holy Mother came to Akita to alleviate confusion which is gripping the Universal Catholic Church. God and Holy Mother planned to revive Catholic faith and unity through a string of supernatural events and messages in Akita that could trigger a revival of our faith in the Real Presence of Jesus in the Holy Eucharist. There were numerous miracles which occurred at Akita concerning the Holy Eucharist which God brought about in order to revive Catholics' conviction in the Real Presence of His Son in this inestimable gift of Divine Love.

2. **Critics of Akita say messages are too gloomy and demanding because Holy Mother requested Catholics to offer up their sufferings, sacrifices and prayers in reparation for sins and insults against God.**

   Today's confusion in the Catholic Church results chiefly from the tendency of Catholics to throw away their crosses out of the windows. Because Holy Mother wanted to remind Catholics of the importance of the spiritual attitude to accept crosses and sufferings in union with the suffering of Jesus and Mary for the redemption of mankind, She showed the prime example of offering Her own sufferings and 101 episodes of weeping of tears from the wooden statue of Herself. God has arranged for the statue to shed tears in order to elucidate the truth that Holy Mother is the Co-Redemptrix, who offered up her supernatural sufferings and tears to co-operate with her Divine Son's work of Redemption ever since the Incarnation. The blood of Jesus which He spilled on Calvary was given to Him from His Heavenly Mother. This resulted in the profound spiritual bond between Jesus and Mary, just as the Holy Father pointed out in his pastoral letter *Redemptoris Mater.* (Mother of the Redeemer)"

3. **Critics say that the apparitions are not authentic, because the First Commission, which investigated it, said they could not prove the supernatural character of the mysterious events.**

The First Commission set up by the Archbishop of Tokyo did not have any legitimacy and validity, because it is the "local ordinary" (*Ordinario Loci*) of the diocese where the apparitions took place that is given **by the Holy See** the canonical authority to hand down the judgment regarding the authenticity of an apparition in question (see "The guidelines and norms of the Congregation of the Doctrine of Faith-regarding the Methods & Procedures for Judging the Alleged Apparitions and Revelations."). The document states unequivocally *"Officium invigilandi vel interveniendi praeprimis competit Ordinario loci."* This means that "The responsibility and work to constantly watch the developments of an apparition and INTERVENE come primarily under the jurisdiction of the local bishop." This document is signed by Franjo, Cardinal Seper, the then Prefect of the Sacred Congregation of the Doctrine of the Faith. Because of this document, the Archbishop of Tokyo, Monsignor Peter Seiichi Shiranyanagi, who was not the local ordinary of the diocese of Niigata in which Akita lies, did not have authority to make a judgment on the apparition.

4. **Critics have made persistent attempts to divert the attention of lay people from the pastoral letter issued by Bishop John Shojiro Ito, who recognized and declared supernatural authenticity of the apparitions in Akita.**

On the authority of the above named document, Bishop Ito said: "After the inquiries conducted up to the present day, I cannot deny the supernatural character of a series of mysterious events concerning the statue of the Holy Mother Mary which is found in the convent of the Institute of the Handmaids of the Sacred Heart of Jesus in the Holy Eucharist at Yuzawadai, Soegawa, Akita. I do not find in these events any elements which are contrary to Catholic faith and morals. Consequently, I authorize throughout the entire diocese, the veneration of the Holy Mother of Akita, while awaiting that the Holy See publishes definitive judgment on this matter."

5. **Critics say that Bishop Francisco Sato, the current local ordinary of the diocese of Niigata, has distanced himself from the apparitions in Akita.**

Bishop Sato said during a sermon to about 400 pilgrims, present at the Consecration of the new convent building at Akita, site of the apparitions, on July 25th, 1993: "Through our example of living, I hope that this place will develop further as a place of pilgrimage." On the previous day, Bishop Sato, joined the rosary procession along with the 400 pilgrims. The procession was led by the miraculous statue of the Holy Mother placed on a beautiful flower-decorated palanquin.

Bishop Sato sent a letter in 1990 to Archbishop of Tokyo, who was then the president of the Japanese Episcopal Conference (CBC Japan). In the official letter of grave providential importance, Bishop Sato declared that he decided to continue Bishop Ito's authorization of the veneration of the Holy Mother of Akita. The letter also pointed to conversions and miraculous cures that have taken place among pilgrims and related persons, according to Bishop John Shojiro Ito, who was attending a conference where the letter was read out to 7 bishops and archbishops. Archbishop of Tokyo received this letter in September 1990. Two months later - on November 29th, - the Archbishop read out the letter to all the seven bishops and Archbishops of the Standing Committee of the Episcopal Conference. After knowing the contents of the letter from Bishop Sato, the Standing Committee, the decision-making panel of the Episcopal Conference, decided to "obey unanimously" the judgment of Bishop Sato, according to the official record of the Conference. The decision was recorded in the form of a typed-out document from the General Secretariat of the Japanese Episcopal Conference (CBC Japan). The document is dated December 4th, 1990. The official statement said the Episcopal Conference decided to obey Bishop Sato's position to authorize the veneration of the Blessed Mother of Akita in accordance with "The guidelines and norms of the Congregation of the Doctrine of Faith regarding the Methods & Procedures for Judging the Alleged Apparitions and Revelations."

The contents of Bishop Sato's letter was revealed for the first time to the world at the Akita International Marian Conference in the autumn of 1992 in front of about 150 bishops, theologians, priests and the faithful from eighty dioceses from around the world, including Father Rene Laurentin, internationally acclaimed Mariologist from France.

The fact that Bishop Sato participated in various devotions in honor of the Holy Mother and the Holy Eucharist during the 1993 two day celebration for the Consecration of the new convent building carries serious importance. The reason is that the document of the Sacred Congregation of the Doctrine of The Faith states unequivocally as follows: "If a bishop of the diocese where the apparition took place reached the conclusion that the apparition is favorable for the faithful, the local ordinary is authorized by the Universal Catholic Church to permit various public manifestations of worship and devotions at the site of the apparition, while continuing to observe the situation always with the maximum prudence. Such episcopal permission is tantamount to declaring the apparition is *"nihil obstare"* in the form of a written document." (The phrase *"nihil obstare"* means that a certain teaching, apparition or message correspond with Catholic faith and morals).

This means that Bishop Sato, in accordance with the Holy See guidelines and norms on apparitions, authorized the public manifestation of devotion at the site of the Marian apparition in Akita. Bishop Sato was the chief celebrant at the Mass and Benediction on July 24th and 25th, 1993 at the Convent of the apparitions.

6. **Archbishop of Tokyo reportedly said that the events in Akita have: "no great significance for the Church" when the "Thirty Days" magazine interviewed him.**

The message of the Holy Mother is the most important, because she delivered it to lift the Catholic Church out of the quagmire that stems from attacks on the Holy Father's doctrinal infallibility and resultant misinterpretation by dissident theologians and some priests of Catholic teachings of salvation. The most serious crisis of faith resulted from the decline in the faithful's ability to recognize the Real Presence of Jesus in the Holy Eucharist. As the loss of reverence for the Holy Eucharist took place, it started preventing the inflow of divine graces into the souls of Roman Catholics. In Akita, God and Holy Mother planned to revive the people's faith in the Real Presence by imparting the Divine lessons about the importance of receiving the Holy Eucharist on the tongue.

On July 26th, 1973, during the Mass celebrated by Bishop Ito, mysterious events took place, preventing Sister Agnes Sasagawa, the visionary nun, from receiving the Holy Eucharist in her hand. Prior to that, the cross-shaped stigmata appeared in the palm of her left hand, inflicting intense pains to Sister Agnes. The bleeding stigmata in the left hand appeared on June 28th, 1973 and continued to pain her until July 27th, 1973. The wound renewed itself every week. On each Thursday the wound started aching. On each Friday it bled profusely. On each Saturday it returned to its original dried-out pink blister. The size of the cross in her hand measured 3 centimeters vertically and 2 centimeters horizontally. Its color bordered on pink.

Sister Agnes explained her experiences with the stigmata in her spiritual diary, in a part dated July 26th, 1973, as follows:

"Mass started a little after 5 p.m. Just as Sister Ishikawa was renewing her vows, my hand started to ache almost unbearably. I almost screamed. It was bleeding and ached just as if someone had pierced my palm all the way to the back with a nail. I tried with my whole strength to bear it. My forehead was in a greasy sweat. At that moment, clinging to Our Lady's medal, I prayed, "Mary, help me"' I tried to endure the pain by thinking of the sufferings of Jesus on the Cross. This all took place in just a short time, but when I was bearing the pain, it seemed like a very long time. I still cannot forget it. At Holy Communion, everyone received in their hands, but since I could not open my palm because of the pain, I received in my mouth."

The mysterious occurrences in Akita corroborate the Holy Father's teachings on the Holy Eucharist. Pope John Paul II said in his pastoral letter, "On the Mystery and Worship of the Holy Eucharist (Dominicae Cenae) issued to all Roman Catholic bishops in the world, Feb. 24 1980:

Pope John Paul II said in the pastoral letter, in his intimate and solemn appeal to all of his fellow priests around the world, as follows;

"Our greatest glory consists in exercising this mysterious power over the Body of the Redeemer, over and above our compliance with the evangelical mission."

"All that is within us should be decisively ordered to this (glorious mission). We should always remember that we have been sacramentally consecrated to this ministerial power and that we have been chosen from among men 'for the good of the people.'"

"We, the priests of the Latin-Roman Catholic Church, should especially think about the fact that our ordination rite added the custom of anointing the priests' hands in the course of many centuries..."

Akita: Mother of God as Coredemptrix

"One must not forget the primary obligation of priests, who have been consecrated by their ordination to represent Christ the Priest; for this reason their hands, like their words and their will, have become the direct instruments of Christ..."

"How eloquently the rite of the anointing of priests' hands in our Latin ordination tells that a special grace and power of the Holy Spirit is necessary precisely for priests' hands!"

"To touch the Holy Eucharist and to distribute them with their own hands is a privilege of the ordained."

Just as Pope John Paul II also stressed in his 1980 pastoral letter *"Dominicae Cenae,"* the custom was introduced for the spiritual "common good" of lay communicants and nuns, whose hands are not consecrated, with sacrament of priestly ordination, by a bishop through whom the Holy Spirit works to sanctify the hands of new priests.

By anointing the hands of a new priest during an ordination rite, a bishop, with the invisible intervention of the Holy Spirit into the rite, gives the priest a privilege of touching and administering the Holy Eucharist to a communicant, according to the Pope.

Pope John Paul II said with his doctrinal infallibility in the pastoral letter, "A special grace and power is necessary precisely for priests' hands."

Now, let's see Pope Paul VI's pastoral instructions *"Memoriale Domini"* (translated from the original Latin text) which first explains — historically — why the universal Catholic Church introduced and mandated the custom of receiving communion on the tongue, in early centuries.;

"...In the following period, after the true meaning of the Eucharistic mystery, its effect, and the presence of Christ in it had been profoundly investigated, the Church introduced the custom by which the priest himself would place the piece of consecrated bread on the tongue of the communicants from a deeper sense of reverence toward this holy sacrament and of the humility which its reception demands."

"In view of the state of the Church as a whole today, this manner of distributing Holy Communion therefore should be observed, not only because it rests upon a tradition of many centuries but especially because it is a sign of reverence by the faithful toward the Eucharist."

The practice of placing Holy Communion on the tongue of the communicants in no way detracts from their personal dignity."

"It is a part of the preparation needed for the most fruitful reception of the Lord's body."

"This traditional manner of administering Holy Communion gives more effective assurance that the holy Eucharist will be given to the faithful with the due reverence, decorum and dignity."

"This manner would enable the faithful to avoid any danger of profaning the Holy Eucharist, in which the whole and entire Christ, God and man, is substantially contained and permanently present in a unique way."

"Finally, the traditional manner would make sure that priests maintain the diligent care which the Church has always requested for the very fragments of the consecrated bread."

"If a particle or fragment of the Holy Eucharist is dropped or lost, perceive it as a lessening of a part of your own body."

"The usage of placing the consecrated bread in the hand of the communicant also includes the following dangers."

"The new manner of administering Holy Communion in the hand of the communicant, then, leads to a lessening of reverence toward the holy sacrament of the altar. The new manner leads to profanation of this blessed sacrament. It also leads to the adulteration of the correct doctrine (of the real presence of Jesus in the Holy Eucharist)."

"Three questions were therefore proposed to the bishops of the entire Latin Church. By March 12, 1968, the following responses had been received."

1) Do you believe the rite of administering Holy Communion in the hand of the faithful should be permitted?
   Yes: 567
   No: 1,233
   Yes, with reservations: 315
   Invalid votes: 20

2) Should experiments with this new rite first be conducted in small communities, with the assent of the local ordinary?
   Yes: 751
   No: 1,215
   Invalid votes: 70

3) Do you think the faithful would accept this new rite willingly, after a well-planned catechetical preparation?
   Yes: 835
   No: 1,185
   Invalid votes: 128

"From these responses received, it is thus clear that by far the greater number of bishops felt that the rule of placing communion on the tongue should not be changed at all. If it were changed, this would offend the sensibilities and spiritual worship (of the Holy Eucharist) on the part of the bishops and most of the faithful."

"The Supreme Pontiff judged that the traditional manner of administering the Holy Eucharist should not be changed, after he considered the observations and the counsel of the bishops whom the Holy Spirit have placed as overseers to feed the Church of God in view of the seriousness of the matter and the importance of the arguments made."

7. **Critics said the message of Sister Agnes' guardian angel on September 28th, 1981, regarding the profound meaning of 101 episodes of weeping of the statue of the Holy Mother is theologically meaningless.**

The guardian angel elucidated the mystery on how the Holy Mother has cooperated with Jesus in the work of Her Son's Redemption of mankind by offering up Her supernatural sufferings and tears ever since the Incarnation. Sister Agnes gave the following testimony on the events and messages of September 28, 1981.

Sr. Agnes suddenly felt the presence of the angel at her side during the adoration of the Blessed Sacrament. She did not see the angel in person but a Bible appeared open before her eyes and she was invited to read a passage. It was a large Bible, very beautiful and surrounded by a celestial light. When Sr. Agnes could recognize the references (Genesis, Chapter 3; V 15) the voice of the angel was heard explaining that the passage had relationship with the tears of the Blessed Mother Mary's statue. Then, the angel continued as follows:

"There is a meaning in the figure one hundred and one, for which the Blessed Virgin Mary shed her Holy tears. This signifies that the Grace of Salvation came into the world through a woman, just as sin came into the world through a woman. The zero between the '1' and '1' signifies the presence of God who is from all eternity until all eternity. The first '1' represents Eve and the last '1' the Blessed Virgin Mary." Then the sister was again instructed to reread the verse, and the angel left.

The verse of Genesis, describing the fight between the Holy Mother and Satan, says, "I will make you enemies of each other. You (Satan) and the woman (the Blessed Virgin Mary) your offspring. It (Jesus) will crush you head and you will strike at its heal (church)." The fact that the profound meaning of these apparitions in Akita were explained and elucidated by this reference to the **Words of the Bible** tells us that the events in Akita is the Divine revelation. The fact also convinces us of the supernatural character of the apparitions and messages in Akita.

The 101 weepings of the statue of the Holy Mother show us that, just as the old Eve tempted Adam to commit a sin, the new Eve, Holy Mother Mary, with her sufferings, became the channel through which the graces of salvation of the mankind by Jesus Christ reached this world.

The tears of Holy Mother's statue is the hard evidence that shows intense fighting is under way between the Holy Mother and Satan. Holy Mother appeared in Akita to appeal to Roman Catholics, the Mystical Body of Christ, to cooperate with the work of Salvation by offering up their prayers, sacrifices and sufferings to God.

8. **Father Garcia Evangelista, a member of the First Commission, invented and spread in Japan (now in the United States), the ectoplasmic theory, by which he alleged Sr. Agnes has the power to transfer her own tears and blood onto the statue, in his attempt to deny the supernatural character of the apparitions.**

When the Medical Faculty of Akita University, a prestigious state-run university, analyzed the blood and the tears collected from the statue in January, 1975, the University identified the blood type of the tears as AB and that of the blood as B. Then in April 1981, Doctor Kaoru Sagisaka, Professor of Gifu University, analyzed the tears from the statue collected with cotton wool and tweezers. He identified the blood type of the tears as type O. If Father Evangelista's theory is correct, the blood types of these specimens of tears and blood must be identical to that of Sister Agnes who has the blood type of B. Father Thomas Yasuda, of the Society of The Divine Word and spiritual director of Sister Agnes said: "God created different types of blood from the same statue on the strength of his Omnipotent power in order to place an absolute refutation on the senseless ectoplasmic theory and defend His work of love in Akita from slanders."

When this writer, Mutsuo Fukushima, interviewed Father Evangelista and asked him why the statue could shed tears whose blood type is different from that of Sister Agnes, he replied: "I do not know. I did not read the medical appraisal documents," which were issued by Akita University and Gifu University.

This priest earlier told Bishop Ito who threw the same question to him, "There must be other nuns who have the ectoplasmic power." However, at the time of the apparitions, there were no nuns with the Blood Type AB.

9. **Critics say Archbishop Aquin Carew, Apostolic Pro Nuncio, in Tokyo, is not favorable to the apparitions in Akita.**

Archbishop Aquin Carew came to the Convent of the Handmaids of the Sacred Heart of Jesus in the Holy Eucharist on September 15th, 1987 accompanied by Bishop Ito and Bishop Sato and four other priests. During the address he delivered, he encouraged the nuns to continue following in the footsteps of Christ by bearing the crosses which God had given to each of the nuns by patiently enduring their daily sufferings, offering them with love to God. Unwittingly the Archbishop was speaking of the central theme of the Holy Mother in Akita who encouraged all Roman Catholics to take up their crosses and follow Jesus Christ. The very day of his visit was the Sixth Anniversary of the one hundred and first weeping of the statue in 1981. After he returned to Tokyo, he sent a heart-warming letter to the convent in which he said "It is a special grace to visit you and to see the place venerated by so many pilgrims gathered to honor Our Lady, Queen of the Universe and Mother of the Church. May Mary cherish and protect you and all visitors during this Marian Year, and bring each and everyone to the everlasting kingdom of Her Son."

10. **Critics have belittled the significance of numerous conversions and miraculous cures pointed out by Bishop Sato and Bishop Ito in their official documents.**

There have been two first class miracles, among many miracles, through the intercession of Our Lady of Akita, which have been thoroughly documented with medical evidence attested by medical doctors of Red Cross Hospital in Akita, and the St. Paul Hospital in Seoul, South Korea (the latter in 1981).